# RISK AND BLAME

University of the
West of England

**FRENCHAY CAMPUS
(BOLLAND) LIBRARY**

**BRISTOL**

Please

# RISK AND BLAME

## Essays in cultural theory

*Mary Douglas*

London and New York

First published in hardback in 1992
Paperback edition published in 1994
by Routledge
11 New Fetter Lane, London EC4P 4EE

Simultaneously published in the USA and Canada
by Routledge
29 West 35th Street, New York, NY 10001

Typeset in Bembo by Intype, London
Printed and bound in Great Britain by
Mackays of Chatham PLC, Chatham, Kent

*British Library Cataloguing in Publication Data*
A catalogue record for this book is available from the British Library

*Library of Congress Cataloging in Publication Data*
A catalog record for this book is available from the Library of Congress

ISBN 0-415-06280-2 (hbk)
ISBN 0-415-11999-5 (pbk)

To James Douglas

# CONTENTS

## Part III Believing and thinking

# INTRODUCTION

These essays have mostly been published in the last five years. They are so dispersed that whoever has seen one of them is unlikely to come across any of the others. For this reason I am very grateful to my publishers, Routledge, for bringing them out as a third collection of my essays, and also grateful to the original publishers in giving permission for them to appear in one volume. Although written for very different occasions, they are not really variegated in their matter. They are all on the same basic theme, a complaint of inhospitality against the social sciences.

Typically an anthropologist tries to see individual persons in their social environment. The anthropological project calls for a holistic view, over a long enough stretch of generations and over a large enough number of persons for some pattern to appear. Using this wider and longer view to capture something about the culture, the anthropologist asks distinctive questions. Sociologists, for example, when they are interested in ritual will want to know if the individual performer is sincere; the anthropologist wants to know how the symbolic actions in one performance match the other performances, and whether there is any fit between the pattern of ritual action and the practical services of mutual support the performers are giving to one another. For anthropologists speculations about the meanings of words are just speculations unless the context of action is taken into account.

The day that anthropologists give up their attempt to ground meanings in politics and economics will be a sad day. The loss will be not so much for themselves as for the social sciences in general. For in the next twenty years or so the social sciences will be looking for just such a holistic approach that they have denied themselves by their methodological individualism. I predict a radical change of heart in the near future.

The idea of risk has recently risen to prominence in political debate, and has become the regular coinage of exchange on public policy. The first of the essays, 'Risk and blame', gives a history of my attempt to find a niche in the growing learned discourse on risk where I could share with other scholars an interest in how danger is politicized. The essay on 'Risk and justice' (Chapter 2) explains why the language of risk is likely to perform that standardizing, centralizing role at the level of public debate. With the political unification of Europe we will find ourselves working out a common language for dovetailing policies. But the public debate needs to be able to refer back to a more or less coherent scholarly debate. It is currently impossible to make sense of the concept of risk in the compartmentalized, individualistic frame of analysis normally employed. It is my belief that the present intellectual fragmentation will no longer be endured. The pressures to speak to each other across national and disciplinary boundaries will grow, and the gravity of the questions posed as comparisons of risk will force the social sciences to make their infrastructure of assumptions coalesce. When that happens, anthropology will be there, ready to meet the demand for an objective, whole view of human action. The first six essays in this volume set the problem and explain the need for a more holistic approach to the subject of risk.

A reason for hoping for such a change is the difficulty of applying the traditional discourse of social anthropology to ourselves. It cannot be done without a radical overhaul, because of deeply entrenched methodological prejudices. Methodology is the one common platform that counters the fragmentation of our knowledge of ourselves, but the accepted methodology starts and ends with the individual. It is my belief that the egocentric theoretical position of most psychology, economics, and cognitive science inhibits their understanding collective behaviour. The essays in Part 2 on 'Wants and institutions' bear witness to the fragmentary state of our received ideas about human behaviour. The normal sociological posture for thinking about institutions is either to leave out the individuals altogether, or to start with an individual threatened by, or controlled by institutions. There is no room for the idea that there may be some individuals who are setting up and maintaining the institutions as part of a process of incorporating other individuals in their own life projects.

A view from inside our own society does not call for theory about the origin of institutions. But the anthropologist is forced by avocation to understand foreign individuals in the act of making their foreign institutions. This is hard enough, but it is harder still to bring home the insights gleaned from abroad. It is tempting to become perpetual tourists, lingering comfortably in the porches of wayside inns. The last essay in this volume turns away from the social sciences and reproaches the anthropologists in their turn. They must not abandon the effort to synthesize what they know about others with what is known about ourselves. For better or worse, because we cannot avoid tangling with the social sciences we cannot avoid social theory.

One of the gaps most difficult to fill in our Western conceptual apparatus is the idea of the self. It is basic to utilitarian philosophy, and to economic analysis, both of which start from the assumption of a person motivated by self-interest. It is basic to psychology in all its branches, especially to cognitive psychology. It is central also to political debate and to the theory of risk, and to theories about credibility. The essay on thought styles (Chapter 12) suggests why the self is so shrouded from analysis that it rates the status of a taboo area. For ideological reasons the self is considered as pure subjectivity, incapable of analysis, insusceptible to theory. But without breaching the taboos, it is possible to write an objective account of how the idea of the self (the idea of it, of course, not the self itself), is treated in the normative debate which is the source and origin of culture.

Balancing the complaints, another theme runs through all the essays, that is a theory of culture. As many of the essays illustrate, cultural theory is a way of thinking about culture that draws the social environment systematically into the picture of individual choices. It provides a method of analysing public debates as positions taken in a conflict between cultures. The background history of this theoretical effort is recorded elsewhere, as shown in the bibliographies of these essays. One of the special strengths of cultural theory is to be able to predict what specific new perspectives appear when a social position is changed, new foregrounds emerge and old worries are backgrounded. The method is continually in process of being strengthened and refined by a scattered group of colleagues whose marks are on every page of this book, and whose support and stimulus I warmly acknowledge.

Finally I return to the topic of the Hotel Kwilu, the last essay in this volume. Academics are tempted to be content with the restricted hospitality of their disciplines. My husband has been tireless in efforts to make me relate the discourse of anthropology to the discourses in economics and political theory. I dedicate this volume to him as the only person I know impervious to the Kwilu effect.

# Part I

# RISK AND BLAME

# 1

# RISK AND BLAME[1]

## MORALS AND DANGER

An American taxi driver in the Mid-West once asked what I did. When I said I was an anthropologist he asked some probing questions which I answered so lamely that I was driven to explain that I was an anthropologist working in the department of Religious Studies. He leapt on this information 'You must be just the person we need in our Bible Group. There is a question we come against every week, and you will know the answer: Who came first, Adam and Eve, or the Dinosaur?' Again I had to excuse myself, saying that it was a proper question for anthropology, but that I could not give much help as my main work was on risk. After a pause he came back hopefully saying that his brother-in-law was a safety officer, and that it would be good to have a talk with me about safety regulations. This is something like the scope and conclusion of my first conversation with Professor Hood. To him, too, I had to explain why an anthropologist in a Department of Religion had come to be interested in risk. It was a matter of retrospection on the book I wrote about pollution a quarter of a century ago.

All the decade that I was researching for *Purity and Danger*[2] I had supposed the task in hand was to vindicate the so-called primitives from the charge of having a different logic or method of thinking. The evidence that there is a distinctive pre-modern mentality allegedly came from attitudes to misfortune. Moderns, the argument went, follow a line of reasoning from effects back to material causes, primitives follow a line from misfortune to spiritual beings.[3] To uphold formally that their thought in itself is different is beset with difficulties. But informally a strong

3

implicit bias holds us to that position, unless we can show that the political uses of natural dangers is a habit with ourselves as well as with others.

In *Purity and Danger* the rational behaviour of primitives is vindicated: taboo turns out not to be incomprehensible but an intelligible concern to protect society from behaviour that will wreck it. When miscreants are accused of spoiling the weather, killing with lightning, or causing storms at sea it is not a flaw in the reasoning process that should interest us, but something about casting blame. With much regret I left the book without making any link between taboo-thinking, which uses natural dangers to uphold community values, and our modern approach. So a gulf was left unbridged: they engage dangers politically on behalf of the constitution, we have disengaged dangers from politics and ideology; and deal with them by the light of science. What explains the difference? I hazarded the idea that their constitutions might be so much more fragile than ours that they needed recourse to blame and taboo, and hinted that the political weakness might be the explanation of what looked on the surface like a weakness in powers of reasoning. Time has passed, and events have made the link that was then so difficult to discern, now easy to assert. But it is interesting to reflect on why it was initially so elusive and why it is still so passionately rejected when the argument of *Purity and Danger* is put into terms of risk.[4]

At the Massachusetts Institute of Technology in 1968 I talked to a friend in political science who, on looking up the word 'pollution' in the new *Encyclopedia of Social Sciences* had been surprised to find my article[5] on ritual defilement. A careful comment on *The Golden Bough* and other misunderstandings of magic and taboo was of little help to him because, at that time, concern for rivers and the survival of water-life had become a major political issue in the United States and he wanted to know what river pollution entailed. I felt he would have liked to have complained to the editors of the encyclopedia about their selection of writers. Polite though he was, this political scientist made it clear that my treatment of pollution was totally unconnected to the burning issues. For a long time the connection between river pollution and taboo seemed to be contrived merely by the happenstance of language, as if one word, 'pollution', was doing duty for two different concepts: pollution of the environment and religious defilement. But now the clock hand has come full circle:

4

taboo is relevant to risk and the one word, 'pollution', is right for both.

There is for me a satisfying sense of the dinosaur biting back, for the 1940s anthropology in which I was trained is quite antediluvian now. The theme, well known to anthropologists, is that in all places at all times the universe is moralized and politicized. Disasters that befoul the air and soil and poison the water are generally turned to political account: someone already unpopular is going to be blamed for it. This forensic theory of danger comes out of the 1940s anthropology in which I was trained at Oxford.[6] It is so established that when I write about it my colleagues' reviews complain that it is all well known so, with added confidence, I go on to develop the implications. The questions start with how people explain misfortune.[7] For example, a woman dies; the mourners ask, why did she die? After observing a number of instances, the anthropologist notices that for any misfortune there is a fixed repertoire of possible causes among which a plausible explanation is chosen, and a fixed repertoire of obligatory actions follow on the choice. Communities tend to be organized on one or another dominant form of explanation.[8]

One type of explanation is moralistic: she died because she had offended the ancestors, she had broken a taboo, she had sinned. Following this kind of explanation the action is expiatory; some purification rituals are called for. To avoid the same fate the community is exhorted to obey the laws. If this is the dominant form of explanation, the community which accepts it is organized very differently from one that does not blame the victim.

An alternative way of explaining misfortune is to attribute it to the work of individual adversaries. The moral will be that a survivor needs to be smarter than her rivals: they will say that the reason she died can be traced back to her not having been quick enough or clever enough in looking after her own interests; rival magic was more powerful than hers. The rivals who killed her are hardly being blamed when the finger of causation points to them, for there is not much moral concern: everyone is expected to do the same to promote their interests. The postmortem decisions set up a community in which each member expects to be beset by rivals, and where the call to action will be for compensation at least, and probably vengeance – a community organized by the tit for tat of individual competition.

Different again in its impact on the community is the explanation of misfortune that blames an outside enemy. In this case the answer is that she died because an enemy of the community got her, not necessarily one who actually comes from outside but a hidden disloyal traitor. The action following the diagnosis is to seek out and inflict a communal punishment on the foe and to exact compensation.

These three types of blaming influence the system of justice. Or rather, the influence goes both ways, the blaming and the system of justice together are symptoms of the way the society is organized. There are communities, barely earning the name, which are not organized at all: here blame goes in all directions, unpredictably. Anything might just as plausibly have been the cause of any misfortune: flying saucers, Martian invaders, witchcraft, moral failure, technical failure; if there is no standard diagnosis, it follows there will be no standard action required. In short, the stronger the solidarity of a community, the more readily will natural disasters be coded as signs of reprehensible behaviour. Every death and most illnesses will give scope for defining blameworthiness. Danger is defined to protect the public good and the incidence of blame is a by-product of arrangements for persuading fellow members to contribute to it. Pollution seen from this point of view is a powerful forensic resource. There is nothing like it for bringing their duties home to members of the community. A common danger gives them a handle to manipulate, the threat of a community-wide pollution is a weapon for mutual coercion.[9] Who can resist using it who cares for the survival of the community?

In this light, the rare community which does not cast blame at all can only survive by a heroic programme of reconciliation. Such a community would have to avoid casting blame. I used to think that this type was theoretically impossible. I was convinced that the process of making a community inherently involved the members in mutual criticism and in using misfortune as a lever to raise the level of solidarity.[10] This thesis is an extension of Durkheim's thesis about the political uses of crime to the political uses of misfortune. I was sceptical that a community could be founded on a resolute refusal to blame anyone, neither the victim nor rivals or enemies. When evidence was proposed, I used to treat it with suspicion, expecting to find the fieldwork unconvincing, and the research not sufficiently aware of conflict going on. I was even disposed to believe that scale was a factor, that very

6

small communities could achieve this benign result. Now I have learnt vigorously to resist theories that peace-loving is possible for a community if it is small in scale.[11] Michael Thompson has persuaded me otherwise by his accounts of the Buddhist Sherpa communities in Nepal,[12] and also by his developments of cultural theory to take account of a fuller range of attitudes to danger and blame.[13] Cultural theory does not propose that persons who form a community consciously decide to have one or the other pattern of blaming. It expects that dangers affecting life and limb are drawn into the constitutional dialogue spontaneously and fall into regular patterns according to the kind of constitution that is being maintained.

In the late 1950s there was a general mood of rejoicing that nuclear power would usher in permanent prosperity for the world. This was why the idea was acceptable that the only people to use danger forensically were those that anthropologists study. This mood of enthusiasm for technology accounts for why the difference between them and us appeared to be a cognitive problem, a matter of knowing the real causes of things. Somehow, it was thought that science had really made things different for us. We were supposed to be able to recognize real dangers, whose causes are objectively identified, backed by the authority of valid experiment and theory. Chance, mystery and malice lurked in small corners not yet claimed by science but, generally speaking, thanks to our accurate knowledge of the world and our powerful technology, our blaming behaviour went direct to real causes instead of being deflected to the constitution-supporting function it performed elsewhere. For us, the line of reasoning implied, what you could call 'real blaming' was possible. Real blame was so guaranteed by its objective basis in knowledge that it could not be harnessed to the sordid work of ideology. This assumption was never challenged by critics of *Purity and Danger*, who presumably thought that way themselves.

Though I felt forced to accept that the difference between taboo and risk assessment was a matter of knowledge, I ardently scanned the 1950s literature on the sociology of knowledge for small exceptions. My object was to gather up any snippets of information about distorted reception of messages. I imagined there would still be residual cases of nature having been politicized even in our modern industrial democracy. I was interested in how information leaves open options for the receivers to interpret.

7

This was already a popular topic in psychology. I was impressed with Frenkel Brunswick's experiments with telling stories where the ideological signals were mixed up, for example sometimes the black man doing good and sometimes doing harm: she found that children could not remember the story at all unless they had first sorted out the roles into acceptable parts.[14] Misreading evidence was an important theme in the history of science, where the same evidence was sometimes used to support alternative theories. In philosophy of science, and in the psychology of perception, and in the information theory that was budding then, interpretive control was fully recognized. In spite of all this current interest in perceptual focus, I found nothing to encourage me to suppose that blaming in modern society could be analysed under the same rubric as blaming anywhere else. It was unquestioned that in this respect we are uniquely different. This is why the sections in *Purity and Danger* which refer to the theory of perception have only a weak connection with the main argument. They are there to show that at least I tried to check.

At the same time, psychologists were developing attribution theory to study how individuals allocate blame. Nearly all the work that I read then on perception was focused on individual cognition. With a small shift of attention to institutional design there should have been an opening for experiments that assessed individual attitudes for cultural influence. Such research might well have shown that we moderns have every bit as much scope as they, the primitives, for politicized reading of danger. The time was ripe in the 1960s for a radical change in our understanding of cognitive processes so as to make proper allowance for the social component in the human make-up. Both economics and psychology were at a great height of esteem and both were using basically the same individualist cognitive model. In the early 1950s individualist theory became sacralized by its incorporation into artificial intelligence theory.[15] There was at that time no scope for recognizing how blaming behaviour is geared into the making of community consensus. But now, encouraged by their having proved to be so wrong, I would propose even more radically that not just blaming but all cognition is politicized.

Looking back, there is a lot of irony. However liberal their political outlook, and however radical their political affiliation, anyone who at that time had an opinion on why the primitives were backward would propose a mental stagnation model, some version of the natives being locked into thought ways that were appropriate for their environment. But to get the discussion of primitive thought going seriously, we would have had somehow to unlock our own thought. One of the obstacles to good conversation on this topic was the low priority attached to bridging the gulf between *The Golden Bough* and modern technology.

To explain the difference between their attitude to pollution and ours, our civilization and theirs, the prevailing idea was that Western advances in knowledge had dissolved a tie that everywhere once used to connect morals and danger: with us morals are soberly enforced by moral persuasion and danger is known by technology; formerly lack of technology allowed the wildest accusations of blame to be hurled right and left and strange spiritual agencies to be invented to cover the cracks in plausibility. Magic and taboo were due to ignorance. Some complacency in these assumptions was our heritage from Hegel's philosophy of the self-realization of Spirit, and they came to sociologists through a closer inheritance of Hegel through Max Weber. Increasing self-knowledge and fuller awareness were thought to come along with increasing technical control. That conception of history still ruled in 1968 when I wrote the pollution article in the *Encyclopedia*.

In conceding that superior knowledge and better communications had dug a gulf between us and the tribal societies, I was in good company. Implicitly many colleagues still subscribe to something like Toynbee's theory of moral advancement. (Academic ethnic prejudice can go no further, but I find that condemning prejudice does not draw sympathy for my theme. In spite of venerating toleration, students of postmodernism draw an irreducible line between historical periods, which makes illegitimate the comparisons I am still interested in.)

Then suddenly technology itself came under attack as the source of danger. Everything changed. It became plain that the old link from danger to morals was not made by lack of knowledge. Knowledge always lacks. Ambiguity always lurks. If you want to cast blame, there are always loopholes for reading the evidence right. Science has not produced a run of people who do not wish to dominate one another. Industrialization has not produced a race of human beings disinclined to use danger in the rhetoric that protects the public good. The difference is not in the quality of knowledge but in the kind of community that we want to

make, or rather, the community we are able to make, or I should
say, the community that technology makes possible for us.

When I went to work in the United States in 1977 I still held,
uncomfortably and in default of an alternative, the ethnically
biased view. In fact, it was so obviously unsatisfactory that
although I had spent two decades researching it I had turned to
other problems.[16] The political uses of danger were put on to a
back-burner in my research. By that time a new profession of
risk analysts had been established, responding to the contemporary need to deal with the overt politicization of risk. The topic
of public perception of danger had burst upon everybody's awareness. The forensic uses of risk were everywhere to be seen. On
the one hand, it was an open attack on industry callous towards
workers' injuries, an attack on government for not curbing industry, a defence of natural resources, of the environment, and of
human rights. On the other hand, calculations of risks were being
made by the accused, to defuse anger, to show that the public
were exaggerating, that the public did not realize what risks they
were incurring every day, when they crossed the road, when they
drank a bottle of Coke, or just sat in the sun. Risk became an
academic growth area, and it still is. I felt very nervous. The
subject in which, for years, I had been trying in vain to interest
people, became suddenly hot, too hot. Like many who take up
anthropology, I had never wanted to engage in politics. I felt like
the safety officer confronted with fighting he ought to have been
able to sort out, but somehow unable to get the combatants to
listen. I don't know about the safety officer's feelings, but I was
not even sure that I wanted to be heard. Waving *The Golden
Bough* was pointless and I had no idea of how to say anything
useful.

Aaron Wildavsky, when he became the ex-President of the
Russell Sage Foundation, taunted me: is all this anthropology just
museum stuff? What is the use of all these theories about pollution? Are they just for the tribes? Does anthropology work for
history but not for today? He touched the sore point: is pollution
behaviour really different in tribal society? Are we above all that
sort of thing? Gradually he helped me to work out a more abstract
statement, embracing both us moderns and them, the tribes, in
a single forensic theory of danger.[17] We hoped it would be welcomed as a shaft of light in a murky area. But if you thought
that the profession of risk analysis would rejoice to see a radical

new contribution,[18] you would have been mistaken. These views about purity and danger in modern times are regarded as very controversial. The explanation has to do with concerns for the purity of the risk analysis profession and the danger of moving out of the favoured paradigm of individual rational choice.

Contemporary risk analysis started out by bundling the forensic uses of risk out of sight. When I tried to engage established risk analysts in conversation I soon gathered that to emphasize these dubious uses of risk is perverse, a dirty way of talking about a clean scientific subject. Though they recognize that the grime and heat of politics are involved in the subject of risk, they sedulously bracket them off. Their professional objective is to get at the real essence of risk perception before it is polluted by interests and ideology. The risk analysts have a good reason for seeking objectivity. Like all professionals, rightly and properly, they do not wish to be politically biased: this is important for their clientele. To avoid the charge of bias, they exclude the whole subject of politics and morals. To see them studying risk-taking and risk-aversion in some imaginary pure state is disappointing to anyone who has been attracted to the dirty side of the subject. It is especially frustrating for an anthropologist of my generation to find that, when danger at last emerges in the social sciences as a subject of study in its own right, it is defined to exclude interest in cultural differences in the distribution of blame.

Risk research has uncovered many conundrums and paradoxes.[19] It has found that 'the public' definitely does not see risks in the same way as the experts. The gap between lay and expert opinion has given rise to a whole new sub-branch of the psychology of risk, a whole new specialized branch of adult education, and a whole new sub-discipline for communicating about and labelling risks, and a whole industry for cataloguing them. But the baffling behaviour of the public, in refusing to buy floodplain or earthquake insurance,[20] in crossing dangerous roads,[21] driving non-road-worthy vehicles, buying accident-provoking gadgets for the home, and not listening to the education on risks, all that continues as before.

The single cause of why the subject is swathed in bafflement is the practitioners' commitment to methodological individualism. This follows from the way they see their need for objectivity. To start from the individual, and to stay with the individual to the bitter end, this is their chosen escape route to objectivity.

11

Nothing sticky or messy, the subject of the laboratory experiment must leave his personal experience outside, and try to display his cognitive processes by calculating numbers of balls in urns or other well-contrived problems in questionnaires. He (or she, because the subjects used in Oregon were often drawn from the League of Women Voters) is supposed to deal with questions that do not stir his/her emotional and political commitments. All capacity for moral outrage is supposed to stay outside the booth. Absence of motivation on the part of the subjects matches the purity of the researcher's motives. But it will not guarantee objectivity. For that is not how risky decisions are taken, not even trivial ones, but least of all major ones. Anger, hope, and fear are part of most risky situations. No one takes a decision that involves costs without consulting neighbours, family, work friends. These are the support group that will help if things go wrong. However, they tend to give conflicting advice. One of the interesting questions in risk studies would be to know how consensus is reached. Placing all the focus on individual cognition excludes the problem. The risk perception analysts say practically nothing about intersubjectivity, consensus making, or social influences on decisions. When they venture into these topics it is without benefit of the considerable finesse now achieved in the more social of the social sciences.[22]

Perhaps because of the same bias towards individual cognition, when risk analysis is applied to institutions it is weak in its treatment of something called 'the human factor'. On the one hand, everyone agrees that the human factor is central. On the other, it is thought difficult to assess. This may be to do with its being defined as the point at which the reliability of a machine is at the mercy of the erratic emotional life of the operator, in other words, a completely inadequate concept of the human factor. For the psychologist the human factor is an individual person. For an anthropologist the human factor would mean the general structure of authority in the institution. It is not difficult to assess what this is like; there are symptoms, clues, lines of communication, incentives and sanctions, all of which can be investigated quite systematically with bearing on the perception of risk. Institutions could be graded quite objectively as safety-ensuring systems. Charles Perrow's analysis of 'normal accidents' is a step in this direction.[23] But he did not focus on the 'human factor', either at the individual level, or at the level of institutional authority. He concentrated on an industrial typology. Two institutions in the same industry, handling the same materials, dealing in the same markets, can have quite different blaming patterns, for example, two universities, two publishers, two boatyards, two docks. Although sociological research on organizations is highly sophisticated, it is not used to illuminate the concerns of risk analysts, again because of their way of protecting their objectivity.

Anthropologists would generally agree that dangers to the body, dangers to children, dangers to nature are available as so many weapons to use in the struggle for ideological domination. There is nothing at all new about that. It underlies Michel Foucault's critical analysis of the 'discourse' which lays its disciplines on the body. It would be strangely innocent nowadays to imagine a society in which the discourse on risk is not politicized. Such a society would have to be lacking free debate about values. It would have to be without a forum for generating a shared ideology. In such a society the isolated members would themselves fulfil the ideal of the human person figured in the psychological theory of risk perception. Mercifully, that person is quite unreal.

When he brackets off culture from his work, the well-intentioned risk analyst has tied his own hands. He wants to be free of bias, he would rather pretend that bias is not important than sully himself by trying to categorize kinds of bias. Claiming that the standardized incidence of blame has got nothing to do with perceiving danger, he has no incentive to overcome his own bias, and no conceptual tools. Thus he has exposed his work to the full blast of local bias. Wishing not to be accused of racism, wishing not to imply cultural superiority, or political right or left-wingedness, he innocently asserts the hegemony of his own culture. But this is not the time for innocence. His method assumes that all humans have the same responses and preferences that are enshrined in the utilitarian philosophy. Instead of objectivity, we find ideological entrenchment. Warm-blooded, passionate, inherently social beings though we think we are, humans are presented in this context as hedonic calculators calmly seeking to pursue private interests. We are said to be risk-aversive, but, alas, so inefficient in handling information that we are unintentional risk-takers; basically we are fools. The charge of irrationality has come home to roost. Personally I doubt that we need to be explained to ourselves by professional risk psychologists. I do not doubt that danger is with us, and very real, but for heaven's sake, how could we have survived on this planet if our thinking is so inherently flawed? 'Purity' and 'danger' are condensed arguments passionately flung against opponents in every dialogue that every community has about its own constitution.

It appears that in Japanese there are words for danger, damage, harm, also the full vocabulary for probability analysis, but no word for risk. So we do well to ask why the word risk has come to its recent prominence and why the concept allows a new articulation of ideas. It is not a new word, of course; it has its origins in gambling theory and the mathematics of probability, but it certainly has acquired new uses.[24] A member of my family recently went for a test to the maternity clinic and discovered that she had a one in two hundred probability of bearing a Down's Syndrome baby. The news was given on the telephone. She was offered a further test, but warned that the amniocentesis held a one in a hundred probability of damaging the foetus. Why the shift to the language of probability? In the old days the choice before her would be given by the family doctor in simple terms of relative danger. The invoking of probability is a symptom of cultural change. When she burst into tears, they told her to make up her mind quickly whether she wanted the test or not, because it was nearly five o'clock and they had to go home.

The language of danger, now turned into the language of risk, often makes a spurious claim to be scientific. But the matter is not just linguistic style. The possibility of a scientifically objective decision about exposure to danger is part of the new complex of ideas. Disputes about risk have become endemic and self-generating. Every institution is now aware of its liability to prosecution for exposing its employees to risk. In response, every institution must try to make users of its facilities liable for damage they cause. A library used to hand out a guide to the catalogues, but now it presents the new reader with a list of misdemeanours to avoid. Everything has to be spelled out. Protecting against one category of risk exposes to another. For example, preventing risks of fire or riot requires open access to the premises; but risks of stolen information call for restricted access: you can have one, or the other, but not both. Scales of vulnerability that used to turn against victims of medical malpractice are turned against the doctors themselves. The doctors, knowing that they are going to be sued if they give the wrong advice, have to practise a more cautious medicine, their manners have to be formal and distant, they watch their words, and resort to objective probabilities to explain the choices that face their patients. They must not advise in these choices, as they may be sued for the wrong advice. The scientific language of risks allows them to let the patient choose for herself.

How to explain the new concern with risk? It is partly a public backlash against the great corporations.[25] A generalized concern for fairness has started us on a new cultural phase. The political pressure is not explicitly against taking risks, but against exposing others to risks. It is a generous political mood, generous to the private person, harsh to the large conglomerate. When we ask why risk has become central to our behaviour the answer has something to do with our moving into a global society, as Ernest Gellner explains.[26] Interested in the rise of nationalism he focuses on how industrialization draws members of small local communities into larger regional, national and international spheres. For new social relations they need new concepts, new words, new schooling and new loyalties to bring themselves up to the appropriate level of inter-community discourse. The nation emerges as a concentration of the loyalties, with new concepts responding to industrial and political pressures. To move out of the local community means defying its tyranny. The escapee is often glad to shuffle off its tedious constraints, and makes light of its old compensations. I would add that liberation from the small community also means losing the old protections. The markets suck us (willingly) out of our cosy, dull, local niches and turn us into unencumbered actors, mobile in a world system, but setting us free they leave us exposed. We feel vulnerable.

At the national level of operations, the nation has to provide new kinds of protection. At the international level, some generalized weapon of defence will be required, to fill the needs of justice and welfare. The idea of risk could have been custom-made. Its universalizing terminology, its abstractness, its power of condensation, its scientificity, its connection with objective analysis, make it perfect. Above all, its forensic uses fit the tool to the task of building a culture that supports a modern industrial society. Of the different types of blaming system that we can find in tribal society, the one we are in now is almost ready to treat every death as chargeable to someone's account, every accident as caused by someone's criminal negligence, every sickness a threatened

15

prosecution. Whose fault? is the first question. Then, what action? Which means, what damages? what compensation? what restitution? and the preventive action is to improve the coding of risk in the domain which has turned out to be inadequately covered. Under the banner of risk reduction, a new blaming system has replaced the former combination of moralistic condemning the victim and opportunistic condemning the victim's incompetence. This approximates remarkably well to the situation among so-called primitives where the idea of a natural death is hardly entertained. In the early half of this century, as we have seen, this was taken to be a failure to apprehend the stochastic nature of events, but now we can see how peculiar was the idea of natural death, and appreciate that its rejection was not due to a failure of intellectual power but to a form of moral concern.

It is exciting to live in an adversarial culture, politics suddenly becomes the talk of everyone. It is challenging; indeed, continual contestation makes it a sight too challenging half the time. When closure on the boundaries turns the community in on itself, we find ourselves in a conspiracy-minded, self-destructive atmosphere. The mood is generous, with painful aspects. Resort to the law in itself engenders mistrust. We have to get used to these anxieties, this mathematics of probability intruding into our intimate concerns, this bogus objectivity, this coding of risks in our present culture. If anyone ever thought that the complex coding of taboos was more restrictive, the work of the modern safety officer should give them pause.

Of the possible types, it might be nicer if we could hope to move out of both the adversarial patterns of blame allocation and the moralistic one, into the pattern where no one gets blamed at all. The kind of plateau we might hope to reach would be that one already inhabited by the Sherpas of Nepal in whose villages every member exerts conscious pressure on the others to compose their quarrels peacefully.[27] They try to reduce their rivalries. They have strong, informal, procedures for reconciliation. If these fail, one of the disputants will leave the village; it is not disastrous for him; he can probably go and work for a cousin who owns a big tourist hotel, so there is no drama of scapegoating or stripping the deviant of citizenship. We need to know more about the conditions for these delightful no-fault cultures. I would like to persuade enthographers to be more concerned with an agenda to explain how blaming is controlled in terms that we can apply to our own predicament. If only we could believe in capricious demons and do exorcisms it might be easier.

Instead of looking to the small and exotic examples for explaining us to ourselves, this time it is worth facing the other way, and using our own case to understand how the foreign one works. Guido Calabresi's path-breaking book on the law of accidents[28] starts with the view that the most dramatic reform of accident law would be to abolish it altogether.[29] He sees the main problem as how to compensate victims adequately and inexpensively. Laying the cost on the party at fault is expensive administratively and in litigation, and in spite of its high cost it produces too little compensation to rehabilitate victims. No-fault road accident insurance has now been introduced and successfully applied in certain states and in some other countries. We have now got a no-fault divorce law. No-fault medical insurance is being discussed. As between justice and mercy, it seems that laying blame accurately is much less important for maintaining public safety than the generous treatment of the victim. Paradoxically, it is cheaper on the collective purse to be generous to victims than to bear with the long drawn out legal feuds and other hidden costs that we are getting to recognize in our new-found litigiousness.

Turning back then, to Sherpas and other peoples who, without advanced technology or benefit of science, have nevertheless achieved a no-fault culture, the same solution seems to apply. They irrigate their social system with a lavish flow of gifts. This can be seen as a kind of social insurance. They are taxing themselves as a collectivity to ensure that no one is neglected, and that victims of accidents are not impoverished or discriminated against. Forgiveness would then be easier to preach, and blame easier to check. It would seem that a no-fault culture is only possible on a sound insurance basis.

According to cultural theory, there are four types of culture which can be easily distinguished, based upon four kinds of organization structures, whose systematic identification would satisfy the most devoted love of objectivity. No need to say now what these types are, and how they differ in generating different patterns of blame allocation.[30] Colleagues are researching these issues and developing this frame of reference for various problems.[31] All that needs to be done today is to list some features of risk perception that obviously need to be studied in the perspective of cultural comparison.

For example, risk depends on time-span. Our understanding of the time-span depends to some extent on features of the social structure. Economists are aware that the organization of the firm affects perception of the long term. Individuals have a much shorter term to their expectations than firms.[32] Does living in an organization that has a long view of the long run affect the private decisions of its members? It could be important to risk studies to know. There are a number of basic methodological questions. For example, when a subject is given a questionnaire on risk, how much of his preconceptions about the world will be brought into the experimental booth with him? How realistic is it to suppose that he can leave the framework of his normal thinking behind? Psychologists have broken the ground.[33] If the average person has a well-justified expectation that he himself is not a jack-pot winner, is he not likely to bring this experience of randomness into his reading of the puzzles that the psychologist asks him to answer?[34] These are problems inherent in the focus on individual cognition.

For example, the control of rumour is central to risk perception. Going back to the 1940s again, the young Theodore Caplow[35] when he was in the army in the Second World War did research on different regimental structures considered as vehicles of information. In some regiments rumours snowballed wildly, and even disastrously. Others always knew accurately what was going to happen. The latter had a clear internal structure, ranked and bounded, with one or two persons who were unofficially treated as accredited go-betweens with the outside. In these regiments there was prestige to be had for passing on valid information, and loss of regard for one who passed on deceiving news. Thus each person was spontaneously grooming himself to be a sensitive censor of wrong rumours. From the informal, spontaneous screening, practical criteria of acceptability were worked out. For any rumour, the first thing to know was its source. Was it a creditable authority? Second, every bare piece of news needed two circumstantial items to give it context: the reliable rumour was tripartite. By these means the men of this regiment always knew before the commanding officer whether they were going to go home for Christmas, whether the enemy were planning an attack, whether the General's scheduled visit had been postponed.

It is very much in the spirit of cultural theory to treat the institutions themselves as the monitors which determine what is going to count as information. Along these lines cultural theory can say a lot that is useful about the control of knowledge, the emergence of consensus and the development of expectations. Those of us who work in this field have varied interests and different agendas. Of course we do not agree on everything. Personally I am interested in cognitive theory. My own idea of the psyche is of an intelligence that is primarily social. The social preoccupations of the person, infant or adult, would be like control gates through which all information has to pass. Blaming is a way of manning the gates through which all information has to pass. Blaming is a way of manning the gates and at the same time of arming the guard. News that is going to be accepted as true information has to be wearing a badge of loyalty to the particular political regime which the person supports; the rest is suspect, deliberately censored or unconsciously ignored. From this standpoint, the proper way to organize a programme of studying risk is to start with studying institutional design.

# NOTES

1 This lecture was delivered at the London School of Economics Seminar on Risk, convened by Professor Christopher Hood, 21 February 1991. I wish to acknowledge a very helpful and informative discussion with Dr Huggins, the Director of Administrative Services in University College London. The first part has been translated as the introduction to a new Spanish edition of *Purity and Danger*.
2 Mary Douglas, *Purity and Danger, An Analysis of Conceptions of Pollution and Taboo* (Routledge & Kegan Paul, 1966).
3 Lucien Lévy-Bruhl, *How Natives Think* (translated from 1910, *Les Fonctions Mentales dans les Sociétés Inférieures*) (Princeton University Press, 1985).
4 M. Douglas and A. Wildavsky, *Risk and Culture* (California University Press, 1982).
5 Mary Douglas, 'Pollution', *International Encyclopedia of the Social Sciences* (1968).
6 Mary Douglas, *Edward Evans-Pritchard* (Fontana Collins, 1980).
7 E. Evans-Pritchard, *Witchcraft, Oracles and Magic among the Azande* (Clarendon Press, 1937).
8 Mary Douglas, *Natural Symbols, Explorations in Cosmology* (Pantheon, Penguin, 1970).
9 Mary Douglas and Marcel Calvez, (1990) 'The Self as Risk Taker: A Cultural Theory of Contagion in Relation to AIDS', *The Sociological Review* 38(3): 445–66.

10 E. Durkheim, *De la Division du Travail Social* (Presses Universitaries de France, 1893), pp. 74–6.

11 Mary Douglas, *How Institutions Think* (Syracuse University Press, 1987).

12 Michael Thompson, 'The Problem of the Centre: An Autonomous Cosmology', in Mary Douglas (ed.) *Essays in the Sociology of Perception* (Routledge & Kegan Paul, 1982), pp. 302–28.

13 Michael Thompson and Michiel Schwartz, *Divided we Stand* (Harvester Press, 1990).

14 Else Frenkel Brunswick, (1949) 'Intolerance of Ambiguity as an Emotional and Perceptual Personality Variable', *Journal of Personality* 18:108–43.

15 Mary Douglas, *How Institutions Think* (Syracuse University Press, 1987).

16 Mary Douglas and B.C. Isherwood, *The World of Goods* (Basic Books, 1979).

17 Mary Douglas and Aaron Wildavsky, *Risk and Culture* (California University Press, 1982).

18 Michael Thompson and Aaron Wildavsky, 'A Proposal to Create a Cultural Theory of Risk', in Howard Kunreuther and Eryl V. Ley (eds), *The Risk Analysis Controversy: An Institutional Perspective* (Springer-Verlag, 1982), pp. 146–61. Michael Thompson, 'Post-script: A Cultural Basis for Comparison', in Howard Kunreuther and Joanne Linnerooth (eds), *Risk Analysis and Decision Processes: The Siting of Liquefied Energy Gas Facilities in Four Countries* (Springer-Verlag, 1983).

19 Mary Douglas, *Risk Acceptability According to the Social Sciences* (Russell Sage/Routledge, 1986).

20 Howard Kunreuther (ed.), *Disaster Insurance Protection, Public Policy Lessons* (Wiley-Interscience, 1978).

21 John Adams, *Risk and Freedom, The Record of Road Safety Regulation* (Transport Publishing Projects, 1985).

22 Mary Douglas, 'Introduction' to the Italian edition of *Risk Acceptability According to the Social Sciences, Come Percepiamo il Pericolo* (Feltrinelli, 1986).

23 Charles Perrow, *Normal Accidents: Living with High-Risk Technologies* (Basic Books, 1984).

24 Mary Douglas, (1990) 'Risk as a Forensic Resource', *Daedalus* 119(4), pp. 1–16 (Fall).

25 James Coleman, *The Asymmetrical Society* (Syracuse University Press, 1982).

26 Ernest Gellner, *Nations and Nationalism* (Blackwell, 1984), pp. 37–8.

27 C. von Furer-Haimendorf, *The Sherpas of Nepal* (John Murray, 1964), *Himalayan Tribe: From Cattle to Cash* (University of California Press, 1980).

28 Guido Calabresi, *The Costs of Accidents: A Legal and Economic Analysis* (Yale University Press, 1970).

29 Calabresi: 6.

30 A good bibliography as well as a sophisticated introduction to the

subject is given in Michael Thompson and Aaron Wildavsky, *Cultural Theory* (Westview Press, California, 1990).

31 Anyone interested in applying it to organization theory could benefit from the articles by David Bloor in *Essays in the Sociology of Perception*, edited by Mary Douglas (Routledge & Kegan Paul, 1982). For a fieldwork model, see J. Gross and S. Rayner *Measuring Culture: A Paradigm for the Analysis of Social Organisation*, Columbia University Press, 1985). Jonathan Gross, Columbia University Maths and Statistics Dept. has been doing pioneering work, as yet unpublished, on applications to artificial intelligence and to electronic-mail communities.

32 Lola Lopes, (1981) 'Notes, Comments, and New Findings: Decision-making in the Short Run', *Journal of Experimental Psychology* 7: 377–85.

33 Ward, Edwards, (1953) 'Probability Preferences in Gambling', *American Journal of Psychology* 66: 349–64, and (1954) 'The Theory of Decision-Making', *Psychological Bulletin* 51:380–417.

34 Lola Lopes, (1982) 'Doing the Impossible: A Note on Induction and the Experience of Randomness', *Journal of Experimental Psychology* 8: 626–36.

35 Theodore Caplow, (1947) 'Rumors in War', *Social Forces* 25.

# 2

# RISK AND JUSTICE

## FROM 'CHANCE' TO 'DANGER'

The word *risk* has acquired new prominence. One popular explanation is that risks from technology have greatly increased. They
have indeed, in all the industrial world. But some other risks
have decreased, at least if the figures for mortality and morbidity
mean anything. So perhaps what needs to be explained is the
greater political awareness of technology in America, greater
awareness than in France,[1] and presumably greater than in Russia
before Chernobyl. Some would explain the new use of the
vocabulary of risk in American politics by the revival of laissez-
faire liberal economics. Theodore Lowi has shown how the nineteenth-century idea of the merits of individual risk-taking have
been reintroduced into American politics.[2] Praise of risk-taking
invokes the virtues of frontier morality to interrupt the long,
slow move to establish collective responsibility for accidents.
However, this ideological change itself needs to be explained.
American political history does not account for the market ideology renascent in Britain, and in China, and more recently in
Russia and Eastern Europe. The question is why a changed political debate goes across national boundaries, couched in terms of
risk. The answer here suggested is that a culture needs a common
forensic vocabulary with which to hold persons accountable and
further that *risk* is a word that admirably serves the forensic needs
of the new global culture.

The object of this essay is to situate the notion of risk by
comparing its current usage with similar concepts in other times
and places. In becoming a central cultural construct in America,
the word has changed its meaning. It has entered politics and in

doing so has weakened its old connection with technical calculations of probability. In the nineteenth century, when the theory of risk-taking became important in economics, humans were thought to be risk averse, because they were supposed to be making their choices according to the hedonic calculus. The owner of a firm needed a special profit incentive for risk-taking or he would not invest. Going further back, in the eighteenth century the analysis of risk had important uses in marine insurance. The chances of a ship coming safely home and making the fortune of its owner were set against the chances of its being lost at sea, bringing ruin. The idea of risk in itself was neutral; it took account of the probability of losses and gains. Going further back still, the concept originally emerged in the seventeenth century in the context of gambling. For this purpose a specialized mathematical analysis of chances was developed. *Risk* then meant the probability of an event occurring, combined with the magnitude of the losses or gains that would be entailed. Since the seventeenth century the analysis of probabilities has become the basis of scientific knowledge, transforming the nature of evidence, of knowledge, of authority, and of logic.[3] Any process or any activity has its probabilities of success or failure. The calculation of risk is deeply entrenched in science and manufacturing and as a theoretical base for decision-making. Clearly, probability theory has provided a modern way of thinking.

According to Ernest Gellner, the course of transition to modern industrial society imposes cultural homogeneity 'by objective, inescapable imperative':

> Culture is no longer merely the adornment, confirmation and legitimation of a social order which was also sustained by harsher and coercive constraints; culture is now the necessary shared medium, the lifeblood or perhaps the minimal shared atmosphere, within which alone the members of the society can breathe and survive and produce. For a given society it must be one in which they can *all* breathe and speak and produce; so it must be the same *culture* . . . it can no longer be a diversified, locality-tied, illiterate little culture or tradition.[4]

On this line of argument the risk concept would have come to the fore in politics because probabilistic thinking is pervasive in industry, modern science, and philosophy. Risk would have become the idiom of politics as part of the homogenizing process of moving to a new world level of interaction. However, the risk that is a central concept for our policy debates has not got much to do with probability calculations. The original connection is only indicated by arm-waving in the direction of possible science: the word *risk* now means danger; *high risk* means a lot of danger.

In this essay Gellner writes particularly about the role of education and shared culture as part of the necessary infrastructure of nationalism. He does not say how the 'inescapable imperative' imposes its commands, or where it finds its authority: the homogenizing process results in the production of key words which cover agreed concepts. But why should this process prise risk away from its original meaning to become one of the key words?

The answer is that the fulcrum of change is a debate about accountability that is carried out incessantly in any community. This dialogue, the cultural process itself, is a contest to muster support for one kind of action rather than another. Decisions to invest in more technology, or less, are the result of the cultural dialogue. Decisions to invade, to refuse immigration, to license, to withhold consent, all these responses to claims need support from institutions of law and justice. The cultural dialogue is therefore best studied in its forensic moments. The concept of risk emerges as a key idea for modern times because of its uses as a forensic resource.

To perform well in a new culture, a word must have a meaning consistent with the political claims in vogue. When the direction of change is the shift from little local communities to a larger world community, the key words need to justify leaving the old constraints and commitments. The new sense of the word *risk* works because it can be strongly biased toward emancipation. The context of a shared commitment to emancipation bends its meaning to refer only to danger. Whereas originally a high risk meant a game in which a throw of the die had a strong probability of bringing great pain or great loss, now *risk* refers only to negative outcomes. The word has been pre-empted to mean bad risks. The promise of good things in contemporary political discourse is couched in other terms. The language of risk is reserved as a specialized lexical register for political talk about the undesirable outcomes. Risk is invoked for a modern-style riposte against abuse of power. The charge of causing risk is a stick to beat authority, to make lazy bureaucrats sit up, to exact restitution for victims. For those purposes *danger* would once have been the right word, but plain *danger* does not have the aura of science or afford the pretension of a possible precise calculation.

## SINS AND TABOOS

All historical cultures are in transition. Cultural stability is short-lived, homogeneity achieved with difficulty and always about to dissolve. Staying within his own culture, a person is apt to see no culturally standardized forms around him: transgression against the norm is more visible than conformity. The inside experience of culture is an experience of choice and decision, scrutinized and judged by neighbours and press. The local view obscures regularities, but as soon as the local moves abroad, he is forcibly struck by the standardized behaviour of foreigners. The innocent view of culture is that we don't have it at home; it is only abroad that people are culturally hide-bound. A special effort of sophistication is necessary to see our own culture. We normally operate within its unnoticed intellectual confines as we ourselves intervene passionately in the dialogue about justice and what the world is likely to do to people if they disregard its real conditions. One way to overcome culture-blindness is to be attentive to the way that claims of authority and solidarity are being treated. In the regular ongoing cultural debate about justice and the world, some idea of danger is usually invoked. The debate sways between pressures for emancipation from the old institutional constraints and pressures to sustain the institutions in which authority and solidarity reside. The claims of justice and danger are rhetorical resources for all parties. On this fulcrum concepts of liability and tort are continuously at stake, always in process of revision. In this respect moderns should not think themselves different from anyone else. They are inescapably in a cultural debate and pressuring one another to cultural conformity.

Most little local cultures develop some common term that runs across the gamut of social life to moralize and politicize dangers. In the preindustrial West, Christianity used the word *sin*. The fact that a word like *sin* would be commonly understood is a sign of the cultural homogeneity achieved. A major sin would be expected to unleash dangers on the community at large, or to afflict the sinner's nearest and dearest. Before the bad event the sinner on the brink of transgression could be reminded of his responsibilities and checked in time; when the bad event happened, it would be traced back to the known sin. Before Christianity, the Bible is full of such interpretations: the defeats of the Israelites by foreign armies, destruction by earthquake, plague, and drought, were attributed to God's anger for sins. The public discourse on sin's dangers mobilized a moral community. This would seem to be a far cry from the modern, sanitized discourse of risk.

Taboos and sins belong to the discourse of religious faith. Because it promotes the opening of closed communities and the free movement of individuals, industrialization also promotes religious scepticism as part of that same cultural homogenizing process. The two cultural contexts for risk and sin would seem to be quite incompatible. If Western industrial democracy were ever to build a homogeneous culture using a uniform vocabulary for moralizing and politicizing the dangers around, it could not use the vocabulary of religion. The neutral vocabulary of risk is all we have for making a bridge between the known facts of existence and the construction of a moral community. But this is why the public discourse about modern risks has fallen into an antique mode. Risk, danger, and sin are used around the world to legitimate policy or to discredit it, to protect individuals from predatory institutions or to protect institutions from predatory individuals. Indeed, risk provides secular terms for rewriting scripture: not the sins of the fathers, but the risks unleashed by the fathers are visited on the heads of their children, even to the *nth* generation.

Risk is certainly not the same as sin or taboo. The differences are not quite what they would seem at first sight. From our modern, sceptical, secular standpoint we have the illusion that taboos and sins work backwards: first the disaster, then the explanation of its cause in an earlier transgression. By contrast, risk seems to look forward: it is used to assess the dangers ahead. This is not a real difference between the discourses about risk and sin. The observer's standpoint deceives. Looking from a secular perspective at sin and taboo, we draw upon our own knowledge about the lack of connection between moral misdeeds and the weather or the spread of disease. The connection the religions used to make between the sins and the disasters is given to them along with the rest of their construction of nature. The model of how the world works is in continuous production and sins work forward just as well as risks. The very name of the sin is often a prophecy, a prediction of trouble. So for the people living together first comes the temptation to sin, and then the thought of future retribution, then warnings from friends and relations, attacks from enemies, and possibly a return to the path of righteousness before the damage is done. The big difference is not in the predictive uses of risk, but in its forensic functions.

As a community reaches for cultural homogeneity, it begins to signpost the major moments of choice with dangers. The signs say that certain kinds of behaviour are very dangerous. That means that the community has reached some (probably temporary and fragile) consensus in condemning the behaviour. Ready examples would be blasphemy, perjury, treason, sedition, disrespect to elders. A climate of disapproval grounds the belief that certain deeds are dangerous. The foreigners' gullibility for taboo which we find strange arises where information about causes is least co-ordinated. Without professional institutions to narrow enquiry and sustain it on empirical tracks, the forensic uses of disaster triumph. We have similar gullibility for forensic explanations on the outlying fringes of the professional world. This is why the fringes are innovative, and why so little of the innovation can get translated into establishment practice.

There is another reason for the credibility of danger in its forensic uses. Who is going to get caught? The victim is going to have done something unpopular when disaster strikes. There has to be some match between the scale of the disaster and the wickedness of the perpetrator who unleashed it. The risk warning lists a condign series of bad outcomes for the transgressor and his family and friends. If a district is thought to be politically disloyal, the chief and his supporters may lay responsibility for a local drought at the door of local treason. A woman who dies in childbirth is an example of the dangers of promiscuity. The danger itself accuses the defecting individual. There is nothing *post hoc* about a connection that is always there, working in both directions. Only when the community consensus weakens in its commitment to political loyalty, or when kinship obligations or marital fidelity weakens, does the weakness of the causal connection come to view.

Danger in the context of taboo is used in a rhetoric of accusation and retribution that ties the individual tightly into community bonds and scores on his mind the invisible fences and paths by which the community co-ordinates its life in common. By grace of their concern for these lines and boundaries they can share their territory and muster resources to protect it. The modern risk concept, parsed now as danger, is invoked to protect individuals against encroachments of others. It is part of the system of thought that upholds the type of individualist culture which sustains an expanding industrial system. This is why risk is such an important subject for America. The expansion has been enormous: there is some retrenchment; more expansion beckons. The dialogue about risk plays the role equivalent to taboo or sin, but the slope is tilted in the reverse direction, away from protecting the community and in favour of protecting the individual.

This does not give a fair picture of taboo: it does not work only against the individual. The taboo concept may support the popular voice against the power of government, just as well as the risk concept. So long as there is a consensus that individuals need to be protected, there is usually a list of dangers cited to restrain abuse of power. It was the Israelite kings who were accused of bringing defeat, enslavement, and drought, by their dilution of the cult. The Shakespearean cycle of historical plays dealings with kingship during the Wars of the Roses draws on similar ideas about the punishment of royal oppression and arbitrariness. Nonetheless, it is still true that there is asymmetry in the usages. Being 'at risk' in modern parlance is not the equivalent but the reciprocal of being 'in sin' or 'under taboo'. To be 'at risk' is equivalent to being sinned against, being vulnerable to the events caused by others, whereas being 'in sin' means being the cause of harm. The sin/taboo rhetoric is more often used to uphold the community, vulnerable to the misbehaviour of the individual, while the risk rhetoric upholds the individual, vulnerable to the misbehaviour of the community. Edward Burger's essay ('Health as a Surrogate for the Environment')[5] describes how political actions to protect the environment have to be proposed as if they were to protect the personal health of individuals. They look like 'political actions taken under the wrong banner', but they are taken under the only banner that will rally support: protection of the individual. The new dialogue about risks normally does not protect the collective good, and the old dialogue about sins normally did. Burger's essay suggests why France and Russia and England have been less politically alert to risks from technology: it is not directly connected with technology or with danger, but rather implies that America has gone farther down the path of cultural individualism, and so can make more use of the forensic potential of the idea of risk.

## RISK AND REALITY

Note that the reality of the dangers is not at issue. The dangers are only too horribly real, in both cases, modern and pre-modern. This argument is not about the reality of the dangers, but about how they are politicized. This point cannot be emphasized too much. It is astonishing how many intelligent reviewers of *Risk and Culture*,[6] even anthropologists, fell into the trap of thinking that the argument cast doubt on the reality of the dangers.[7] In the pre-industrial world life expectancy is short, often not more than 48 years; mortality rates are high for everyone, but infant deaths may be over 25 per cent. Death of women in childbirth is very high. Starvation, blight, and famine are perennial threats. It is a bad joke to take this analysis as hinting that the dangers are imaginary. The risks in the industrial world are equally real. The cross-cultural argument would not work if the dangers were fictive. The culturally innocent debate would not work if the dangers were not real. The debate always links some real danger and some disapproved behaviour, coding the danger in terms of a threat to valued institutions. For us the valued institution is the liberty of the individual. If heavy taboos hold a woman to her marriage, you will find that the marriage is not a simple partnership of a man and a woman, but a complex series of alliances, the central institution governing processes of production and reproduction. If sedition is thought to unleash climatic disorders, then you can be sure that political solidarity is both precarious and desired.

Standing outside their community as we do, it is easy to see that dangers (real dangers) are being used to give automatic, self-validating legitimacy to established law and order. We see their punitive or deterrent function. But that is only half of what is happening. Those who fear the taboos see dangers and their connection with morality as part of how the world works. If they shake their heads and say of a woman who has died in childbirth that she got what was coming to her, it is because adultery is connected indefeasibly with reproductive disorders as fire is with burning. Taboo works because a community of believers has developed a consensus on the kinds of solidarity that will help them to cope collectively with their environment of disease, accident, and war. They deal with their risks by mustering solidarity, invoking danger to maintain difference. It may be that solidarity is more of a problem for them,[8] or it may be that defection and loss of solidarity affect us less. This would explain why it is so difficult to see ourselves in the same perspective: the sin/taboo discourse is aimed at conserving solidarity, while the risk discourse aims to disperse it and to dissolve distinctions.

Within the cultural debate about risk and justice opponents seek to inculpate the other side and exonerate their own supporters from blame. *Risk* is unequivocally used to mean danger from future damage, caused by the opponents. How much risk is a matter for the experts, but on both sides of the debate it has to be taken for granted that the matter is ascertainable. Anyone who insists that there is a high degree of uncertainty is taken to be opting out of accountability.

## THE INNOCENT MODEL

The innocent model of risk works well when disputants are agreed on the kind of accountability they want to enforce in their community. Questions of fact will suffice to guide on questions of moral preference when goals are not in dispute. Risk analysis can tell you to very fine degrees the probability of a particular event happening, with a one in a million chance, one in a thousand, one in a hundred, and so on. Similar analysis can tell you the costs of averting the event, the costs of insuring against it, the costs of compensating for it, or even the scale of benefits that the event would engender. All of this information is necessary if the parties agree on community goals; none of it will reconcile to a decision that one party fundamentally disapproves.

Consensus does not depend on the facts being recognized. And consensus among a group of scientists does not guarantee consensus among the public. The profession of psychologists which has grown up to study risk perception takes the culturally innocent approach by treating political dissension as intellectual disagreement. Aiming to disregard the contests over power which give rise to differences of opinion about risks, the profession neglects the central issue. It seeks to bring to the assessment of public perceptions the same degree of objectivity aimed at in risk analysis itself, and by similar methods. Unfortunately, the effort is skewed by the culturally innocent assumption that cultural bias is irrelevant for us at home, that culture is something that starts with the Wogs, abroad.

Using the innocent model of risk perception generally leads to the conclusion that there should be more education of the misguided public. But in a democracy education is not expected to change political commitments. It is proper for professionals operating within their own culture to find that the public needs to be better instructed in particular kinds of information, sexually transmitted diseases, and risks to health. It would obviously be helpful for policy on risk if the public were better instructed in many subjects. (For instance, it would be easier to discuss energy problems if many people did not believe that acid rain is caused by nuclear power stations.) But it is most unlikely that better communication and more education would reconcile differences of opinion on risks.

A risk is not only the probability of an event but also the probable magnitude of its outcome, and everything depends on the value that is set on the outcome. The evaluation is a political, aesthetic, and moral matter. In practical life private decisions about risk are taken by comparing many risks, and their probable good and bad outcomes. No risk item will normally be considered in isolation. Nor does intellectual activity happen in isolation. As Aaron Wildavsky and Karl Dake find in their essay quoted above, political bias is the strongest predictor of attitudes towards risk. Essentially, a theoretical framework is needed to transcend the culture in which the risks are being debated.

Cultural theory starts by assuming that a culture is a system of persons holding one another mutually accountable. A person tries to live at some level of being held accountable which is bearable and which matches the level at which that person wants to hold others accountable. From this angle, culture is fraught with the political implications of mutual accountability. Instead of imagining the isolated individual testing every piece of news without bias or moral commitment, the person is assumed to be sifting possible information through a collectively constructed censor set to a given standard of accountability. It is as if a kind of constitutional scanning device inside the person's head were busy testing incoming news. The criterion for assimilated knowledge or rejecting mere noise is whether the new idea or fact will reinforce the subject's preferred political scheme. On this assumption it is futile to study risk perception without systematically taking the cultural bias into account. The subjects of psychological enquiry take into the experimental booth with them an idea about what constitutes a long term, a sense of whether the respondent will be there to enjoy a long term, and a practical experience of long and short odds in everyday life. It would be very feasible to develop questionnaires that sorted experimental subjects according to their cultural bias before embarking on their response to probabilities of loss.

## CULTURE AND KNOWLEDGE

Several important essays in the volume in which this article first appeared (*Daedalus* 119, 4, Fall 1990) indicate that knowledge is falling apart. Alternative knowledge in medicine and law has successfully jostled for a place beside establishment knowledge. No one offers us certainty, even in science. When we lived in a hierarchical culture, we used to think that either a thing was known to be true or it was wrong; a fact was a fact, and as such it guaranteed deductions made from it. Now that we are committed to an individualist culture, the competition is on; knowledge has to be defended at every point; the open society guarantees nothing. Each type of culture is based on a distinctive attitude toward knowledge. Hierarchy, both as a system of governance and a type of culture, assumes that the world is up to a point knowable, and that itself, the hierarchy is organized according to the principles which run the universe. Consequently, the consensus that upholds the political system upholds the authority of facts. Its self-protective political effort goes into protecting the system of knowledge with which it is identified. Confidence in its old knowledge is its hallmark. Individualism as a type of culture pays rewards to new knowledge. Individualism is not a formal system of governance so much as a competitive market system; even for ideas and facts its controlling principles are embedded in market exchange; characteristically the community arbitrates what is permissible through price. New knowledge must perforce discredit old knowledge. Knowing very well why we want new knowledge, we should not be surprised at the uncertainty that is generated.

As Theodore Lowi has outlined, competitive market individualism needs a political base to assure its basic security. In the same way, the hierarchical culture needs an economic base. There cannot be a market without an accompanying political culture and there cannot be hierarchy without economic exchange. This said, the culture of individualism severely constrains how and what the government can do and the culture of hierarchy severely constrains the market. Though they must coexist, the balance is so different in each case that each requires a different world-view to sustain it. The homogenizing educational process that Gellner describes as the infrastructure of nationalism is also the necessary infrastructure of cultural bias, but the effective locus of transformation is the law court, not the schoolroom.

Appealing to degrees of risk assessed by accredited experts, is appealing to an external arbiter, an independent, objective judge of the rights and wrongs of the case. Normally the appeal to professional experts to settle questions of accountability works when their methods and their results are backed by authority. There has to be a Solomon to judge; the evidence does not provide the judgment by itself. In the present circumstances the appeal to science is made because of the absence of respect for any adjudicator. Solomon's role is not acceptable. The very idea that there could be a technical solution to a disagreement about goals and purposes shows that political reconciliation is rejected. The predictable consequence of using science in politics is that both sides consult their own scientific experts. Peter Huber describes how fringe calls to fringe: peripheral movements take technical advice from peripheral science and force a split between centre and frontier.[9] His own vivid warning that frontier science is barren is a form of modified discredit for science itself. When science is used to arbitrate in these conditions, it eventually loses its independent status, and like other high priests who mix politics with ritual, finally disqualifies itself. This process has been powerfully described in Brian Wynne's book on the connection between hazardous waste and the sociology of knowledge.[10]

If the scales of cultural change are tipping toward a more pervasive individualism, it is not because it is being imposed upon us. We who are the debaters in the forum of culture bring it about because we wish it. If the foundations of knowledge have come to seem more precarious, it is because we have been quietly undermining them. In doing so we are responding to the opportunities of the global industrial system. Every small shift in the legal structure can be assessed for its preserving or dismantling the edifice of structured solidarity. Pushing toward the culture of individualism puts knowledge into the forefront of political competition, just because that culture is incompatible with either authority or structure. Whoever bewails the results should consider the alternatives. Harvey Sapolsky's depiction of the political system itself as a health hazard for Americans is wonderfully to the point, but notice that in this perspective every political system is a health hazard, one way or another, for someone or other.[11] The best way to stay cool about health and other hazards is to be self-aware about the choice between cultures.

## MINORITY RISKS

One of the major policy issues that emerges from a survey of the debates on risk is the fear that those who are already disadvantaged will suffer more. The poor who carry the brunt often carry the blame for epidemic disaster. According to Paul Slack, in the Great Plague the majority of the English well-to-do saw the incidence of plague as the sign of God's judgement directed against the sins of the poor:

> The danger of contagion was employed to justify the new social policies of sixteenth century municipalities . . . the isolation procedures taken against the plague would not have been so savage if the poor had not presented a conspicuous target which was subject to attack for other reasons. It is significant that plague regulations were most clearly and strictly formulated when the socially discriminatory disease became conspicuous.[12]

It may be a general trait of human society that fear of danger tends to strengthen the lines of division in a community. If that is so, the response to a major crisis digs more deeply the cleavages that have been there all the time. This will mean that if there is a big inequality of wealth, the poor will suffer more than if the distribution were more equitable. If there is violent xenophobia, the foreigners will be blamed and pogrommed more. Today there is concern about the political scapegoating of homosexuals.

If marginal groups and poor inhabitants of inner cities are specially at risk from sexually transmitted diseases, is there a tendency to forget about them? The answer emphatically is yes, if the culture is individualist. Since it is inherently difficult to be aware of liminal groups in a society organized under the principles of competitive individualism, it is easier to write them off as human derelicts. Hierarchy does not necessarily perform better, but it is capable of being more aware of minority interests, because it is a political system for incorporating subgroups. Each culture discriminates, but the hierarchical one does it overtly, handing out group badges of difference; the individualist one does it covertly, by ignoring the powerless. If the existence of the minority is not acknowledged, even the scale of its problems is not assessable: the figures are not there. A minority in a well-run hierarchy should find it easier to organize its own consciousness of difference. It must be harder to become a vote to be reckoned with in a system that withholds overt recognition to minority segments. For us it is hard to imagine beggars organizing their own union, but in Islamic cities in Africa that is normal practice.

David Richards says of the age-old tendency to moralize danger from AIDS that it:

> adds a patina of public-health justification to what is essentially a kind of heresy persecution of homosexuals as moral heretics to the family . . . The idea of moral plague is today a morally inexcusable failure of elementary standards of intellectual and moral responsibility.[13]

The word *today* in that sentence implies that persecution of moral deviants in the name of the dangers they spread is a primitive form of behaviour which does not belong in the modern world. Similarly, Dorothy Nelkin and Sander Gilman explain stigmatizing of deviants by an individual need to escape reality. Like Richards, they also find it old-fashioned and inappropriate today to moralize and politicize danger: 'Despite the sophisticated scientific understanding underlying conceptions of disease in the late twentieth century, we still seek explanations based on behavior, ethnicity, or social stereotypes.'[14] There is nothing old-fashioned or exclusively primitive about social stereotyping. To assert that it is anomalous in our day is sheer cultural innocence. They are objecting to culture; they are saying that it should not still be with us. In asking for the discourse on danger to unload its ancient moral freight, they are innocently asking for the community of perfect love. Are they asking us outright to stop all exclusionary behaviour, or are they asking us to try not to notice the stigma?

An individualist culture finds ways of making its disadvantaged members disappear from sight. To stop stigmatizing would be another way of making them invisible. It would only help the stigmatized if there was a welcoming community into which they could be incorporated. In default of that welcome and alleviation of wrong, removing stigma could only make the privileged members of the community feel more comfortable. It would have the effect of drawing a veil over the sorrows of aliens and the poor and the deviants. For them to be unclassified would result in their being unrecognized[15] but then their harms would remain unremedied. In a society organized by wealth, how hard it is to bring down barriers between rich and poor, to propose laws against residential zoning or to find work for the unemployed. There are real wrongs, and stigma is not the worst of them.

Stigma is interesting as a self-fulfilling prophecy. Prejudiced and exclusionary behaviour validates itself. The urban poor are housed in crime-infested districts with unpoliced subways, ill-lit streets, damp walls, and malodorous drains. They are more infectious in their bodies, more exposed to disease and mutilating accidents at work, with a shorter life expectancy. The stigma is not a false symbol of contamination: the sign is true and it is the condition of the stigmatized to be contaminating.

The underlying problem in talking about exposure to risk is still justice. Cultural analysis is a countervailing vision which warns what categories in each kind of culture are most likely to be at risk, who will be sinned against, and who will be counted as the sinner exposing the others to risk. It is true, as Charles Rosenberg says:

> Cultural values and social location have always provided the materials for self-serving constructions of epidemiological risk. The poor, the alien, the sinner have all served as convenient objects for such stigmatizing speculations.[16]

What is not true is that the same speculations are found in all cultures. In an individualist culture, the weak are going to carry the blame for what happens to them; in a hierarchy, the deviants; in a sect, aliens and also faction leaders. It behooves us therefore to try to know as much as possible about the different cultures in which the idea of risk is put to use even if it is only in order to know whether we are saying the same as everyone else.

## ACKNOWLEDGEMENT

This article first appeared in *Daedalus, Journal of the American Academy of Arts and Science* 119 (4), Fall 1990, Risk.

## NOTES

1 Denis Duclos, *La Peur et le Savoir: La Société Face à la Science, la Technique et leurs Dangers* (Paris, Editions de la Decouverte, 1989).
2 Theodore J. Lowi, 'Risks and Rights in the History of American Governments', *Risk, Daedalus* 119(4) (1990): 17–40.
3 Ian Hacking, *The Emergence of Probability, a Philosophical Study of Early Ideas about Probability, Induction and Statistical Inference* (Cambridge, Cambridge University Press, 1975).
4 Ernest Gellner, *Nations and Nationalism* (Oxford, Basil Blackwell, 1984), 37–38.
5 Edward J. Burger, Jr., 'Health as a Surrogate for the Environment', *Risk, Daedalus* 119(4) (1990): 133–54.
6 Mary Douglas and Aaron Wildavsky, *Risk and Culture* (Berkeley, University of California Press, 1982).
7 Langdon Winner, 'Pollution as Delusion', *New York Times Book Review* (August 1982): 8, 18; M. Kaprow, 'Manufacturing Danger: Fear and Pollution in Industrial Society', *American Anthropologist* 87 (1985): 357–64; Brandon Johnson and Vincent Covello, 'The Social and Cultural Construction of Risk: Essays on Risk Selection and Perception' (Netherlands: Reidel, 1987), viii: 'According to this view, risk is not an objective reality.'
8 Mary Douglas, *How Institutions Think* (Syracuse, N.Y., Syracuse University Press, 1986).
9 Peter Huber, 'Pathological Science in Court', *Risk, Daedalus* 119(4) (1990): 97–119.
10 Brian Wynne, *Risk Management and Hazardous Waste, Implementation and the Dialectics of Credibility* (Berlin, Springer, 1987).
11 Harvey M. Sapolsky, 'The Politics of Risk', *Risk, Daedalus* 119(4) (1990): 83–96.
12 Paul Slack, 'Response to Plague', *Social Research* 55 (3) (1988): 433–53.
13 David A. Richards, 'Human Rights, Public Health and the Idea of Moral Plague', *Social Research* 55 (3) (1988): 492–528.
14 Dorothy Nelkin and Sander Gilman, 'Placing Blame for Devastating Disease', *Social Research* 55 (3) (1988): 378.
15 Paul Starr, 'Social Categories and Claims in the Liberal State' in Mary Douglas and David Hull (eds), *How Classification Works* (Edinburgh, Edinburgh University Press, 1992).
16 Charles Rosenberg, 'The Definition and Control of Disease', *Social Research* 55 (3) (1988): 329.

# 3

# RISK AND DANGER

## RISK AND SOCIETY

As I write,[1] a shipment of toxic waste hailing from Canada is
being returned to its port of origin. The Port Authorities of
Liverpool have refused to handle it, although the Minister of the
Environment declares that we have facilities for disposing of it
safely. The argument is about danger, and morality. If it be
dangerous, why should English ministers be happy to make this
country the dumping ground of other nations' toxic wastes? If it
were really safe, why would the other nations want to ship it to
us? Is taking in other people's waste a fitting way for us to be
earning our living among the nations? Other shipments are said
to be on their way and other ports in England are rejecting them
in advance. This political dilemma is typical of many. A lay
person might well think that if the experts meet quietly and come
up with a technical answer, either that it is safe, or that it is not
safe, the disagreement would be speedily settled. Either the waste
can be disposed of safely, or not. But, no; the problem involves
low probabilities and high levels of uncertainty. The experts may
be able to agree on the technical questions, but not on the issue of
desirable margins of safety. On this issue of acceptability nothing
decisive can be said by experts. Here lies the first major knot of
muddles. The experts on risk do not want to talk politics lest
they become defiled with political dirt, one way or the other.
They see their professional interest in keeping clear of politics.
You will find that the dominant psychological theory of risk
perception gives little clue about how to analyse political aspects
of risk. Indeed, reading the texts on risk it is often hard to believe
that any political issues are involved. But while the risk experts

keep their hands clean, the public does not refrain from politicizing the subject.

British water supplies have recently attracted attention because of the discussions surrounding plans to privatize the water utilities. They have been declared to be at unacceptably high levels of pollution by the European Community. While those responsible are hastening to remedy the fault, on our national television channels the inevitable riposte to Europe's criticism is building up. In programme after programme the public is given a comparative survey of levels of water safety in different European countries. In the media the risk of contaminated supplies is treated like a football league table in which we are working out where the British stand – the best, middling, or the worst as far as this, that, and another pollution risk is concerned. Though the rhetoric is cast in the language of risk the political thinking is quite simplistic. Neither accuracy nor articulateness is served by using the word 'risk' in these debates. The word 'dangerous' would be accurate enough most of the time, supplemented with some derogatory epithet such as 'dirty', 'polluted', or 'unacceptable'.

The probability theorists who developed risk assessment as a purely neutral, objective tool of analysis, must find that it is much transformed as it moves into national and international politics. Though the public seems to be thinking politically in terms of comparative risks, the number-crunching does not matter; the idea of risk is transcribed simply as unacceptable danger. So 'risk' does not signify an all-round assessment of probable outcomes but becomes a stick for beating authority, often a slogan for mustering xenophobia. The Japanese have had parallel experience of the use of the word 'risk' to express international concern for the whale as an endangered species. Since there is no Japanese word for 'risk', national concern about siting of airports and nuclear installations is presumably expressed directly in terms of the moral and political concerns which 'risk' language obfuscates. The dangers are real enough, and terrifying too. Furthermore, action taken to avoid one, provokes another set of dangers. Choices between dangers are not simple and it would usually be preferable to have the choices directly presented as political questions, instead of sanitized and disguised in probability theory terms.

The political need is to see various uncertainties in the context of a whole system of probabilities. The original technical sense of 'risk' suggests that such a holistic presentation would be possible. 'Risk' is the probability of an event combined with the magnitude of the losses and gains that it will entail. However, our political discourse debases the word. From a complex attempt to reduce uncertainty it has become a decorative flourish on the word 'danger'. Without using the word 'risk' the Japanese can discourse very precisely about formal probability, technical limits of certainty, degrees of safety, and, of course, about the most primitive idea of all, danger. They obviously do not need the word 'risk' in its new political sense. It is doubtful whether Europeans or anyone else need it in that sense. When the public are told there is a 10 per cent probability of something bad happening, or 0.01 per cent probability, the formula is a poor guide to action and still poorer when the probabilities are reduced by several orders of magnitude.

To invoke very low probabilities of a particular dangerous event makes surprisingly little difference to the understanding of a choice. This is not because the public does not understand the sums, but because many other objectives which it cares about have been left out of the risk calculation.

Having done without it so far, it is unlikely that the Japanese should want to develop or adopt this word in its present uses. However, a better, more rounded and balanced conception of risk in political analysis would be useful for us all. I will argue that it is specially difficult for Europeans to make available to political debate a concept of technically sound probabilistic comparisons of good and bad outcomes. The reasons lie in the history of the theory of probability, and in the history of the industrializing process. What has gone wrong is that the public response to risk has been individualized. Public perception of risk is treated as if it were the aggregated response of millions of private individuals. Among other well-known fallacies of aggregated choice, it fails to take account of persons' interaction with one another, their advice to one another, their persuasions and intersubjective mobilizations of belief. As I will try to show below, the analysis that fails to register risk perception as a culturally standardized response misses the central part of its problem. Japan might be a good base for developing a revolution in the social sciences' use of probability. It might also be able to provoke risk perception theorists into studying risk-taking and risk-aversion in a cultural framework. There would be two far-reaching innovations in social thought that could come out of this conference.

## PERSONAL SAFETY AND PUBLIC HONOUR

Risk assessment as currently practised can account for high-risk economic decisions in terms of the expectation of a probable high gain. But it cannot account for danger-seeking political action. We can give no account of the motives of men and women of the ancient Teutonic civilization of northern Europe, nor of the regions surrounding the Mediterranean where honour is a prime motivation, nor of the Plains Indians, nor of Islamic Fundamentalist groups, nor of the PLO or the IRA terrorists who take danger into their hands, for themselves as for their victims. But the assumptions of risk assessment can give no account of deliberate political and physical risk-taking. In default of a theory they have to be entered in the same column as hang-gliding and other dangerous sports, as voluntary risk-taking, on which, like tastes, there can be no argument. In spite of evidence to the contrary, avoiding loss is written into the psychology textbooks as the normal, rational human motive. But all that this means is that the commercial, risk-averse culture has locally vanquished the risk-seeking culture, and writes off the latter as pathological or abnormal. To ignore such a large segment of the human psychology tells us more about assumptions upholding the modern industrial way of life than about human nature's risk-taking propensities.

The cultural bias in psychology ought to be corrected. At present we think about ourselves, or rather our professional psychologists think about us, in terms that are cruder and more artificially distorted and inapplicable than those which any so-called primitive culture affords for self-knowledge.[2] Without removing the bias, we cannot answer the prime question about risk: how safe is safe enough? Some cultures demand public commitment from individuals, while some expect individual self-interest to be the dominant motive; some judge their members on purity of motive, others expect nothing of the sort; some respect compromise that enables all disputants to seem to have won, others fiercely reject ambiguous solutions. The question about risk has to be: how safe is safe enough for this particular culture? Asked in that form the question focuses choice more realistically than when perception of risk is referred to an imaginary culture-free individual.

## HEROIC AND BOURGEOIS FICTION

To make the context for this, permit a digression on the idea of political and professional purity. I select three works of fiction on the theme of personal involvement in politics. Gustave Flaubert's *The Sentimental Education*, written in 1869, sets a student hero in Paris, at the time of the revolutionary turmoils of 1848. Sartre's *Les Mains Sales*, published in 1948, is a comment on the idealism of young French radical revolutionaries. Yukio Mishima's *Runaway Horses*[3] was written about the same theme of compromise and commitment as the other two novels, but with triple emphasis: the student hero lives in the turmoil of Osaka and Tokyo in the 1930s, while action in the story is deliberately plotted upon an earlier failed uprising of 1873, and the author is situated in the aftermath of the world-wide student revolts of 1968. (I apologize for the fact that as a European my interpretation of Mishima's great book must seem inevitably clumsy and even false to Japanese readers.)

All three writers deal with the theme of revolutionary ardour and political compromise. In Flaubert's story the young hero accommodates only too easily to the tarnished loyalties and venal consciences around him. The treatment is unheroic; no one has pure motives or takes personal risks and the country is eventually plunged into war. In Sartre's story the young hero vows to carry out a political assassination to prove to his fellow conspirators his perfect commitment to their common revolutionary cause. He discovers his friends' duplicity and though at the end of the story he commits the promised assassination, his reasons for doing it have changed so that he cannot regard it as an act of patriotism – but it is unscrupulously used as such by the co-conspirators who betrayed him. The treatment is cynical, but with more contained passion than Flaubert musters. For Sartre, as for Flaubert, the society is not admirable in which commitment is scorned.

Mishima's story, about the extreme of total commitment, reserves biting scorn for compromise and self-serving. The Japanese student, brilliant, articulate, and dedicated, finds himself caught in a web of contradictory obligations. In his mind the problem is very simple: Japan is in deep trouble, the Emperor is badly served, the gods are insulted, the farmers are ruined, unemployment is rife. The solution is equally simple: a loyal band must assassinate the enemies of the nation, and give themselves a glorious death by *seppuku*. Through the story successive betrayals and fallings away do not shake the hero's resolution. Then to his dismay he finds that his father has for years been a secret pensioner of the villain he has vowed to assassinate. Now he faces the dire conflict of duty, impossible to honour his vow without dishonouring his father, and so defiling himself. His dilemma is resolved when he eventually discovers that it was his own father who originally betrayed him to the police. Then he goes forth with a clear conscience to murder the man who is the cause of all Japan's pain and of his father's dishonour, thus purifying himself and his father at the same stroke. All three tales, Flaubert's, Sartre's, and Mishima's, are social commentaries which condemn the society for which risks are not worth taking.

## THE CULTURAL DIALOGUE

At the inception of any community a debate is opened about the future form of the society. This is an ongoing normative debate about values and beliefs about the world.[4] It never stops. It is not conducted at special sites, like town meetings or law courts, or parliaments, or at fixed times. Whenever anyone makes a claim against anyone else, any kind of demand on their time and resources, the response is defended in terms of values and beliefs. In the normative debate the claims of society against its members are asserted, and accepted or denied. The novels I have quoted above are not to be read as expressions of national culture, but as claims entered into the normative debate. Opposing views will certainly be found in other writings of the time.

Perhaps the clearest way to see the normative debate in action is to compare two contemporary authors expounding opposite views. Saicho Maruya's domestic comedy, *A Singular Rebellion*,[5] displays the whole theme of commitment and purity of motive (Mishima's theme), from the point of view of an elderly businessman who has fallen in love with a fashion model. Not passionate but compassionate, not clarifying or separating but ambiguating and reconciling, funny and moving, it sympathetically describes the students' revolt while commending order and compromise.

A writer of fiction can easily enter opposing claims in the same story, as James Joyce or Dylan Thomas who write both nostalgically and disparagingly about bourgeois values. Recalling this background of heroic and unheroic fiction should be enough to point my complaint against the pretensions of a risk analysis that is supposed to be a politically neutral analysis of culture-free individuals.

Since we live in a modern industrial culture we can recognize around us a number of deep cultural divisions, even within the same national boundaries. Consequently it should not be difficult for us to agree that a workable model of risk perception needs to take account of culturally distinct attitudes to authority and order. Risk analysis that only allows the cautious, risk-averse behaviour to be rational is convicted of crippling cultural bias. To correct this bias Mishima's extraordinarily powerful book should be read by anyone (and especially by risk analysts) who thinks that risk-aversive behaviour is normal and rational, and by anyone who assumes that risk-taking is a trait of individual personality and not a culturally shared attitude. And it should be read by anyone who wants to understand the culture of terrorism amidst which we have been living for some decades. Sartre, and Flaubert before him, signalled the imminent disintegration of ideals in an industrial culture which knows no national boundaries or moral constraints. Like Mishima, they questioned the possibility of remaining pure by standing forever on the sidelines.

## RISKS ARE ALWAYS POLITICAL

Risk analysis that tries to exclude moral ideas and politics from its calculations is putting professional integrity before sense. Looking for the wrong kind of purity it gets enmeshed in the impurities it seeks to avoid. The point to be made here is not that the risk analysts cannot achieve purity nor that they cannot stand forever on the side lines. They probably could, but at the cost of relevance. They are employed by corporations and governments who want to know something more than the technical calculation of probabilities. The political question is always about acceptable risk. By shunning that question, they shirk the professional task.

Furthermore, the political aspect of risk cannot be concealed any longer. This point is central to the treatment of risk by two

European writers. Ulrich Beck's *Risikogesellschaft* is an ambitious and original attempt to rewrite the whole of political science and economics in terms of risk. His idea is that this shift of focus is inevitable, that our modern industrial society has undergone changes which result in the old moral questions about the allocation of wealth being transformed into new moral questions about the allocation of risks. Like the general public, he uses the word 'risk' as danger, disregarding its origins and its technical applications and its intimate present connection with probability theory and the theory of rational choice. Risks, as Beck uses the term, are uncontrollable scientific, technical or social developments which were started long before their side-effects or long-term consequences were known. In earlier phases of the transformation to modernity consciousness was achieved and innocence lost. The 'risk society', having lost innocence about causes of misfortune, focuses with a new political intensity on the distribution of risks.[6] Beck's analysis of power, wealth and differential vulnerability to risk gives rise to profound reflections on social justice. He has brought the experts' arcane discussions of individual perception of risk full into the light of politics and into the impassioned intellectual debates on consciousness in modernity and postmodernity. His reproach to science is precisely that its pretensions to innocence are often invalid, and usually wrong-headed. Science also must admit its involvement with the world, become conscious of itself, and bring its own dealings with politics under conscious control.[7]

The second author, Denis Duclos, has provided an original treatment of the theme by comparing the institutions for dealing with technological risks in France and America.[8] A French comment on how the theme has developed in response to famous disasters in America, it is very fascinating. Duclos writes within the French sociological tradition, with special interest in the bases of knowledge. To this end he contrasts the attitude of scientists, engineers, government, industrialists, and the lay public. Again, within the French sociological tradition, he asks about the sources of collective fear, and raises the question of whether the confrontation with major industrial risk produces a sense of the 'sacred'. A very different treatment from that of Beck, it also goes straight to the political question. He sees the denunciation of technological risks as revealing two kinds of fear of technology, not primarily the fear of death and disaster, but fear of oppression by authority

45

overmasteringly empowered by new technology, and fear of transparency in social life, nothing hidden from new electronic means of scrutiny.

There will certainly be other books to follow that will further philosophize about the politicization of risks. The days of a neutral, individualistic experimental science of risk perception are numbered. But it will be a pity if it were to die out before taking the chance to develop a more effective instrument for assessing culturally standardized responses to risk.


## A CULTURAL THEORY OF RISK

The very word 'risk' could well be dropped from politics. 'Danger' would do the work it does just as well. When 'risk' enters as a concept in political debate, it becomes a menacing thing, like a flood, an earthquake, or a thrown brick. But it is not a thing, it is a way of thinking, and a highly artificial contrivance at that. Thinking probabilistically is very different from thinking in terms of proximate causes. Thomas Kuhn has compared the new forms of explanation in physics with the shift between the two causal theories described by Aristotle, the first concerned with efficient causes, and the other with final causes.[9] The former method of explanation discovers relations between parts or between parts and wholes, without specific interest in the general shape of the systems within which the effective connections are being made. That there is a connection is the interesting discovery. The latter is a mode of explanation based on features of whole systems as such. The history of science has seen several shifts, as between one discipline and another, or at one time and the next, between concern with efficient, proximate causes and concern with final causes or systems. In the social sciences, of course, both interests are well represented, with plenty of famous system builders and systems analysts. However, the beneficial possibilities of analysing perception of risk as part of a probabilistic system of social relations have not been realized.

If we want to do comparative research on risk perception there are four questions which need examination at the outset. One, but not necessarily the first, is about the bearing of the particular risk on the individual risk-perceiver's purposes, whether it is seen as integral to them, or peripheral. Another is how much the community is part of ego's purposes, integral or peripheral. How

46

to assess these crucial points is well explained in the handbook by Rayner and Gross, *Measuring Culture*.[10] A third is whether the risk is thought to affect the individual or the collective good. This depends on what kind of community it is. There is no way of proceeding with analysing risk perception without typifying kinds of communities according to the support their members give to authority, commitment, boundaries, and structure. According to the theory of culture that is being developed the analysis may use three, four, twenty, or hundreds of cultural types for comparison. As *Risk and Culture* argues, a cultural theory with only three political types can provide a very powerful explanation of attitudes to risk.[11] Each culture is designed to use dangers as a bargaining weapon, but different types of culture select different kinds of dangers for their self-maintaining purposes.

The types chosen for analysis are familiar in the traditional political thought of Europe: hierarchical, individualist, and sectarian. Return to the comparison I sketched above of the two novels, *Runaway Horses* and *A Singular Rebellion*. Anyone reading either book can recognize representatives of the different extremes of cultural types. Hierarchy, sect, and individualism are richly represented, though with difference in moral colouring, to be sure, because the authors are putting opinions into the mouths of characters whom they depict as inhabiting different cultural spheres. In the mind of the student bent on an exemplary deed of selfless heroism, the entrepreneurial businessman who is not bound by loyalty to person or country and who expects to be able to buy out any opposition to his plans is the primary villain. The tension between them is the tension in any complex social system between the individualist and the sectarian culture. Corrupt self-seekers also appear in the other novel, the comedy written from the point of view of a member of a large hierarchical business. Here the individualist is an assiduous builder of networks for private gain, but he is not a wealthy industrialist. His crime is to have tempted away the faithful, old domestic servant of the narrator to run one of his café bars, seducing her with false expectations of sexual fulfilment. Since it is second nature to novelists to deploy the cultural typology so familiar to their readers, the problem for sociology is the technical matter of finding measures of solidarity, and measures of structure in social relations. Cultural theory does this work. Consequently it is available for self-analysis. Any citizen can use it to ascertain where his own cultural preferences lie, and thus become better prepared to enter political debate.

This analysis of attitudes to risk treats the system of society as one: the community, its political behaviour, its theory of how the world is, the strengths and weaknesses of its forms of solidarity. Integrally part of the system, as one of the sources of its viability, is its public attitude to risks. So far this approach to risk perception persuades social scientists slowly and with difficulty. This is to some extent due to the preference in the social sciences for explanations based on efficient or immediate causes. Psychology produces the causes, albeit vaguely, and its theorizing stops at the individual. It has no sociological explanations. Probabilistic analyses are used in the social sciences for individual reactions within a population, but the full power of probabilistic thought has not been tried. The latter will involve seeing the community and its debate about conflicting beliefs and values as a system. When the community is presented as a world which can be described by the higher probabilities of various interactions, differences in risk perception can begin to be accounted for.

## UNCERTAINTY

Supposing such a shift to probabilistic description of whole cultures takes place, it will be for the social sciences like the invention of the printing press or alphabetic script, a so far unimaginable transformation of our thinking about human activities, which will bestow new sophistication on our demands for certainty.[12] There is no intrinsic reason why the analysis of risk perception should not engage in comparisons of culture. As I said, there are ways of measuring cultural differences and explaining them, and of making predictions on the basis of whether they are risk-averse, or risk-taking, varying according to what property or whose lives are at risk, and especially varying according to the levels of solidarity and structure maintained.

We witness some irony of timing. Probability analysis arrives at politics in the form of a word, 'risk'. The word gets its connection with probability squeezed out of it and put to the same primitive political uses as any term for 'danger'. Even if it were still representing a form of scientific analysis, it arrives just at the moment in which it cannot deliver what politics most wants of it. Politics requires from science its authority – certainty. In the 1950s, in the hopeful years after the Second World War, science was very confident. Fifty years ago its methods did seem to promise certainty. Perhaps as a result of being used to arbitrate in momentous political issues, and further as a result of trying to fill in the chinks that show up between different grounding assumptions, science now shows signs of a new mood. Superbia is gone; the mood is modest, cautious, insisting on vast areas of uncertainty. Scientists are being pressed to take the role of ultimate arbiter in political contests when there is no hope of die-hard adversaries coming to agreement. This thankless role can only embroil science and bring it into disrepute, as Brian Wynne has shown with devastating clarity in his study of the administration of industrial waste disposal.[13] The problem for science is the same as for risk theorists in general: how to avoid being used politically without refusing political responsibility.

Philosophers are now interested in risk as an applied and politically important branch of the theory of knowledge. A brilliant example is Isaac Levi's *The Enterprise of Knowledge* whose subtitle is *An Essay on Knowledge, Credal Probability, and Chance*.[14] Its appendix: 'A Brief Sermon on Assessing Accident Risks in U.S. Commercial Nuclear Power Plants' reviews the statistical arguments used in the Nuclear Regulatory Commission's report, *The Reactor Safety Study*. Levi considers quite simply that the conclusions of the report were based on inadequate data and that there had never been a proper basis for making estimates of chances of accident. Furthermore, Levi regards the construction of the argument as one 'incapable of rendering a negative verdict on the practice of evaluating risks of a serious accident in nuclear plants. . .' This is a serious criticism which Levi follows with a plea for admitting ignorance:

> The moral of the story is that we should learn to suspend judgment. . . But although we should prize precision when we can get it, we should never pretend to precision we lack; and we should ever be mindful of our ignorance even when it hurts (pp. 441–2). . . Scientists and technologists should not pretend to a knowledge they do not have because a government or public demands that they be supplied with answers to questions for which there is insufficient evidence. And the public and government should understand and

respect the limits on what they can expect of responsible scientists and engineers. They should refrain from putting unreasonable pressures on investigators to subvert their better judgment (p. 444).

While they suspend judgement on their own researches, it will not help scientists or us to allow them a politically dust-free habitation. That would involve scientists in the pretended innocence that Ulrich Beck rejects. His expectation of the new 'risk society' is that all, and especially scientists, should lose their innocence, no longer pretend to be apolitical, but instead try to possess fuller consciousness. This would mean trying to know both where the political stakes lie and also where the individual stands in relation to them. Beck exhorts rather than proposes a method for achieving this consciousness. But cultural theory is such a method.

## CONCLUSION

An open discussion on risk with Japanese scholars is challenging. This must be a uniquely privileged occasion for questioning European habits of thought in an international perspective. The above criticisms of European risk analysis are focused on the unfortunate effects of methodological individualism, which results from our particular intellectual and social history. I am led to hope that Japanese psychologists and philosophers could resolve various contradictions and anomalies in the risk debates in Europe. Our usual analysis of how people behave in face of risks is wrong, just because it abstracts a particular risk issue from the moral and political issues in which the person normally sees it embedded. We need a way of putting the isolated risk issue into the context of the larger system.

For us the concept of risk has emerged slowly from a specialized mathematical development of probability theory in gambling.[15] A concept of expectations based on patterns of frequencies has taken over from older theories of causality in all the sciences. There is an idea current among risk analysts that the ordinary lay person, the man in the street, is weak on probabilistic thinking. In Europe mechanical theories of cause and effect have given way late and with difficulty to statistical inference and formal probability theory. But though the formal principles of probability theory are a complex artifice which the lay person finds exceedingly arcane, humans have to be able to size up probabilities informally, or they would not have survived even through the paleolithic periods of archaeology. There is surely a natural, informal way of thinking probabilistically. Anyone whose livelihood has depended on understanding the weather or tides, any sailor or fisherman, is used to taking a huge number of factors into account and has rules of thumb for trying to reduce uncertainty.

Modern science first developed by a meticulous isolating of particular causes and their effects, particularly isolating them from metaphysical and moral principles. A separating, disembedding process of analysis had to go completely counter to the kind of thinking which assumed the connectedness of everything in the universe, as pairs or as opposites of everything else.[16] Many intermediate steps had to be taken to provide transferable, abstractable symbolic structures for articulating and communicating, and all had to happen long before scientific thought as we know it. The phonetic alphabet, for example, and arabic numerals, are complex notation systems which, like syllogistic reasoning, and like the patient tracing of immediate cause and effect, are methods for decomposing experience. They are powerful tools of thought because they break down the synchronous systems of relations.

When it arrived in the seventeenth century probability theory changed ideas about valid reasoning and relevant evidence by working in the other direction: not by decomposing but by constituting complex events as patterns of frequencies. Although ordinary persons undoubtedly scan frequencies and assess them in their everyday decisions, the way they think is not like causal theory before the advent of probability, nor like probability theory either. It is something different and yet an effective tool of decision-making. Cultural theory brings us somewhat nearer to understanding risk perception of lay persons by providing a systematic view of the widest range of goals that the person is seeking to achieve. Instead of isolating the risk as a technical problem we should formulate it so as to include, however crudely, its moral and political implications. Is it possible that the Japanese have a cultural advantage in probabilistic thinking? The reasons would be to do with the teaching of mathematics, with the form of literacy, and with the ancient form of society.

To start with the abacus, it is an apparently simple device

which performs complex mathematical operations. In Japan, as in Korea and other South Asian countries, every man, woman and child can learn the abacus, and in fact a large percentage go to abacus summer school. I understand that it would be controversial to claim that early familiarity with and regular use of high powered mathematical transformations would make for a special facility for thinking in terms of complex systems. I am told[17] that Professor Takeshi Hatta's research suggests, to the contrary, that proficient abacus users work like touch typists, automatically and without giving any thought to the process that they have mastered. Even so I am loath to give up the idea that the little Japanese children are in a habit of systems thinking which puts them ahead of little European children if they were asked to solve formal probability problems.

Second, writing based on ideogrammatic characters instead of on phonetic script involves a totally different method of thinking. As I only too vaguely understand it, a Chinese or Japanese character is an exemplar, rather than a symbol standing for something else. A European child becomes literate by learning to break down words into component sounds and transcribing sounds into letters and from this decomposing process then to start to recompose letters into words and words into sentences and ideas. A Japanese child learning a character, learns an exemplar, an instance of a class. A symbol carries meaning by pointing to something else other than itself, so it is intermediary between the understanding and the thing it signifies, whereas a sample is an instance of the things in the same class as itself.[18] Scientific thinking builds analogies from exemplars.[19] The process of arriving at abstraction from symbols is reductive, it sheds possible other meanings; but the intellectual process of abstracting from exemplars does not narrow down richness of meaning. On this argument, reading and writing based on ideograms would provide an intellectual discipline more hospitable to the sustaining of paradigmatic models, whole systems, rather than focusing on part-to-part or part-whole effects. Because of these two fundamental pedagogic differences I would expect that probabilistic reasoning would come less painfully to a wider group of the public in Japan than in Europe.

Third, Japan is a country whose hierarchical and heroic traditions have only recently been subjected to the challenge of the individualistic culture that goes with industrialization. Her philosophers are perhaps new to the individualist philosophy that starts and ends its moral enquiry with the good of individuals. A hierarchy is a notion of a whole, of a system which includes the good of the individual. A member of a hierarchy has an ingrained habit of referring moral issues to the whole. Solidarity usually implies hierarchical forms of thought, a symbolism of microcosmic models, a disposition of honourable rewards and dishonouring penalties that induce loyalty. This means that the older Japanese would have the experience of hierarchical solidarity as a system deeply informing their moral and political thought. Hierarchy sets communal goals in the minds of persons confronted with a major risk. In the older Japanese citizen, therefore, the perception of a risk would be, as with everyone, an informal assessment of the probability of the event occurring and an informal assessment of the probable damaging consequences, not only to the individual but to the community, and also an informal assessment of the probable benefits, both to the individual and to the community.

Dimly apprehended ideas of this kind lead me to suppose that Japanese philosophers would have a better start for the task of intellectual synthesis around the idea of political risk than European culture which has been embarked on three hundred years of effort to focus on individuals, and has ended by turning the word for 'risk' into a word for 'danger'.

## ACKNOWLEDGEMENTS

I acknowledge the suggestions of Thomas Crump, Professor of Anthropology at the Free University of Amsterdam, concerning the implications for cognitive theory of populations trained to use the abacus. I am grateful to Margret Hagemann for guidance on the German discussion of risk, and to Denis Duclos for the discussion of risk perception in France. They are not responsible for the use I have made of their work.

This paper was given at the Euralia Research Commission Conference of European and Japanese scholars on Risk in Human Activities (1989). An Italian version appears in the translation of *Risk Acceptability According to the Social Sciences, Come Percepiamo Pericolo* (Feltrinelli, 1991). I am grateful to Harry Gow for permission to print the English version.

# NOTES

1 September 1989.
2 Ruth Finnegan and Robin Horton, *Modes of Thought* (London, Faber, 1969).
3 Yukio Mishima, *Runaway Horses* (London, Secker & Warburg, 1973).
4 Mary Douglas, 'Culture and Collective Action', in Morris Freilich (ed.), *The Relevance of Culture* (New York, Bergin and Garvey, 1989).
5 Saicho Maruya, *A Singular Rebellion* (Tokyo, Kodansha, 1986).
6 Ulrich Beck, *Risikogesellschaft: Auf dem Weg in eine Andere Moderne* (Frankfurt on Maine, Suhrkamp, 1986).
7 I gratefully acknowledge the help of Margret Hagemann in discussing this author.
8 Denis Duclos, *La Peur et le Savoir: La Société Face à La Science, La Technique et Leurs Dangers* (Paris, Sciences et Société, Editions de la Decouverte, 1989).
9 T.S. Kuhn, 'The Concepts of Cause in the Development of Physics', Ch. 2 in *The Essential Tension, Selected Studies in Scientific Tradition and Change* (Chicago, University of Chicago Press, 1977).
10 Jonathan Gross and Steve Rayner, *Measuring Culture* (New York, University of Columbia Press, 1984).
11 Mary Douglas and Aaron Wildavsky, *Risk and Culture, An Essay on the Selection of Technological and Environmental Dangers* (Berkeley, California University Press, 1982).
12 Henri Atlan, *A Tort et a Raison, Intercritique de la Science et du Mythe* (Paris, Seuil, 1986).
13 Brian Wynne, *Risk Management and Hazardous Waste, Implementation and the Dialectics of Credibility* (Berlin, Springer-Verlag, 1987).
14 Isaac Levi, *The Enterprise of Knowledge, An Essay on Knowledge, Credal Probability, and Chance* (Cambridge, MA, MIT Press, 1980).
15 Ian Hacking, *The Emergence of Probability, A Philosophical Study of Early Ideas about Probability, Induction and Statistical Inference* (Cambridge, Cambridge University Press, 1975).
16 G.E.R. Lloyd, *Polarity and Analogy; Two Types of Argumentation in Early Greek Thought* (Cambridge, Cambridge University Press, 1966).
17 Thomas Crump has been kind enough to discuss this with me from his vantage point as an anthropologist working in Japan, but he is in no way responsible for my interpretation.
18 Nelson Goodman, *Languages of Art* (Cambridge, Hackett, 1976).
19 Mary Hesse, *Models and Analogies in Science* (London, Sheed & Ward, Newman History and Philosophy of Science, 1963).

# 4

# MUFFLED EARS

## INTRODUCTION

An issue in risk perception studies is whether and how individuals can perceive low probability events.[1] It is a peculiar issue which only arises because such events are recognized to be on our horizon right now – so evidently some people can perceive them. Those who do the perceiving rely on an extraordinarily advanced and arcane technology of assessment. So the question is how individuals who are not competent in that technology may come to accept warnings about such dangers and endow the warnings with credibility. The answer will be to expand the sociological context of perception. Humans are social animals and we use social as well as spatial, temporal, and bodily reference schemes. The approach I am using focuses on how physical disasters get systematically used in the micro-politics of social institutions. The processes of blame and exoneration are central to the problem.

In tribal societies there is often a lively expectation that unspeakable horrors will be triggered by low probability events or that rare individuals may wield catastrophic evil powers. So the ability to consider low probability disasters is not beyond human ken. I shall start with the alleged finding that individuals have difficulty thinking probabilistically at all. Questioning some of the charge against individuals and conceding some of it, I shall develop an anthropological line of thought which suggests that individuals always transfer the relevant part of their decision-making to the institutions in which they live.

This statement has an old-fashioned ring about it. Indeed, it is a long time since it was said by Simon and March that the organizational and social environment in which the decision maker finds himself determines what consequences he will anticipate, what ones he will not; what alternatives he will consider, what ones he will ignore. In a theory of organization, these variables cannot be treated as unexplained, independent factors, but must themselves be determined and explained by the theory.[2]

All the language in which Simon's theory of bounded rationality has been expressed is entirely sympathetic to my argument. The rational chooser's definition of a situation is not to be taken as given: the selective elements are the outcomes of psychological and sociological processes, including the chooser's own activities and the activities of others in his environment. Yet, in spite of this apparently common starting point, I will argue that questions about human perception of disaster have never yet been directly addressed to the characteristics of the social institutions which blinker and focus the individual rational agent. I therefore suggest that the major part of the enquiry about rational choice is applied to the wrong units, to individuals instead of to institutions. The missing piece in the puzzle is the way that institutions mobilize moral concern to engage their members' sustained support. None of the typologizing that I have scanned to find a link between the anthropologists' and the organization theorists' work gives systematic attention to this process. My feeble forays into this highly developed and central field of Western social thought requires some apologies. But I hope that in spite of my ineptitude, the descriptions of my search will provoke others to address themselves more effectively to the question of which kind of organization is best equipped to alert its members to low probability, high consequence risks.

## THINKING PROBABILISTICALLY

Until recently it was widely agreed among psychologists that individuals have difficulty in giving rational answers to problems. The trend that came near to calling us all irrational has been stemmed by a recent declaration that irrationality can never be demonstrated. Jonathan Cohen argues that the conditions for rationality are so flexible that by invoking the full array of assumptions from which an individual starts and the full array of motives and goals to which he subscribes, any decision (but *any* one) can be exempted from the charge of irrationality.[3] The argument is complex but essentially it expects rational thought to be exercised through two kinds of competence, one a universal pan-human competence in logical operations (avoiding contradiction and expecting coherence and consistency) and the other a culturally acquired competence in recognizing, assembling, and sorting particular elements. Cohen dubs the combination 'intuition'. Since the input from culture can never be determined, there is no way of proving any choice or decision to be irrational. Before this rather weak vindication of our rationality was declared, risk perception had already tempered its terminology and we had been hearing not that individuals are irrational, but that they are weak in probabilistic thinking.[4] This weakness may explain why we do not take reasonable precautions in the face of low probability, high consequence risks which the experts reveal to us.

But when we look at what understanding probabilism requires, it does not sound so difficult. Apparently, we only need to grasp three principles: randomness, statistical independence, and sampling variability.[5] Furthermore, when we consider any technical activity whatever, we find that any of us is capable of using all three principles. This is without regard to formal schooling: any tribe of hunters or fishers or any profession of farmers or sailors use their grasp of probabilism to assess their materials, the predicted behaviour of fish or sheep or tides or weather. They know all about random variation in the accuracy of their instruments, they disregard inferences from too small samples, and without knowing statistics they know a lot about the practical equivalent of statistical independence. If they did not, they would not be craftsmen or navigators or merchants.

Since scientists who explicitly use probability theory also fail in these tests that floor less formally trained subjects,[6] we need to look more closely at the questions in the psychology experiments. When we do so, we suspect that they all relate to a particular field of expertise, that of probability theory as such. In other words the culturally learned intuitions which guide our judgement for any of our fields of competence, teach us enough probabilistic principles but they are heavily culture bound. We are all lost when we venture beyond the scope of our culturally-given intuitions and presumably the technically competent proba-

57

bilist would be equally lost if asked to predict outside his skilled intuitions.

Though this may prove that individuals are not weak in thinking probabilistically, it leaves the general position unchanged. The issue of perceiving low probability, high consequence risks concerns inexpert perceivers. If people can only think probabilistically from a position of expert competence and if there is no way for all or any of us to become experts in weaponry or nuclear power, the problem of how we are to make a political judgement of such risks is still the same.

The dilemma arises because our Western tradition of thinking about judgement and choice leaves cultural influences out of account. The upshot of much anthropological research on cultural bias suggests that individuals do not try to make independent choices, especially about big political issues. When faced with estimating probability and credibility, they come already primed with culturally learned assumptions and weightings. One could say that they have been fabricating their prejudices as part of the work of designing their institutions. They have set up their institutions as decision processors which shut out some options and put others in favourable light. Individuals make the basic choices between joining and not joining institutions of different kinds. They then engage in continuous monitoring of the institutional machinery. The big choices reach them in the form of questions whether to reinforce authority or to subvert it. Whether to block or to enable action.

If we want to understand rational behaviour, we should examine this monitoring process. It consists of applying two kinds of tests to the institutional structure. One is the matching of promises to performance. For instance, we are promised that our jobs are safe, then someone gets fired; are we to trust the firm's guarantees of security or not? The other test is applied to the principles of justification: Is their logic strong? What are the principles of classification? Are the rules contradictory? How coherent is the whole system of rules by which the institution works? Mishaps, misfortunes, and threats and disasters provoke endless challenges and cogitation about the structure of institutional life. It is not difficult to see that this monitoring process establishes for any institution some agreed norms for acceptable and unaccepable risk over all precedents.[7] But then, the unprecedented event will never have been brought into its purview.

So the question about perceiving very low frequency events seems to be just as unanswerable, even if we take institutional factors in perception into account. However, I am going to argue, from experience as an anthropologist in central Africa, that some forms of organization are adapted to recognizing low probability dangers. My problem of exposition is to transcend the local peculiarities of the central African case, so I will turn for help to organization theory to find a general analysis of kinds of organizations; but first let me explain further the kind of lead that comes from research on perceiving danger in African societies.

## PERCEIVING DANGER

The central method of enquiry is to fasten attention on misfortunes.[8] The underlying assumption is that any major mishap in an organization sparks an internal battery of questions about responsibility. If the organization has been established long enough to have taken a particular form, the questions are not going to be random. Still less will the answers seem credible unless they reinforce the members' concerns about the form of the organization they live in. For example, if people in an organization dislike the way that top authority has been exercised, it will be credible that the responsibility for accidents be pinned at the top; in the course of being made answerable, the harshness and arbitrary weight of authority will be investigated and criticized. Or for a reverse direction of concern, if the majority of members in an organization are worried about the disruptive behaviour of their junior members and fearful of a possible challenge to traditional authority, then minor and major misfortunes will seem very plausibly to have been caused by the young Turks. The battery of enquiries following on misfortunes represents the normal exercise of individual rational thought: the focus being on institutional norms and values, everyone is acutely concerned to hear the excuses and justifications for the harm that has happened and to pass judgement. But they are not merely enquiring dispassionately. They bring to the tests of logical coherence all their culturally loaded intuitions about what the ideal organization ought to be, influenced by their memory of past investigations and precedents. Whether the institution has been developing in one direction or in another, the search for a culpable agent will be biased accordingly. This is how man-made and natural disasters become enmeshed with the micro-politics of institutions. Processes of blame-pinning or exonerating from blame strengthen the pattern of the organization and are actually an integral part of it.

To follow the argument, first purge from the mind any assumption that it is easy to set up an organization and make it endure over time; remember authority is always fragile and power always held precariously. The smaller the organization and the less the capital investment in it, the harder the conditions for stability. If we should come across an institution in which power is seen to flow smoothly through legitimate channels, instead of taking it for granted we should marvel and ask how such stability has been achieved. In such a case, watch to see how these people attribute responsibility for misfortune and how they control envy and the spread of alarm and mutual blaming.

This type of enquiry is familiar to anthropologists. Yet it is not applied to organizations in modern industrial society. In textbooks on political or economic organization, the various appeals to danger are not considered systematically as one of the regular solutions for regularly recurring problems. Historians, to be sure, cite cases of statesmen beleaguered by their local rivals who save their own skins by sounding the tocsin for foreign alarums. But they are treated as not quite honest or at least as unusual ploys, whereas I would maintain they are the normal strategy of statecraft. It is as if the Renaissance or the War of Independence or some other huge divide too obvious to name separates the modern mind from the mystic mentality of pre-moderns. But I maintain that this is a false assumption on which modern ideas of modernity are misleadingly based. The task for this essay is to reduce that apparent divide. Big questions about perception of risk can only be treated trivially in default of some theory about the deployment of threats of danger in different political regimes.

## LATENT POWERS

The kinds of enquiry into disaster will vary according to the kinds of legitimated authority being sought. Each distinctive kind of regime[9] will invoke a distinctive set of active powers in the universe to do three things, one cognitive, to explain disasters, one political, to justify allegiances, one system-maintaining, to stabilize the distinctive workings of the regime.

I will assume that a regime will only survive by the moral commitment of its members. This usage gives the word a special sense. As a first step, I need to take extreme cases so as to distinguish different types of regimes for a well-contrasted comparison. The main exercise is to examine the rhetoric of explanations, persuasions, and excuses in so far as it sustains the political regime by appeal to active principles in the universe. The comparison has to be general and abstract enough to encompass together, within the typology, regimes reported by anthropologists and those conceived by policy analysts and organization theorists.

The first example of a distinctive regime rests upon the principle of individual freedom to negotiate. That is the competitive individualist society described for certain polities in New Guinea which corresponds to the description of the market place in socioeconomic analyses.[10] If this kind of regime is to survive the interpretations of misfortune, it must uphold the individuals' freedom to contract. Explanation tends to appeal to personal resources that are attributed to a successful person. Let me class them all under the head of fetish power, using the term broadly to cover the power that a living individual may claim to use for controlling mysterious powers or agencies, whether the power be purchased, or gifted by an ally, or a charisma innate in the person's own self.

Each actor, pursuing his private ends, is busily making or breaking up coalitions: unsuccessful operations get driven down and out of the market, a few big ones emerge for a brief period of glory. Such a society continues in being only if everyone is committed to its underlying principles. When they enquire into the causes of a grave mishap, no one will let it be said that refusal to abide by ancient tradition was its cause. No one is going to accept a coroner's verdict which implies that daring innovation, new forms of brokerage or free negotiation has attracted punishment. Some more morally flexible principle is needed. What I am here calling fetish power supports the successful leader and permits something like a free market in leadership; so it admirably suits the regime.

In the course of attracting allies or intimidating rivals, individuals in this regime will have been boasting of their powerful sponsors, personal talents, and secret resources, others will have been assessing their claims and choosing alignments accordingly.

When a misfortune needs to be explained, plausible reasons are ready. If the leader argues that his rival has more charisma, more powerful sponsoring demons, or stronger magic technology, his own charisma will inevitably be diminished. A theory of personal resources works to maintain the fluidity of this kind of society because it justifies the change in alignment that everyone is always making.[11] Wanting to leave Y who is a weak ally and to join X who is currently successful, they can justify the switch of allegiance because X has obviously got bigger battalions, better secrets, bigger guardian spirits, or luck working for him; and when X starts to fail, the same theory allows his supporters to drift away, seeing that his technology has run down, his demon has deserted him, or his luck has run out. This may sound like a worrying kind of society to be living in, but it is more worrying for the prominent leaders than the others. The man who controls the biggest fetish power has been claiming to be the biggest source of danger on the horizon. Since everyone knows who he is and since he wants recruits, anyone can join his side and earn his protection. If he does not deliver his promises, they can wait until some new disaster can be made a crusading point for another leader to challenge his fetish power. By crediting fickle fetish power with causing its major physical dangers, the society can maintain itself as a free and open system, like Napoleon's army, not with a general's baton in every knapsack, but with high expectations of personal mobility, large social rewards, and social oblivion for those who fail.

By contrast a more stable constitution is supported by people who either pin blame for misfortunes on politically disapproved elements or pin responsibility on the victim so that blaming is checked. No one would be seen to be doing the adjudicating: the explanation of mishaps would uphold authority diffusely and obliquely, thanks to a tacit consensus that it is to be protected. The graver mishaps will be classed as a radical intervention from some higher than human authority or as a self-invited punishment: X died because of his contempt of rules, Y had this accident because he spread subversive rumours. In the ideal system no one needs to stick his own neck out by personally giving judgement against contempt or subversion: the damage will be seen to have been caused by an invisible agent imbued with moral concern and armed with enough power to vindicate the community.

It is obvious how a row of punitive ancestors is an effective control in a society of a tradition-loving kind. When a disaster befalls, it is plausible in such a regime to claim that the victim had entered forbidden territory or breached an ancient rule and so had brought his troubles on himself. That the ancestors are by definition dead makes it more certain that the only convincing interpretation of what they like will be one that commands the widest consensual support.

These two kinds of explanations are mutually exclusive in so far as neither one can be used to support the other regime. It is possible to characterize two exclusive sets of explanations that appeal quite differently to ultimate principles in the universe and that guide the individual's attributions of danger in diametrically opposed ways. Since none of this will seem very problematical to the Western social scientist, I can perhaps take the opportunity of pointing out the central deficiency of so-called attribution theory in that it tries to explain individual attributions of characteristics to others without systematically incorporating the bias of institutional structures in the cognitive scheme.[12]

The drift of my argument so far is that everyone thinks probabilistically in the fields of their normal competence and acts accordingly. But such fields of competence tend to be circumscribed and do not provide a model for appreciating how people think of other kinds of grave risks outside their normal competence, especially those which involve complex social judgements of value. Such big decisions I argue, are not analysed and assessed dispassionately on their merits by individuals. Rather the onus of choice is shifted away from particular issues to a choice between kinds of social institutions. Physical disasters are keenly studied in every community deserving the name and occasion is taken to score the performance of community institutions: blame falls in such a way as to reinforce the local community ideal. Far from being steadily analysed, from the start danger is roped into the work of showing up villains or maintaining morale. As Robert Merton said of a rain ceremony, its manifest function refers to the objective requirement of changing meteoric conditions, but it may have the latent effect of reinforcing group identity.[13] The manifest intention of any enquiry about disaster is to limit future dangers, but it also has latent functions for the social unit, which need to be understood.

The distinction between latent and manifest seems at first to offer a handhold for the question at issue. After all, I am allocating perceptions of danger among the unintended consequences which regularly follow when the social unit adopts a certain political regime. I could rephrase the discussion of ancestors and fetishes as beliefs latent in particular kinds of manifest organizational objectives. This might be a way to present my case. My task is to expose different types of unintended consequences which control perception and to classify them according to the types of officially recognized institutional forms from which they emanate. The simple contrast of market with bureaucracy is merely a start. How to make a relevant typology of institutional forms is the problem.

## THE TWO KINDS OF ORGANIZATION

Though extravagantly rich in typologizing exercises, organization theory is poor in explanations of institutional blindness. The actual typologies that emerge in a well-developed way are surprisingly few. By typology I mean something rather more elaborate than comparison developed along a single dimension (such as the famous shift from status to contract). A number of incipient typologies fragment and get lost. For example, one popular contrast distinguishes large from small organizations, implying also that the large are complex and the small are simple. This never develops very far, because the small organizations quickly get discarded from the exercise. Indeed, organization theory seems unduly obsessed by the idea that problems are created by increase in scale. The prejudice may be enhanced by the fact that large organizations employ decision analysts as consultants, and subsequently small organizations may seem to have few problems. It is assumed that complexity is a function of scale:[14] increase in scale leads to devolution, centralization, compartmentalization, and these lead to overloaded channels and problematical communications. Indeed it surely does. But in the experience of anthropology, some very small organizations can have very grave problems that lead to factions, fission, and fizzling out, while others equally small, survive with a high degree of internal complexity, devolution, and compartmentalization. I get the impression that the importance of scale has been much exaggerated.

Principles of sociological classification derived from Max Weber provide slightly overlapping typologies. First, the contrast between charismatic leadership and routinized procedures, based on the distinctive roles of prophet and priest, has haunted so much of Western social thought. But is it the leader who has charisma, or is it thrust upon the leader in certain kinds of political regimes? The charismatic leader fits closely to the anthropologist's descriptions of rule by competing big men (who tend to have recourse to fetish power in some form or another). The routinized society has some affinity with the traditionalism of the ancestor cults. This contrast of leadership styles would be useful to my present purpose if the literature on charisma (whether on party leaders or on personality cults) did not treat the leaders too much apart from the analysis of political regimes.[15]

The other classificatory principle developed by Weber which dominates our thinking about society, gives the contrast between market (dominated by means-end rationality) and bureaucratic rationality (dominated by procedural rules and hierarchical values). Whereas routinization tends to lead to bureaucracy, charisma tends to float outside of both market and bureaucracy and we have the illusion of three types. Whereas if charisma studies were well integrated with interest-group studies it might well appear that we only have two types still, bureaucracy on the one hand, with its routinization, and market on the other, certain phases of which develop scope for charismatic leaders to build fragile coalitions, bring them up to climax and predictable collapse.

Perhaps two strongly contrasted types are enough for most theorizing. Perhaps social reality is like that and two is the sum of all there really is. Perhaps it is hubris to look for more complex typologies that will help to bridge the regimes that anthropologists study and those studied by organization theorists. It is easy to construct the imaginative link between the individual operating in the market with all its mysterious advertising and sales gimmicks and powerful trade secrets, and the kind of society that expects all its effective operators to be using fetish powers against each other. It is equally easy to relate bureaucracy to societies observing ancestor cults. Bureaucracy is oriented towards its own vision of life, expressed in its traditions and in the procedures which enshrine them. *The ancestors* are not only adjudicating instruments between rival factions. They represent a whole version of the beginning of time and how the universe started, how they emerged and constituted the segments of human society.

They stand for *a synoptic vision of order and justice* which their cult makes actual for their descendants. In its organization of segments bureaucracy fabricates buffers which allow members of the organization to override or forget their personal differences. The market thrives on confrontation, bureaucracy plays it down. Bureaucratic procedures insulate members from outside political forces. One unintended consequence of setting up a successful bureaucracy that is strong enough to endure over time's jolts and scares is that its viewpoint tends to be insensitive to political outcomes.[16] On the other side, market, being focused on individual profits, is myopic to larger effects. Bureaucracy is insensitive to warnings of dangers it has not met already; market foresees danger only from the individual perspective. Neither is a form of organization that can train its members to be sensitive to low probability, high consequence events. The two kinds of horizon are both restricted. The market regime is hopeful about the ultimate successful working out of its constitutive principles. Bureaucracy is hopeful about the power of human reasoning. Institutional hopefulness blunts concern for distant disasters.

Though these two types are the recurring favourite contrasts in Western social thought, they are not always used consistently, nor is the link between institutional structure and associated mode of thought made clear. Sometimes no link is made, sometimes the historical factors are worked hard, sometimes a psychological bias is implied. For my task of relating the kinds of perception to kinds of organization, these two grand types simply stand around, as a backdrop to generalizations made in organization theory and political analysis.

One major exception needs to be noted. That is Gabriel Almond's and Sidney Verba's[17] pioneering study of the civic culture, its influence on the political culture, and the consequences of their interactions for the stability of democratic society. Here, certainly, typologies abound. Political culture is taken to be based initially on four variables: (1) how much the political system is perceived by the individual as a general object; (2) what knowledge he has of the structure and roles of political elites and the upward flows of policy-making; (3) what knowledge he has of policy enforcement as its downward flows impinge upon his life; (4) what are the norms of citizen participation in these processes that he acknowledges. From this three types of political culture emerge. Negative answers on all these issues gives the parochial type of political involvement; second, knowing the system as a general political object and himself as a point on which policy impinges gives the subject type of political culture; the third type is the case of the participant political culture in which the citizen has a good knowledge of the general political powers, is aware of himself as a subject and object in it and actively participates. This approach, with its emphasis on political consciousness and participation, seems at first to be very congenial to my present enterprise. This is especially so since the main purpose of the typology is to contrast degrees of subjective competence (that is the citizen's sense that he can influence the political process) with his degree of active participation. The assumption is that a successful democracy needs to be stable and that stability requires a mismatch of a kind such that citizens who perceive themselves subjectively to be in a political system in which they could effectively intervene also feel sufficient trust in the ways of its workings that they rarely do bother to intervene. Participation tends to engender trust and trust ensures stability, but not necessarily. The authors lean heavily on local political history for understanding how the different mixes have arisen and to explain anomalous cases.

Reading back on that work of only twenty years ago, one is struck by what an ambitious scheme it was and how quickly it became dated. It shows on every page the mark of its period, the heyday of functionalism with the unquestioned assumptions that balanced equilibrium will be the mark of a successful system and that stability is what every democracy should seek. One is also struck by how fast the frontiers of knowledge and understanding on that subject have moved. Subsequent reappraisals have raised most of the issues that now seem problematical which then were dormant.[18] Above all, the difference made by socio-economic status in the attitudes of respondents could not now be brushed under the carpet, or the circularity of the argument, which tests the subjective sense of competence against the subjective reporting of political involvement, and the subjective sense of political satisfaction with the overall system. Alas, for my hope to find here some sophistication about how social structures fix perceptual blinkers on individuals. This huge research effort never tackles the question of how the subjective experiences relate to real life, except historically. Evidently, once upon a time, events impinged upon and changed people's perception, but then subsequent events combined to fix the angle of vision. Since I want to investigate this process of stabilizing the political vision, with regret I leave aside this brave exercise.

## KINDS OF DECISION-MAKING

When we turn to decision analysis, we find a formidable literature that assumes that kinds of thinking are related to kinds of organization. Be not surprised that there are only two kinds of decision-making organizations generally considered. The seminal article which sets the terms for the comparisons that are still being made is Lindblom's 1959 criticism of decision and organization theory.[19] Here he contrasts Root style of decision making with Branch style (see Table 4.1).

In this Table, the left-hand column, Root, makes experts its butt and on the right-hand column the ordinary bumbling organization proceeding by limited comparisons and trial and error seems to be the good guys, the firm which is out there in the market place, receiving advice from the experts. In much subsequent research inspired by this contrast we have seen two kinds of budgeting contrasted, comprehensive or Policy Programming and Budgeting versus incremental budgeting,[20] two kinds of policy formation, cogitative and interactive.[21] The good guy sometimes changes from one side to the other – as for example, when the level is raised from government departments to whole national governmental styles. In *Politics and Markets* Lindblom seems to favour his Model 1, the intellectually guided society, against his Model 2, the interaction type.[22] No matter, we have two types, and they still correspond closely to the ancestor cult (Lindblom's Model 1, with its famous founders, synoptic vision of world history and human nature, and top-down formalities of precedence for organizing political behaviour) and Model 2, the fickle fetish-holding market interaction, with its negotiating and coalescing for strength and arriving at fragmentary, practicable decisions on a short-term basis.

Several thinkers have tried to propose a *third type* of decision-making. On closer inspection, their typologies tend to reduce to two. Allison[23] offers three models of government decision-making; the first is based on the individual behaving according to classical utility theory: the government is presented as if it were a single rational agent, able to know and rank its goals and

*Table 4.1*

| Model I Root | Model II Branch |
|---|---|
| Rational-comprehensive (Root) | Successive limited comparisons (Branch) |
| 1a. Clarification of values or objectives distinct from and usually prerequisite to empirical analysis of alternative policies. | 1b. Selection of value goals and empirical analysis of the needed action are not distinct from one another but are closely intertwined. |
| 2a. Policy formulation is therefore approached through means-end analysis: first the ends are isolated, then the means to achieve them are sought. | 2b. Since means and ends are not distinct, measured analysis is often inappropriate or limited. |
| 3a. The test of a 'good' policy is that it can be shown to be the most appropriate means to desired ends. | 3b. The test of a 'good' policy is typically that various analysts find themselves directly agreeing on a policy (without their agreeing that it is the most appropriate means to an ageed objective). |
| 4a. Analysis is comprehensive, every important relevant factor is taken into account. | 4b. Analysis is drastically limited:<br>(i) Important possible outcomes are neglected.<br>(ii) Important alternative potential policies are neglected.<br>(iii) Important affected values are neglected. |
| 5a. Theory is often heavily relied upon. | 5b. A succession of comparisons greatly reduces or eliminates reliance on theory. |

*Source*: C.E. Lindblom, 'The Science of Muddling Through', *Public Administration Review* 19 (1959)

solve its problems, according to a rational appraisal of costs and benefits; the second echoes Lindblom's descriptions of actual organizational muddling through, contrary to the behests of theorists. The big difference between Model 1 and Model 2 is the importance of standard operating procedures in the latter, the constraints on seeking information, the sequential and fragmented dealing with policy problems. In Model 2 the different elements behave as a loose alliance of semi-independent organizations; internal conflict is reduced by the recourse to fixed plans and routines. Model 1 and Model 2 correspond closely to Lindblom's two models cited above. Allison's Model 3 is a more complicated version of the utility theory used for Model 1, in which the whole market of individual agents are bargaining, compromising, and making coalitions. If you see Lindblom's Model 2 as a system based on market interaction, then Allison's Model 3 takes it to a further stage. So in effect, instead of providing three distinct types, Allison is working with the usual two basic models.

Steinbruner[24] tries to have three models of cognition in organizations: a classic utility model (which corresponds roughly to Lindblom's rational comprehensive Root style of policy formulation and to Allison's Model 1) which he calls analytic thinking; second, a pragmatic interactive model (which roughly corresponds to Lindblom's Model 2); and a cybernetic model with bureaucratically restricted focus at a lower level of organization which has much in common with the emphasis on fixed goals and routines in Allison's Model 2. So the distinctions that would justify claiming more than two basic models are not convincingly worked out. Both Steinbruner and Allison are interested in the central problem that concerns us here, that is how the prior mental set affects interpretations of events. But neither stops to ask where the mental set and its assumptions come from. They imply that the answer will refer to national culture or individual psychological make-up. I am arguing that the kind of organization itself generates the decision-making and perceptual bias, but I do not get enough help from typologies used in discussing organization behaviour for developing my project.

Furthermore, given the heavy use of the idea of rational behaviour in the classical theory of organization, one would expect the differences between the individual decision-taker and the organization to be fully spelled out. A recent survey[25] shows that the paradigmatic scheme of the organization as if it were an individual is full of loose ends and not at all as well understood as one might expect of a central tool in decision theory. The two incomplete models which prevail either treat the organization as an individual within a market environment or as a market in which its constituent parts are individuals. This limited vision of what kinds of different organizations there may be is unable to provide ideas about institutional blinders.

# MARKET, BUREAUCRACY, AND VOLUNTARY COMMITMENT

Two swallows do not make a summer. Two regimes do not make a typology. Search as I may in the theory of organizations, I do not find any consistently developed typology that does more than embroider upon the basic two models, and absolutely nothing that suggests how the political culture selects institutional forms and supports them with beliefs about responsibility. To make the transfer between the anthropologists' materials and the subject matter of Western political thought I need to find at least a three part scheme,[26] articulated so as to show how blame is attributed to sustain different regimes.

One formulation of the difference between market and bureaucracy seems particularly well adapted to this purpose. This is the market failures framework which, whatever its limitations may be, takes my argument out of the static periphery of Western social thought to which anthropological observations are generally consigned.

Market transactions are contractual relations of varying degrees of long-term commitment. Market failure is an analytic device which considers the cases in which costs of individual transactions may be too high for maintaining the conditions of completely contractual market relationships. Williamson[27] has used the idea of market failure as a conceptual framework for comparing the strengths of markets as opposed to bureaucracy.

Suppose all transactions can be mediated by market relations, then ask what conditions will cause some of these market relations to fail and come to be replaced by bureaucratic mediating forms. This argument assumes every bureaucratic organization to be an example of market failure. When transaction costs mount for one reason or another, a bureaucratic organization offers an employment relation which can produce trust, develop expertise, and provide flexible continuity, and these combined can outweigh its inefficiencies. Ouchi has suggested a third organizational form from within this conceptual scheme.[28] He calls 'clan' a structure which he derives from Durkheim's idea of organic solidarity, in which a total congruence of goals allows for much more informality and a less explicit statement of rules (see Table 4.2).

The difficulty about this nice scheme is to know how commitment to common goals arises. Ouchi sees the clan as emerging

Table 4.2 An organizational failures framework

| Modes of control | Normative requirements | Informational requirements |
|---|---|---|
| Market | Reciprocity | Prices |
| Bureaucracy | Reciprocity, legitimate authority | Rules |
| Clan | Reciprocity, legitimate authority, common values | Traditions |

Source: W.G. Ouchi, Table II, p. 138 Administrative Science Quarterly (25.1.1980)

in response to failure of bureaucratic organization. 'When a bureaucracy fails, then due to excessively ambiguous performance evaluation, the sole form of mediation remaining is the clan, which relies on creating goal congruence.'[29] He claims that clans do not require explicit auditing and evaluation, because of the subtle, mutual monitoring of intimate co-workers. He may be right in seeing 'clans' formed in the course of rejecting bureaucracy's rules. But his enthusiasm for implicit unmediated forms of communication lets him down. The clan idea needs more analysis. Like Rosabeth Moss Kanter,[30] whose work he cites in evidence, he is telling us that moral commitment to common goals is an independent factor. If he can assume that moral commitment arises so easily, just from disappointment with the workings of bureaucracy, why can we not also suppose it preceded market relations and then ask why it became superseded in turn? Ouchi skips out of the central dilemmas of political theory in which the issue over the centuries has been how shared moral commitment ever emerges and how it is sustained. The 'clan' as described is not the promised third branch of a typology starting with individual rational agents transacting with one another and then avoiding excessive transaction costs by developing employment relations.

Using the mechanisms of accountability and blame allocation as principal organizers of our scheme, we may start again with the two recognized types, bureaucracy and market, as shown in Table 4.3. The morally punitive universe in which ancestor power is an element can be identified with bureaucratic or hierarchical regimes and the belief in secret weaponry such as fetish power or charisma can be identified with market regimes.

These two contrasted regimes with their latent cosmic forces

Table 4.3 Two forms of risk-perceiving organization

|  | Hierarchy | Market |
|---|---|---|
| Organized by | Individual-subordinating to group protective, compartmentalizing, top-down principles of command | Individual exchange, profit-maximizing, bottom-up principles of consultation and influence |
| Latent goal | Secure internal structure of authority | Preserve individual freedom to contract |
| Invoke benefits | Of tradition, of connections, of territorial heritage and material symbols of group | Of esoteric techniques and personal qualities |
| Invoke dangers | Of loss of morale, loss of commitment | Of personal power and feelings of rival individuals |
| Disasters interpreted | To support group control over individuals | To magnify competition of leaders |
| Action justified | Stabilize patterns of segmentation | Shifts of allegiance |
| Latent cosmic forces | Ancestor power, taboos in a punitive universe | Fetish power, charisma, and equivalent personal weaponry |

would seem to be an acceptable extension of political thought to include the regimes of Africa and the ancient world under the same contemporary rubric. But they do not touch upon a certain type of regime that anthropology records, in which warning of horrible, unprecedented dangers is the usual recourse for resolving micro-political crises. There is a third organizational type, quite distinct, which solves its difficulties of allegiance neither by boasting of control of fetishes nor by appeal to dead ancestral vengeance but by threat of being destroyed by an evil conspiracy of living outsiders. Fortunately, I can develop this third type of regime including both African exemplars and modern political analysis within the theory of rational choice by drawing upon Mancur Olson's analysis of *The Logic of Collective Action*.[31] Markets and hierarchies survive, thanks to the commitment of members who expect to enjoy selective benefits for themselves. Olson indicates a third type, the voluntary organization that is not protected by coercive power and does not afford individual selective benefits. The difference is a matter of degree; the less that individual selective benefits are available, the more the organization encounters grave problems of commitment, leadership, and decision-making – so much so that Mancur Olson expects it to have difficulties in producing any collective good at all.

According to Olson, when there is no coercion and no selective individual benefits, a group is going to be bothered by free-rider problems. Each member will expect to be able to enjoy the public benefits created by the others without anyone noticing whether or not he puts in his bit. If there is a difference between big and small stake holders, the latter will tend to blackmail the former, threatening to withdraw and so gaining a paralysing veto power over the whole group. Leadership is thwarted; even on the principle of a hundred per cent participation, endless bargaining blocks the decisions of endless committees. Such a group has a problem even in raising funds for its minimum organization costs and must be judged to be specially fragile and especially vulnerable to internal dissension.

The first step towards a solution for this kind of organization when trying to collect contributions and prevent secessions is to draw a clear boundary around members against the outside world, painting the latter as a corrupt and nasty place. Second, it will need to keep the hundred per cent participation rule so as to prevent any one member from seeming to reap more benefits than the others and so creating discord. We can supplement Olson by adding that the organization works better if an ambitious power-hungry member is said to reveal those very corrupt tendencies which make the outside world so threatening. Being committed by internal political needs to make a virtue of equality, this organization will be led to associate ambition with inequality, corrupt stratification, and the inhumane machinations of the outside world. So long as there are no internal crises, this is enough of a shared metaphysic to promote latent intentions that the organization should survive. But this voluntary organization is prone to factionalism. Faction leaders are a threat; one way to control them is to accuse them of teacherous alliance with the bad outside world. The more the internal crises heat up, the more it suits the latent goals of the organization for everyone committed to it to shade their eyes, staring at the horizon, spotting there the signs of conspiracy and cosmic disaster which can only be staved off for the world if everyone converts into the egalitarian doctrines of the sect. In a more extreme case, the disasters on the horizon justify expelling the unpopular faction leader.

I have done a stint of fieldwork in Central Africa and am familiar with its pre-colonial history and its processes of adaptation to colonial rule. Before 1890 caravans of ivory and slave traders over the Nyasa Region brought prosperity to some and disaster to others in a country largely organized upon the market type of regime.[32] After Pax Britannica was established, there was an end of raiding and a beginning of district tribunals, taxes, cash cropping, and labour migration, all poorly paid economic enterprises compared with what had been. The one thing that the colonial government did not interfere with was who lived with whom in what village. But the villages had no fixed assets to attract a permanent core of residents. Over and over again, the anthropologists and district officers reported the highly fissile nature of the society; the tendency of villages no longer threatened by marauders to split and spread; the periodic and regular thwarting of any leader's ambition to hold his village together.[33]

The villages moved around every decade or so. There was no fixed territory whose boundaries the ancestors could guard or centres for their shrines. No fixed land rights were maintained in the slash and burn cultivation system; endemic tsetse fly would kill livestock and there was nothing to inherit that would constrain the footloose to choose to stay in one village rather than in another. The active young men were apt to use the threat of withdrawal effectively to get forgiveness for any misdeeds. Always the shared belief that it is good to live in a stable, peaceful village was strained by quarrels which burst into general conflagration after a succession of misfortunes had caused a witch to be identified in their midst. The alleged witch's friends would find themselves in a faction counterpoised against the accusers. The quarrels would have been festering over decades until solution by the exile of the witch or the splitting of the village. In practice the populations were remarkably stable, shedding dissident elements to nearby areas and welcoming their offspring home in the next generation. The anthropologists' micro-political analyses of this self-maintaining process is convincing.[34] Until I read Olson, I had not seen any general theoretical analysis in which the central African predicament and solution could be included.

But it is plausible that being without strong selective benefits to induce their members to bear the insults and tensions of living together, they used the accusation of witchcraft and threat of distant dangers to solve their organizational problems. I am using the term cosmic plot to correspond to witchcraft and sorcery when they are politically usable ideas. The function of the witch or sorcerer in the regime that sees itself at risk in a cosmic evil plot is diametrically opposed to that of the ancestor and to that of the fetish-holding leader. The latter claims his magic powers explicitly and thrives or fails according to his success in justifying his claims. The magic is an accelerator of his destiny. If plague and drought strike his enemies and spare his friends, he will himself claim responsibility and he will have to carry the blame if his friends suffer. Unlike fetish power, both witchcraft and ancestral powers are attributed indirectly through the working of the political process. The ancestor is too dead to claim credit himself and the witch has to be a live person visibly in the thick of the political scene so as to be the target of factional abuse. Unlike the ancestor, who mediates the moral justice of heaven or its equivalent, the witch is distinctively a traitor, allied to alien conspirators, plotting evil against good citizens. Unlike ancestors or the fetish holder, the witch is hard to identify, masked in deceit. The idea of the ancestors is employed by the collectivity to suppress moral deviance, but the idea of witches is used for factional fighting. The political essence of the witch is the outside threat which he insidiously supports. The more terrifying the outside threat, the more the sense of factional solidarity and opposition is reinforced.[35]

Beliefs in fetishes, ancestors, and cosmic plots are here presented, each as the indirect political manipulation appropriate to a distinctive kind of political regime. Each regime animadverts differently at post mortems, inquests, and other inquiries into disaster. First, the fetish beliefs point directly to where power is actually located. Power is not veiled or frustrated in such a regime and the fetish theory gives it such legitimation as it needs for its maintenance. Second, the ancestor beliefs uphold authority and help to channel power to legitimate office holders. Attributing deaths and accidents of all kinds to the corrective surveillance of the dead removes from live office-holders the unpopularity of meting out punishment. Third, the cosmic plot provides an idiom for bringing hidden hostilities into the open. At one point the threat of being accused controls and at another point it fuels factional discord, allowing the social unit to slough off elements it cannot contain peacefully.[36] In all these cases, disasters, natural and man-made, trigger the enquiries which trace the real distribution of power and its challengers.

Perhaps this language is too dramatic to bridge the gap between anthropological work and the current bemusement about perception of risk. But fetish power, ancestors, and cosmic plot are not more dramatic than what we commonly read about impending catastrophe or the vituperations against the deceits of the tobacco industry, advertising interests, the industrial-military complex, and the aggressive ploys of the nuclear industries. The language of civic criticism should be dramatic.

Another reason why the bridge is difficult is that this sort of analysis takes the focus off physical dangers and turns it inward to the state of trust in political life. Just as we are being asked to attend to the physical dangers on the horizon, this argument turns to the kinds of political contests in which they are made to figure. The key point is the way that nature is politicized and engages in the legitimation and delegitimation of power.

I argue that organizations which are most keenly alert to low probability, high consequence danger are religious sects and communes (which are notoriously millennialist and apt to prophesy doom) and also political lobbies, new political movements, and public interest groups. The more difficulty they have in holding their membership together and getting common dues paid, the more they are tempted to call in cosmic plot as a low-cost solution to their organizational problems. The different elements in the environmental movement show more or less alarm about the future of the world according to the way their organization fits between the middle and the right-hand column of Table 4.4.[37]

Now we have a real typology in which each of three levels has been identified by the distinctive principles of moral solidarity which are required for maintaining the type of regime. It seems to follow the programme of Durkheimian analysis to which Ouchi's paper refers, but looking for social commitment in all parts of the scheme instead of only in the clan. It adds a corrective element to Ouchi's idea of the clan, since he has rather idealistic notions of what it feels like to be in a small group in which all roles are ambiguously defined. This scheme suggests reservation about the satisfactions of living in a universe that is

Table 4.4

| ORGANIZATIONS | | |
|---|---|---|
| With selective benefits | | Without selective benefits |
| Market | Bureaucracy | Voluntary group |
| **Latent goal** Preserve individual freedom to contract | Secure internal structure of authority | Survival of group |
| **Disasters interpreted** To magnify competition of leaders | To support group control over individuals | To damp dissidence or clarify factions |
| **Latent cosmic forces** Secret weaponry | Punitive universe | Cosmic plot or betrayal |
| **Accusation** Leader has lost power | Group has lost commitment | Individual treachery |

thought to be threatened by cosmic plot. The merit of the typology is that while it is consistently derived from individual rational choice calculations, it also adds the cultural dimension which is missing from approaches to risk perception from the cognitive sciences.

# CONCLUSION

To go back to the beginning of this argument, I have now illustrated how individuals transfer their decision-making to the institutions in which they live. I have tried to make a bridge between organizational theory and anthropology, to show how different kinds of organizations provide different controls on the perceptions of their members. The bridge is very faulty and weak, but I hope just interesting enough to be worth further attention. It suggests a sad predicament. Of three kinds of organization, one is well adapted to pick up and relay warnings of low probability, high consequence disasters because its internal structure creates problems which are habitually solved by identifying distant dangers and associating them with large-scale conspiracy with which one or other of their members may be charged with colluding. Unfortunately, the other two kinds of organizations are fitted with blinkers and ear mufflers so that it is extremely unlikely that they will even hear warnings. Why three? Three is not the limit or a magic number. Michael Thompson uses three or five in his typologies of cultural bias. It is merely that these three and combinations thereof have attracted most of the typological thinking in organization theory, with the third lagging far behind the first two in the attention it has attracted. Second, three gives enough to provide a lot of explanation. Each of these types of organization demands and provides itself with symbolic reinforcement. Once it has produced the cosmological beliefs that can be used to maintain the form of the regime, the extra degree of coherence between institutions, beliefs, and actions will reinforce stability. Any other organizations that provide further examples of how danger is used to stabilize social systems can be added to develop the comparison.

One upshot of this argument is that accepting risks is part of accepting organizations. The risk analysts and risk perception psychologists try to strip the idea of acceptable risk free of political adhesions, but the problems of risk perception are essentially political. Congresses and parliaments give away their rightful territory when they hand over such problems to risk experts. The public debates about risk are debates about politics. They should be read as a sailor reads the movement of the sails to know which quarter the wind is in. To read the risk debates would make explicit a need for more trust here and more watchfulness there. Treating risk acceptability as a technical question disperses sovereignty. Congresses and parliaments should repossess themselves. Through studying risk perception as an institutional effect, the latent purposes of the nation as a whole can be protected. Studying risk perception as an individual cognitive exercise conceals the action of constituent elements in the nation, each solving their own institutional problems in the name of dangers.

Finally, the deeper implications of this essay have less to do with risk perception than with theories of knowledge.[38] It is presented as a link between Michael Thompson's essay on decision-making with regard to dangers from liquid natural gas and James Douglas's essay on how a plurality of options are funnelled into the form of coherent choices through the political process.[39] Parliaments and voting are certain kinds of filters on political perception. Organizational structures are other kinds again and it befits the twentieth-century intellectual promises to reach self-consciousness for us to be aware of these funnels and blinders that we ourselves create.

## ACNOWLEDGEMENTS

I thank the International Institute of Systems Analysis in Laxenburg, Austria, for two workshops which stimulated the writing of this paper, in May and December 1981, and particularly Howard Kunreuther, then Chairman of the Risk Analysis Conference, and Ed Loser, librarian, for stimulating criticism. I also thank the SSRC of England for providing for a visit to the Experimental Psychology Laboratory of Oxford for a conference on Explanation in March 1982 and especially Mansur Lalljee who thought of inviting me. I also thank Robin Hogarth, Jack Knotts, and Aaron Wildavsky for commenting and suggesting reading.

This paper was originally published as 'Perceiving Low Probability Events', in *Social Choice and Cultural Bias*, Collaborative Paper 83–4 by James Douglas, Mary Douglas, and Michael Thompson, International Institute for Applied Systems Analysis, A–2361 Laxenburg, Austria, 1983: 31–68.

## NOTES

1 Howard Kunreuther, *Disaster Insurance Protection, Public Policy Lessons* (John Wiley, 1978).
2 James G. March and Herbert A. Simon, *Organizations* (John Wiley, 1958).
3 L. Jonathan Cohen, (1981) 'Can Human Irrationality Be Experimentally Demonstrated?', *The Behavioral and Brain Sciences* 4:317–331 and see the following open peer commentary:331–370.
4 Paul Slovic, Baruch Fischhoff and Sarah Lichtenstein, 'Informing People About Risk', in Louis A. Morris et al. (eds) *Banbury Report, 6: Product Labeling and Health Risks* (Cold Spring Harbor, 1980).
5 Robin Hogarth, *Judgment and Choice, The Psychology of Decision* (John Wiley, 1980), pp. 16–17.
6 Ibid. p. 18, quoting work by D. Kahneman and A. Tversky (1972) 'Subjective Probability: A Judgment of Representativeness', *Cognitive Psychology* 3:127–131.
7 E.E. Evans-Pritchard, *Nuer Religion* (The Clarendon Press, 1956) p. 315. Writing of cultural analysis: 'The test of what is the dominant motif is usually, perhaps always, to what a people attribute dangers and sickness and other misfortunes and what steps they take to avoid or eliminate them.' See also Mary Douglas, *Evans-Pritchard* (Fontana Modern Masters, 1980).

8 E.E. Evans-Pritchard, *Oracles, Witchcraft and Magic Among the Azande* (The Clarendon Press, 1937).

9 I use the word 'regime' with acknowledgements to the use made of it by Aaron Wildavsky in his unpublished studies of political regimes and political cultures.

10 A short bibliography of Polynesian and Melanesian political studies can be cited to support this usage. See *Cultural Bias*, by Mary Douglas, Royal Anthropological Institute (occasional paper No. 35, 1978).

11 Ernest Gellner, analysis of how *baraka* or holiness can perform this function in *Saints of the Atlas* (Weidenfeld and Nicolson, 1969).

12 Here I acknowledge the generosity of the SSRC which enabled me to attend an important conference organized by the department of experimental psychology in Oxford in March 1982 on the topic of 'Everyday Explanation', one object of which was to compare the kinds of explanations considered in attribution theory with others in different branches of the social sciences, such as psychology, law, philosophy, science, and anthropology. If this did not confirm my impression that the approach here advocated is not well known and well tried, I need only refer to Herbert A. Simon's Bicentennial Address to the American Academy of Arts and Sciences (see Bulletin 35, No. 6, March 1982) which summarizes the state of the art in cognitive studies.

13 R.K. Merton, 'Manifest and Latent Functions, Toward the Codification of Functional Analysis in Sociology', *Social Theory and Social Structure* (enlarged edition, Free Press, 1968) Ch. 3:73–138.

14 Todd R. LaPorte, *Organized Social Complexity: Challenge to Politics and Policy* (Princeton University Press, 1975).

15 Here I acknowledge suggestions on an early draft of this paper from Jack Knotts (currently Research Fellow of the Russell Sage Foundation) who made this point, among other acute criticisms.

16 See Karl Mannheim, *Ideology and Utopia: An Introduction to the Sociology of Knowledge* (Harcourt, Brace, 1936) pp. 106–7. And see the account of hierarchy in Ch. 5 of *Risk and Culture*, Mary Douglas and Aaron Wildavsky (California Press, 1982).

17 Gabriel Almond and Sidney Verba, *The Civic Culture: Political Attitudes and Democracy in Five Nations* (Princeton University Press, 1963).

18 Gabriel Almond and Sidney Verba, *The Civic Culture Revisited* (Little Brown, 1980).

19 Charles E. Lindblom, (1959) 'The Science of Muddling Through', *Public Administration Review* 19:155–69.

20 Aaron Wildavsky, *Budgeting, A Comparative Theory of Budgetary Processes* (Little Brown, 1975).

21 Aaron Wildavsky, *Speaking Truth to Power: The Art and Craft of Policy Analysis* (Little Brown, 1979).

22 Charles Lindblom, *Politics and Markets: The World's Political-Economic Systems* (Basic Books Inc., 1977).

23 Graham T. Allison, *Essence of Decision, Explaining the Cuban Missile Crisis* (Little Brown, 1971).

24 J. D. Steinbruner, *The Cybernetic Theory of Decision* (Princeton University Press, 1976).

25 Robin M. Hogarth, 'Decision Making in Organizations and the Organization of Decision Making' (unfinished draft, unpublished, kindly lent to me by the author).

26 A four-fold taxonomy would better suit the model of social factors influencing beliefs and values on which the cultural bias approach depends and for which I am seeking here to provide an introduction. See *Cultural Bias* (Mary Douglas, Royal Anthropological Institute, occasional paper No. 35, 1978). But a three-fold taxonomy takes us well into the argument as Michael Thompson has shown elsewhere.

27 O.E. Williamson, *Markets and Hierarchies: Analysis and Anti-trust Implications* (Free Press, 1975).

28 William G. Ouchi, (1980) 'Markets, Bureaucracies and Clans', *Administrative Science Quarterly* 1, 25:129–41.

29 Ibid.

30 Rosabeth Moss Kanter, *Commitment and Community* (Harvard University Press, 1972).

31 Mancur Olson, *The Logic of Collective Action: Public Goods and the Theory of Groups* (Harvard Economic Studies) (Harvard University Press, 1965).

32 For a summary of the literature on which this judgement is based, *Peoples of the Lake Nyasa Region*, by Mary Tew, Ethnographic Survey of Africa (International African Institute, East Central Africa, 1949).

33 Max Gluckman, John Barnes and Clyde Mitchell, (1949) 'The Village Headman in British Central Africa', *Africa* 19, 2.

34 Clyde Mitchell, *The Yao Village* (Manchester University Press, 1956). M. G. Marwick, (1952) 'The Social Context of Cewa Witch Beliefs', *Africa* 22:232.

35 John Middleton and E.H. Winter (eds) *Witchcraft and Sorcery in East Africa*, see Introduction.

36 Marwick ('The Social Context of Cewa Witch Beliefs', *Africa* 22) uses some vivid expressions for this function: witchcraft beliefs 'dissolve relations which have become redundant' and 'blast down the dilapidated parts of the social structure'.

37 See Chapter 7 in *Risk and Culture* (Douglas and Wildavsky, California Press, 1982).

38 See *Essays in the Sociology of Perception*, edited by Mary Douglas (Routledge & Kegan Paul, 1982).

39 James Douglas (1983) 'How Actual Political Systems Cope with the Paradoxes of Social Change', *Social Choice and Cultural Bias, Collaborative Paper* 83–84:1–30 (International Institute for Applied Systems Analysis, Laxenburg, Austria).

# 5

# WITCHCRAFT AND LEPROSY
## Two strategies for rejection

## INSIDIOUS HARM

This article will discuss two strategies of rejection, both accusations of causing injury, but neither normally linked with the other. They are two varieties of insidious damage, accusations of witchcraft on the one hand, and on the other, diagnoses of hidden infectious disease. Infection and causing occult harm are both hidden from observation; a carrier can transmit disease to others without showing any signs of infection; a witch looks like anyone else. From their hiddenness both forms of harm afford the same kind of opportunity for accusations and exclusions. To historians the anthropologist's analysis of witchcraft appears in antique fancy dress, as if the subject is cast to be played in skins or the clothes worn by their own seventeenth-century dramatis personae. However, combining witchcraft with infectious disease as two strategies in the same process of exclusion and rejection may shed light on some shady corners of medical history. The argument that follows will summarize some of the anthropological analyses of witchcraft accusations in order to apply the same approach to the supposed epidemic of leprosy in northern Europe in the twelfth century.

In recounting the history of witchcraft accusations we generally take a sceptical attitude. It is curious that we treat a reported outbreak of leprosy as another matter. We do believe what the people thought of it at the time, even though the evidence is dubious. For what follows, the reality or unreality of the cause of harm makes no difference: it is enough that the people believe in it. Personally, I take my stand against the reality of witchcraft. To believe in witches would contradict too heavily everything else that I believe. By contrast, infectious diseases qualify for me as real dangers. The case of infection is different; I know that everything that was once thought to be infectious is not necessarily so, but in general infections exist. They wipe out populations, cripple, mutilate, and kill. The significant fact is that a person who is carrying infection does not necessarily show it. Unless the infected are required to wear a badge, or unless they are confined to restricted areas, or made to declare their condition publicly, the contact with the infection can be unperceived. Infectious diseases therefore come into the class of insidious causes of damage. In European belief witches were thought to be difficult to recognize. Both witch and carrier of infection are liable to go unsuspected. Both have a capacity to deceive. The hidden power of causing injury that they have in common justifies their being treated together as potential weapons in strategies of rejection.

The comparison has been inspired by a remarkable article in *Annales* (Pegg 1990) by a young medievalist, Mark Pegg. He has compared the attitudes to leprosy in very much the same spirit as the anthropologists compare reports of witchcraft. The problem which he addresses is why in Western Christendom it should have seemed utterly shocking that a king could be a leper, while in the Latin Kingdom of Jerusalem in 1174 Baldwin IV, a known leper, was actually anointed and crowned. Pope Alexander III sent out an Encyclical, *Cor Nostrum*, in which he deplored the coronation of a sinner, and anticipated disaster for the Holy Land which would not be able to be held against the infidel with a sinner on the throne. The answer Mark Pegg gives is to do with the imputing of sin to lepers. As soon as immorality is associated with infectious disease the syndrome of social exclusion is buttressed with accusations of causing insidious harm. The problem which is raised by his study is whether it would not be as well to exercise the same scepticism in face of accusations of leprosy as we exercise in face of witchcraft accusations. The alleged twelfth-century outbreak would have been a curious epidemic from a medical point of view because the bacteria of Hansen's disease do not normally flourish in the cold climate of northern Europe. Moreover there are not enough lepers' skeletons in the graveyards exclusively reserved for inmates of twelfth-century leprosariums to support the idea of a widespread epidemic. Another kind of explanation is required, and it is possible to suggest that the comparison with witchcraft accusations may provide it.

# TECHNIQUES OF REJECTION AND CONTROL

Sociologists tend to lump techniques of rejection together as ways of dealing with marginal categories. However, the comparisons that follow show that the topic is more complex. Sometimes the person who is to be rejected is not marginal at all: an unpopular leader, a young tyrant, an ageing monarch. It is necessary to realize that the same strategies of rejection may sometimes be used against the powerful. There has to be consensus. There has to be an imputation of immorality. The scale of infamy starts with imputing minor moral weakness to unimportant candidates for degradation, and rises to the full imputation of filthy living. This range of slander is the common backdrop to the slurs and slights of 'orientalism' and the derogatory definitions of feminine gender to which critical studies of the past twenty years have made us sensitive. To cause a person's civil claims to be rejected, libel on its own is not enough, it has to be supported by an accusation of causing damage so that the victim can be classed as a public nuisance.

The benefit of considering witchcraft and infection together is that the parallel with witchcraft gives insight into disease as a resource for maintaining particular cultural regimes. British social anthropologists of the post-war era made powerful analyses of the uses of witchcraft accusations in African villages and chief-doms for maintaining patterns of authority. This essay will suggest that a historian of medicine could make similar analyses of the use of infectious disease as a resource for controlling designated public enemies. For such an analysis, medical diagnosis would have to be brought into a common category with 'accusation', and note taken of the destructive effect of some diagnoses on civic status. The result would be a sociological model of the treatment of infectious diseases.

There are various reasons for this synthesis having been delayed. The spectacular European witch trials distracted historians' attention from close correspondences between infectious disease and occult harm, perhaps because of their focus on Satanism. Another reason is what William James called 'medical materialism', the reluctance of students of medicine to consider illness as an accusation, and so their reluctance to consider a social epidemiology of accusations.

## THE LIBEL

The regular strategy of rejection starts with the libel. The simple food libel (foreigners eat disgusting foods), and the sex libel (the demeaned category is promiscuous, effeminate, incestuous), escalate to violence and perversion, and if the determination to exclude is fixed, it resorts to the blood libel (the enemy is murderous, and even murders children). The culminating infamy that incites ethnic persecution combines blood, sex, food, and religion. In the Bible the Canaanite enemy was accused of child sacrifice and sexual orgies in honour of the anti-god. In medieval Europe the Jews were accused of child sacrifice and ritual orgies. Tracing the rise and fall of imputed filth, it is remarkable that the arrow of accusation shifts over time from one target to another (Douglas 1970). Sometimes the accusation points upwards to betraying leaders who can be removed if the libel musters enough anger. Sometimes disfranchised masses or hordes of refugees attract the libel, so that they can be put under restraint. Imputing filth to the victims enables them to be rejected without a qualm.

We shall see below that at certain times and places the European lepers attracted a version of the blood libel. But the first task in this paper is to insist that witchcraft and sorcery accusations are examples of the full libel, blood, sex, and food. Suspected of Satanism and heresy, the medieval witch was also thought to be given to unnatural vice and to an insatiable sexual appetite. Charges of secret sexual deviance, spite, heresy, and occult dangerous powers were combined. Everything significant about the European witch was occult, hidden, unknowable by ordinary means. In other regions of the world, leaving out the component of heresy, a similar bundle of evil propensities characterizes alleged witches and sorcerers: anthropophagy, unnatural vice, treason, spite, general depravity, and insidious damage by occult means.

The cleverer they are in occult knowledge the more incredible the crimes that can be attributed to them. For this reason evidence that might count in their favour was regarded as suspect. English witch trials in the sixteenth century relied heavily on character attributes to enhance the likelihood that an impoverished old widow had sexual congress with the devil: evidence of her importunacy and greedy acquisitiveness would carry the day against her.

An example that I witnessed in the course of fieldwork in the 1950s in the then Belgian Congo will illustrate the closure that is placed upon contrary evidence. Two children had died; their grandmother had been accused of causing their deaths by sorcery magic; in evidence was her quarrelsome personality; in proof was the mess of human faeces alleged to have been found in the crown of a tall palm tree by a young man who climbed it to draw palm wine. Since it was at that time very unusual for the Lele ever to accuse a woman, the traditional constraints on accusations were evidently breaking down. Since women never climbed trees and were thought to be incapable of it, the proof was not prima facie convincing. To the sceptical query about how a woman could have got up there and defecated precariously perched on top of a palm, the clinching answer was that no ordinary woman could: only a witch with occult powers could fly up there and do it. The woman left the village, her in-laws had proved some point, but nothing more was done against her.

Whether the witch is really able to do harm or not, whether the person is really infectious or not, the attribution of a hidden power to hurt is a weapon of attack against them. Attributions of occult injury and hidden infection informally entrench the hierarchy of social categories and warn well-placed persons against indiscriminate social intercourse. There is an element of social discrimination carried in any attribution of occultism, like the common idea that a miasmic harmful influence emanates from certain quarters, generally those inhabited by the poor, on the outskirts of towns. In different kinds of political regime the accusation of insidious harm will be put to different uses. The accusation can be completely outrageous; it will be credible essentially if the political system on whose behalf it is made is accepted. The process of formally accusing, testifying, verifying, and remedying play a crucial part in entrenching the system.

Awareness of insidious harm arouses public concern on behalf of the public good. According to how the public good is conceived, accusations of causing insidious harm will be aimed at different targets. A successful accusation is one that has enough credibility for a public outcry to remove the opportunity of repeating the damage. This preventive action will entail degrading the accused. However, though anyone may accuse, not all accusations will be accepted. To be successful an accusation should be directed against victims hated by the populace. The cause of the harm must be vague, unspecific, difficult to prove or disprove. The crime must be difficult to deny, even impossible to disprove. One accusation that sticks will make the accused infamous, and will collect other infamy. Once defamed, the person will continue plausibly to attract similar charges and convictions. But he or she is not necessarily a marginal person. Insidious harm is an accusation that reaches different targets in different political regimes (Thompson, Ellis and Wildavsky, 1990).

## TARGETS OF ACCUSATIONS IN AFRICA

In the 1950s the anthropologists' studies of witchcraft accusations were mainly focused at village level. The interest was on who did the accusing, who was accused, the relation between the victim, the accuser, and the accused, and changes in the general level of accusations. Now the same analysis is applied at state level (Rowlands and Warmier 1988). Witchcraft is used politically in default of other redress. From one community to another, the pattern of accusation revealed different political burdens, reflecting the lines of political legitimacy. Where the authority structure was normally strong witchcraft accusations were used at a time of transition to sway the balance by defaming a candidate for office, to hasten the exit of one who was already on the way out (Middleton 1960), or to block his choice of successor. They might be used to fuel dynastic wrangles (Schapera 1971). Usually the possibility of accusation would be one among a rich variety of strategies (Forde 1964). When the legitimacy of political office was weak and easily challenged, witchcraft accusations were used continually to disqualify from office holding.

Zambia, Malawi, Zimbabwe, and modern Zaire were at the time of study under colonial rule, the land was sparsely populated, the social system destroyed to a large extent by migrant labour and an ineffectual entry into the cash economy. The old political systems were not functioning as they would if inter-village raiding, capital punishment, self-help, and judicial ordeals were still among the resources of the officials. In that situation, accusing a rival of witchcraft was the surest way of mustering effective popular support for a cause. Sometimes witchcraft accusations disqualified unpopular incumbents of the office of village headman (Mitchell 1956). This was demonstrated in an exemplary study of the Yao in Malawi, by Clyde Mitchell, whose analysis remained the model for the subject.

Among the Yao the alleged victims of the witch were children, his own nieces and nephews, or his sisters, the female support group on which he depended for his hegemony in the village. The accusers were generally related to the accused witch as his nephews or younger brothers, persons who would normally be subject to his authority, but who were the group from which the heirs to the headmanship would be designated in the event of his death. They were bound to him by powerful moral pressures. Only proof of his total depravity would absolve them from their obedience. The accusation that he was a witch and that he killed his own nearest and dearest was further supported by the knowledge that witches get their power by incest, and that it inspires in them a lust for human flesh, preferably decaying flesh exhumed from graveyards; furthermore he belongs to a coven of witches whose members engage each other in flesh debts, each witch being forced by the others to hand over his own kin in return for feasting on theirs.

The horrible stories would not be credible if the accusations were not part of a developing rivalry between the legal heirs of the accused, on the one hand, and on the other the family of his sons who had no formal rights in the succession. The strategy of the headman was to try to reconcile and merge the two lines by marriages of cousins descended from himself and his sisters. While the younger generations were growing up the village would live in peace, but later the two parties, one led by the headman's sons who had no formal rights, and the other led by his legal heirs, his maternal kin, would align in mutual hostility. The village would be riven by strife at some point when its population exceeded a certain size in relation to its resources. It would have to split, one part would have to go away to new land. Accusations of witchcraft against the incumbent headman would hasten the process, bring the smouldering disputes to a head, and conclude by dismissing him from office. In consequence the rate of witchcraft accusations was linked to demography and this to the political cycle of the village structure. Accusations petered out at some periods, and revived at other ecologically and demographically determined points. Mitchell could predict from longitudinal data when a new wave of accusations was due, who would be accused, by whom, and even what the political outcome would be.

## EPIDEMIOLOGY OF INSIDIOUS HARM

Latent stereotyped belief in insidious damage emerges regularly at specific crises (Ardener 1970). It enables the community to restructure itself on previous lines by absolution from certain specified moral obligations. Max Marwick in this tradition wrote of a Central African people that their witch beliefs were a somewhat ruthless way

> to dissolve relations which have become redundant . . . blast down the dilapidated parts of the social structure, and clear the rubble in preparation for new ones . . . maintain the virility of the indigenous social structure by allowing the periodic redistribution of structural forces. (Marwick 1952)

For a contemporary example, in the current epidemic of AIDS there are some who have tried to work the moralizing to boost the constraints of traditional sexual morality.

In Africa there were variations on this pattern. Among the Lele of the Kasai the suspected sorcerers were the whole class of old men, and particularly those who had been initiated into the diviners' guild. They were the doctors and lawyers, as it were, the professionals who knew who the dead sorcerers were, and how they might punish the living for disobeying their wishes, and who had the remedies. But the theory of the unity of knowledge was used to show that those who could cure could kill. The older a man was, the more likely he was, so the common theory ran, to be angry and jealous of the young, and embroiled with his own age group. So age and sex were strong indicators of who would be accused of insidious damage. Women were largely excluded, and young persons completely. It was thought to be a learned skill, which eliminated young men from the range of suspects. The incidence of accusations showed the part played by sorcery beliefs in maintaining the balance between the generations. This was a village community in which many privileges went to the old men. In pre-colonial days the old would have had to defer to the middle-aged and young warriors, but the Pax Belgica had disturbed that equilibrium between young and old. Sorcery accusations restored it. Old men who tried to abuse their privileges, who made exigent demands on the young, or who stole other men's wives would in the old days sooner or later be lined up to take the poison ordeal; at the time of research, since the poison ordeal was forbidden under Belgian law, they were banished from their village. This sounds like a minor disadvantage, but it was grave because they carried their infamous reputation with them wherever they settled. The first death in the village which had given them asylum would cause them to be ousted again, until they became wanderers of no fixed abode, dependent on erratic charity (Douglas 1963).

Forty years later the same people were still convinced of much the same ideas about insidious harm from sorcery, but there were a few changes about who might be doing it. It was no longer thought to be a learned skill, so the old men were no more likely to commit it than anyone else. The range of accusations had widened completely so that it was plausible to accuse young men and women, and even children. The accusations of children against their parents were now taken seriously. The pattern had lost its structure. The little bits of theory about how it worked, which formerly had the effect of making plausible accusations do the public service of reining in the too exigent demands of the old men, had dissolved. Now it had become plausible to accuse anyone. Even the old idea that sorcery would not work at a distance, which used to rule out some suspects because they had gone too far away, and which made it sensible to exile convicted sorcerers, had disappeared. Sorcery danger was unlimited in geographical range. Within the country villages it seemed like a raging epidemic against which nothing would prevail. Living without cash in a newly monetarized economy, such solidarity as might have helped their situations was sapped by the fear of each neighbour's sorcery. But the incidence of accusations in the new epidemiological mdoel was not entirely unstructured. The arrow of accusation was stronger going in the direction from town to country. Townsfolk believed that their kin in the villages were so sorcery-infected that it was dangerous to visit them. The jealousy of the sorcerers was believed to be directed against their well-dressed, well-fed kinsmen in town. It would be very noble-minded if the latter could resist the temptation to use the imputed infamy as an excuse not to respond to the continuous begging of their country cousins.

## EUROPEAN WITCHCRAFT

William Monter may be short-sighted to think, 'All things considered, non-Western social anthropology provides keys that do not fit continental European beliefs', and that 'forays beyond Europe' are useless for understanding European witchcraft (Monter 1976: 11). The historians tend to focus on particular moments, the outbreaks of accusations being treated as one-off events that are exceptions to a more regular appreciation of material cause and effect. The anthropological focus is similar except for a focus on recurring structural problems expected to reproduce the same effects over and over again. Consequently they find that accusations work with other normative pressures.

In European studies the wild rash of witch trials that erupted in the fifteenth and sixteenth centuries and died out in the seventeenth has drawn various speculations. Individual historians have tended to think that their own case studies disprove the reasons advanced to explain mass executions of witches in other regions. For example, William Monter proposes that the French and Swiss border experience contradicts the interpretation of Keith Thomas of English witch beliefs (Monter 1976). But the African experience suggests, on the contrary, that the various explanations could each be right in different places. As a technique of exclusion and control the accusation of the same kind of crime is used to achieve different objectives. The use of torture for obtaining confessions, the demand by the ecclesiastical courts for further denunciations, vows of secrecy from those who denounced others as witches, all these judicial practices made a difference to the way the witch craze developed in different countries.

In early fourteenth-century England occasional witch trials were political and courtly in character: only in the fifteenth century did witch-hunting begin to be directed against the common people (Kieckhefer 1984:10–14). In Scotland and in France there was the same progression from courtly intrigue to mass repression from the end of the sixteenth century. The arrow of accusation, having started by pointing neither up nor down but across palace factions, changed direction.

The historians of seventeenth-century England arrive at the point when the arrow of accusation is pointing downwards, and so pay attention to changes in the economic structure which destituted certain categories and led to their posing social problems at national and neighbourhood levels (Thomas 1979; Macfarlane 1979). European witch trials were more mixed up with heresy than in England (Monter 1976). Although the conception of the witch as the child of poverty much influenced French historians (Palou 1957:50; Muchembled 1978:37) the history of French witchcraft was inevitably more involved with the contest between the Catholic Church and the civil authorities (Mandrou 1968). The Italian accusations tended to be launched by the clerics against rival religious practitioners in the surviving rural cults, humble purveyors of cures and predictions attacked by the dominant religion: a downward pointing arrow (Ginzburg 1983). In Spanish Basque country the Inquisitors found that the clergy themselves were denounced by peasant women, the first victims of accusations: an upward pointing arrow (Henningsen 1980).

Historians of European witch trials confess themselves as much at a loss to account for the decline of the beliefs as for their rise. The nineteenth-century historians saw it as a contest between superstition and reason, and the triumph of the latter (Henningsen 1980:19). A patient piecing together of the state of knowledge at the end of the seventeenth century hardly bears out that consoling picture. The question is not one of intellectual advance, the end of superstition, the demand for new standards of proof following the great scientific developments of the period (Shapiro 1983). There was plenty of superstition around still. Nor did a moral improvement make judges feel so much more kindly that they wished to mitigate the severe punishments that convicted witches received; on the contrary, the Parlement of Paris went on burning other criminals whose cases had nothing to do with magic (Mandrou 1968:353). Nor does it help to consider a wave of witchcraft accusations as a response to relative deprivation, for there are many very deprived populations which resist that resource for settling scores.

The explanation has much more to do with the growth and effectiveness of centralized judiciaries in the European states. The worst witch trial terrors were in the seventeenth century when the Thirty Years war started and ended. As backdrop to the rise and decline of witchcraft national boundaries were realigned, France and England both started and ended a civil war. The end of the century, when the witch craze died away, saw one of the periodic arrivals of the nations of Europe at a new level of centralization and judicial control. The movement to standardize the legal process would have ended resort to insidious harm for controlling rivals. The effective assertion of the rule of law, a single law for the realm, would have been much more influential for the decline of such accusations than any advance in scientific thinking or intellectual practice of demanding proof. The idea of insidious harm, hidden as it is by definition, can best exert its disruptive influence when separate rules are allowed for private and ecclesiastical courts. The comparison with leprosy beliefs that follows pays attention to political effects and especially to the disturbances that follow in the wake of a move to centralize, and that are calmed after it has been achieved. The analysis of authority and responses to authority which will be sketched below in respect of leprosy could well be applied to the variety of situations in which witchcraft was prosecuted.

## IMPUTED LEPROSY CORRECTS ABUSE OF OFFICE

To sum up, we have used witchcraft cases to show how the accusation of insidious harm works with the political balance. We have seen how it changes its direction, and how it is not exclusively used against the poor and the outcast. We have seen how, by inculpating some, it exculpates others. The next step is to discount the spectacular phantasmagoric effects of the witchcraft cases, so as to extend the analysis more widely to all kinds of social context.

Mark Pegg approaches leprosy as a historian working within the framework of the comparison of *mentalités*, as exemplified in other numbers of *Annales*. His first interest is the shift in attitudes to the body through twelfth-century Europe. Evidently, at that period in England and France the body was made into an image of society in a much more thoroughgoing way than before. But why so? Or rather, why in France and England, and not in Jerusalem? His answer deploys a compact and densely argued comparison of three cultural regimes.

The first period is from the end of the eleventh century through to the beginning of the twelfth, roughly to 1125. This would be the time when the tremendous effort to centralize the Church had just begun, in response to the Moorish threat in the Mediterranean, and after the First Crusade. The Crusades were to bring profound upheavals into Europe; new wealth and monetarization of what had been largely a barter economy; new classes: rich burghers rivalling the nobility in splendour, demanding to marry their sons and daughters to noble families but being refused; and a new, large class of poor. A new learned bureaucracy was developing, economic power was concentrating.

By the end of the century the standard ideas of the person, the body and the society were transformed. The secular powers put in hand the centralization of the kingdoms to keep pace with the centralization of the Church. By the end of the century the hierarchical principles were established on a larger scale and more effectively than ever before. But the movement could not have been smooth. In the background of the major transformation, in the small face-to-face societies of rural demesne, little hierarchies were in existence: the little hierarchy of a monastery, of a lord and his knights, a bishop and his priests. The small local hierarchies were threatened by new forms of wealth, new temptations, loss of respect for old obligations.

In this first period of the comparison, to the beginning of the twelfth century, leprosy seems to have been rare. The few recorded charges were always made against persons in power by their own subordinates. Monks complaining of the harsh and arbitrary rule of their abbot, priests complaining of the peculation of their bishop, knights dissatisfied with their lord, would charge the unpopular holder of office with leprosy. The charge is analogous to the charge of witchcraft made against a village head to resolve conflict in the Yao village. Its object was to restore the proper functioning of a small-scale hierarchy. A leper went through a ceremony of ritual death inspired by the Biblical law controlling lepers. He lost control over his property and was automatically and definitively removed from office. Leprosy was associated with sin, it was a chastisement by the hand of God, but as it was not considered to be a source of infection at that stage there were no restrictions on the leper's free movement.

## FILTH IMPUTED TO THE DISENTITLED

In the course of the stressful next fifty years the accusation of leprosy changed its target. New wealth combined with centralization and threw up masses of poor. After 1170 vagabonds, beggars, and heretics were the category charged with leprosy, while the rich and powerful suddenly seem to have become practically immune. Instead of being deposed from office (for they held none) the new class of lepers were segregated into leprosariums, part of the successful attempt to create order that resulted in the highly structured society of the thirteenth century. The comparison with witchcraft has already prepared us for the physical constraints and the systematic vilification of lepers that belongs to this period. The idea of the disease was transformed. Lepers were now held to be highly infectious, the disease was thought to be transmitted by sexual penetration. Endowed with an inordinate sexual appetite, lepers were incestuous, lepers were rapists, lepers sought to spread their condition by forced sexual intercourse with healthy persons. Segregated for the public good, they were not allowed to move freely in London streets, they were not able to prosecute at law, nor to inherit land, nor to transmit land rights that they might otherwise have had by inheritance. They were effectually stripped of citizenship.

It would seem that the discrimination against lepers was a solution to the problem of masses disadvantaged by a new individualism eroding the feudal system. Landless persons whom no one wanted to know about were tidied away in leprosariums. Legislation began to segregate lepers from the rest of the community. The Third Lateran Council prohibited them from attending church with healthy persons; they had to have their own churches and their own graveyards. The segregation and control of lepers was part of the generally increased control on sexuality through the period: marriage laws were tightened up, sexual control over lay persons and clerics was asserted, celibacy for the clergy and continence for the unmarried, fidelity for the married laity. Endowing a leprosarium was a much approved form of philanthropy and numerous leprosaria sprung up in the West. The donors themselves might be classified lepers: fair enough, if they were not allowed otherwise to hold their own property, to endow a refuge for oneself. Living in the controlled conditions of a leprosarium would have been relatively comfortable, but the less fortunate either wandered or lived in segregated leper settlements (Moore 1987:54–5).

By the end of the twelfth century writing about leprosy was so prolific that it is thought to indicate a veritable epidemic (Foucault 1972:16; Brody 1974:103; Turner 1984:66–154, and see also Beriac 1988). However, the anthropological context of imputed filth throws doubt on the idea that a leprosy epidemic in England and France appeared and gradually died away in those seventy-five years. It is hardly credible that the disease itself, which had formerly chosen its few victims among the elite, now chose them in large quantities among the dispossessed, leaving its former victims alone. Since they had not been immune earlier the idea of epidemic leprosy would be more plausible if there was some record of an equivalent number of nobles, bishops, and abbots being afflicted with it in the later third of the twelfth century. Perhaps a soap and water barrier blocked the spread of the disease, perhaps the rich did wash more; it is doubtful. More plausible, the arrow of accusation had changed direction in the same way that it did with witchcraft four centuries later.

## FILTH IMPUTED TO OUTSIDERS

The third leg of the argument developed by Mark Pegg is the extraordinary contrast of the theory of leprosy in Western Christendom and in the Latin Kingdom of Jerusalem in the East. The first surprise is that in the East the disease was known and accurately described. It is a surprise because the weakness of diagnosis in the West could have been attributed to the general lack of medical knowledge at the time. Detailed and precise descriptions of a disease called 'elephantiasis', corresponding in symptoms and prognosis to Hansen's disease, show that leprosy as we know it was known. In the West, though the disease attracted so much attention, there was no precise diagnosis or description. Evidently many kinds of skin disease counted as leprosy: eczema, psoriasis, scrofula, skin cancers, ulcers of various kinds. It is very likely that in France and England poor people who were not infected were herded into leper houses. If there was an epidemic the skeletal remains from leper graveyards should show the marks on deformed and scarred bones, but those who believe in the real increase of leprosy have to contend with the very small archaeological traces it left. Bryan Turner maintains that the people of the period were confusing a real disease with imaginary sins (Turner 1984). It is more likely that they were trying to cure a real social blight by isolating an imagined disease.

In the West the medical diagnosis was not specific, and the infamy imputed to lepers shows the idea of insidious harm being put to political use. In the East the precise diagnosis went hand in hand with moral detachment, for sin was not associated with leprosy. So far from being stripped of civic status, a leper, competently diagnosed in the Kingdom of Jerusalem, had his civic rights safeguarded. There was an order of leper knights, unthinkable in the West. Leper houses were governed by lepers, again something unheard of in the West. There was no theory of the king's body implicating the body politic, and no objection whatever to the anointing and crowning of a leper as king.

To account for the difference, Pegg renews his research into political and economic patterns and finds in the Latin Kingdom of Jerusalem a pattern of control very different from the simple hierarchical kingdoms of Europe at the end of the eleventh century. It was also very different from the economic competitiveness of burghers and nobles in the later period, contained by the centralizing power of the king from the middle of the century. In the Eastern Kingdom he describes the ten noble families sharing power with the king, more as equals. Instead of a hierarchical hill of rank, the polity is a plateau. It sounds like an egalitarian political enclave, the Christian state in the middle of the Muslim world, surrounded by enemies, militarily weak, relatively poor, and very valiant. In those conditions cultural theory would predict that the members of the community would be far more impressed with the need for solidarity than for carving out distinctions among themselves. Indeed, he notes a law to punish severely any Christian having sexual relations with a non-Christian. The external boundary looms so much more significantly in such conditions that infectious disease will not be made into a political weapon for keeping down the system's derelicts, nor will the system be sufficiently hierarchical for there to be occasion to use imputed filth to remove unpopular incumbents of high office.

## CONCLUSION

Thanks to a brilliant article, much richer and far better documented than this summary has suggested, three cultural patterns of response to insidious harm from lepers have been illustrated. They correspond to three of the types of witchcraft accusations identified in Africa. In the first case the arrow points up, against the office holders attempting to abuse their advantages. In another it points down, against the disfranchised majority. In the last it points outwards, against the outsiders who threaten the tight, beleaguered community.

Given his point of departure, the central interest for Mark Pegg is the role that the newly transformed idea of the leper played in a new idea of society that emerged in the West: the leper's diseased body was the reprehensible metaphor of social disorder. But much more than a metaphor, as he shows, leprosy was credited with dangerous effects which had to be controlled. The anthropological analysis supplements the *mentalités* approach of French historians by drawing attention to the context of discrimination. Phrasing the situation in terms of accusations, the idea of contagious leprosy was used to solve social dilemmas by shifting legitimacy into a new pattern. Tracing the resulting benefits for the accusers and loss for the accused reveals the social context in which it was plausible to believe such outrageous libels. Pegg even argues that the change in the direction of accusations against lepers in the twelfth century played an integral role in the process of centralizing Church and State in Western Christendom.

To suggest that the ideas about leprosy enabled hordes of vagabonds, mendicants, and homeless wanderers to be put under control is very much in keeping with the work of Michel Foucault on the disciplines of society. The direction of that work has been to warn researchers to watch out for despotism and take note of attacks against the weak and helpless. The normative implication that the perfect society would be non-persecuting has so strongly gripped the imagination of social science writers (Richards 1990) that it has left no room for a more open-ended comparative framework. It is true that any community whatever is liable to try to control its boundary by accusing the fringes of harbouring infection or limiting the influx of poverty-stricken strangers by a theory of imported disease (Douglas and Calvez 1990). But there is more to be said.

Sociologists are very impressed with the ferocity with which a community constitutes its boundaries and oppresses its marginal members. They recognized at once that accusations of immoral conduct are a technique of control against the weak and powerless (Nelkin and Gilman 1988). This essay has sought to show the more complex uses of accusation. The histories of the definition of a disease call to mind that the community constitutes itself also in a struggle for power between its members. Fears of witchcraft or fears of infection are easily mobilized for sending the blood libel to its target. Within the more complex framework of cultural comparison suggested here, there should be scope for a partnership between cultural theory and medical history. In such a framework we should be able to reconsider the prolonged outbreak of leprosy in a cold climate, that apparently devastated the region, but then cleared up and went away without leaving the marks of its depredations on the population.

## ACKNOWLEDGEMENTS

This paper was prepared for the MIT Conference, 'Epidemics: Perspectives in Cultural Studies', 19–20 October 1990, under the title of 'Infection and Witchcraft as Insidious Harm'. I wish to take the opportunity of thanking the organizers, Kenneth Manning, David Halperin, and David Thorburn for the hospitable welcome and stimulating discussion. A French version was later presented at the Conference AEPS at the *Institut Régional du Travail Social de Bretagne*, at Rennes, 22 November, and again I wish to thank Marcel Calvez and Dr Guihard for hospitality and criticism. I also wish to acknowledge the helpful comments of Robert Moore who read an earlier version of the manuscript, and above all Mark Pegg for many long instructive conversations.

## REFERENCES

Ardener, E. (1970) 'Witchcraft, Economics and the Continuity of Belief', in Mary Douglas (ed.), *Witchcraft Confessions and Accusations*, London, Tavistock, pp. 141–160.

Beriac, Françoise (1988) *Histoire des Lépreux au Moyen Age: Une Société d'Exclus*, Paris, Imago.

Brody, S.N. (1974) *The Disease of the Soul: Leprosy in Medieval Literature*, Ithaca, Cornell University Press, p. 103.

Douglas, Mary (1963) 'Techniques of Sorcery Control in Central Africa', in John Middleton and E.H. Winter (eds), *Witchcraft and Sorcery in East Africa*, London, Routledge & Kegan Paul, pp. 123–41.

Douglas, Mary (1970) *Witchcraft Accusations and Confessions, Essays presented to E. Evans-Pritchard*, London, Tavistock Publications.

Douglas, Mary and Calvez, Marcel (1990) 'The Self as Risk Taker: A Cultural Theory of Contagion in Relation to AIDS', *The Sociological Review* 38,3:445–64.

Forde, Daryll (1964) 'Spirits, Witches and Sorcerers', *Yako Studies*, Oxford, IAI, pp. 210–33.

Foucault, Michel (1972) *Histoire de la Folie à l'Age Classique*, Paris, Plon, p. 16.

Ginzburg, Carlo (1983) *Night Battles: Witchcraft and Agrarian Cults in the Sixteenth and Seventeenth Centuries*, London, Routledge & Kegan Paul.

Henningsen, G. (1980) *The Witches' Advocate: Basque Witchcraft and the Spanish Inquisition, 1609–1614*, University of Nevada Press.

Kieckhefer, R. (1984) *European Witch Trials*, Berkeley, California University Press.

Macfarlane, Alan (1970) 'Witchcraft in Tudor and Stuart Essex', in Mary Douglas (ed.), *Witchcraft Accusations and Confessions*, London, Tavistock, pp. 81–99.

Macfarlane, A. (1979) *Witchcraft in Tudor and Stuart England*, London, Routledge and Kegan Paul.

Mandrou, R. (1968) *Magistrats et Sorciers en France au XVII siècle: Une Analyse de Psychologie Historique*, Paris, Plon.

Marwick, Max (1952) 'The Social Context of Cewa Witch Beliefs', *Africa*, 22,2:120–35; 3:215–33.

Middleton, John (1960) *Lugbara Religion*, Oxford, Oxford University Press.

Mitchell, Clyde (1956) *The Yao Village*, Manchester, Manchester University Press.

Monter, W.E. (1976) *Witchcraft in France and Switzerland: The Borderlands during the Reformation*, Ithaca, Cornell University Press.

Moore, Robert (1987) *The Formation of a Persecuting Society*, Oxford, Oxford University Press.

Muchembled, R. (1978) *Prophètes et Sorciers*, Paris, Hachette.

Nelkin, D. and Gilman, S. (1988) 'Placing Blame for Devastating Disease', *Social Research* 55(3):361–78.

Palou, Jean (1957) 'La Sorcellerie', *Que Sais-Je?*, Paris, Presses Universitaires de France.

Pegg, Mark G. (1990) 'Le Corps et l'autorité: la lepre de Badouin IV', *Annales ESC*, mars-avril, 2:265–87.

Richards, D.A. (1990) 'Human Rights, Public Health and the Idea of Moral Plague', *Social Research* 55(3):433–53.

Rowlands, M. and Warmier, J.-P. (1988) 'Sorcery, Power and the Modern State in Cameroon', *Man* (NS) 23:118–32.

Schapera, I. (1971) *Rain Making Rites of Tswana Tribes*, Cambridge, African Studies Centre.

Shapiro, B. (1983) *Probability and Certainty in Seventeenth-Century England: A Study of the Relationships between Natural Science, Religion, History, Law, and Literature*, New Jersey, Princeton University Press.

Thomas, Keith (1979) *Religion and the Decline of Magic*, London, Weidenfeld & Nicolson.

Thompson, M., Ellis, R. and Wildavsky, A. (1990) *Cultural Theory*, Boulder, Colorado, Westview Press.

Turner, B.S. (1984) *The Body and Society: Explorations in Social Theory*, Oxford, Blackwell, pp. 66–154.

# 6

# THE SELF AS RISK-TAKER
## A cultural theory of contagion in relation to AIDS

## SELF-KNOWLEDGE, A CULTURAL PRODUCT

In a long tradition in economics the individual self is conceived as risk-averse. This is for no better reason than that the theory of rational choice assumes that the individual will always choose according to his own self-interest, and that so choosing is the essence of rational behaviour. At the same time the theory gives no guidance for knowing how that interest is conceived. The thesis here to be proposed is that the self is risk-taking or risk-averse according to a predictable pattern of dealings between the person and others in the community. Both emerge, the community and the person's self, as ready for particular risks or as averse to them, in the course of their interactions. The person who never thought of himself as a risk-taker, in the unfolding of the drama of his personal life, and under the threat of the community's censure, finds himself declaring a commitment to high risk.

The relevant behaviour for identifying this process is in mutual scanning, judging, reproving and excusing, blaming and retaliating against blame. No subtle or subjective concept of the self is to be used here. Psychology, emotions, or aesthetics play no part. It is an outside view of the self. It is an ethnomethodological-sociological view for which all the evidence comes from listening to claims the ego makes in the name of self-knowledge, or from listening to ego's deploying self-knowledge for rebutting other's claims.

This concept of the self can be used to combat the established theories of individualist psychology. The latter are vindicated by empirical research; this concept is equally empirical. It relies not

102

at all on intuitive, subjective sources of knowledge about own self or other selves, but on systematic observation. If a person is heard to reject advice about safety and to take grave risks in the name of his knowledge of his own self, the evidence about himself is stronger than anything which he puts on record replying to questionnaires and doing tests in the psychological laboratory: stronger because the person is putting his life where his mouth is. When action and talk support each other, you have something to go on. Theorizing about differential ratings for intelligence becomes irrelevant. A homosexual may be advised by the doctor to give up certain practices because of the danger of AIDS, he may be warned that he is risking his life by retaining these practices. If he replies that he has never been a cautious person, and that the high-risk way of life is what he prefers, he is deploying information about himself to support his claim to be left alone, to do as he likes, to be free of well-wishers' interference. A refusal to take sound hygienic advice is not to be attributed to weakness of understanding. It is a preference. To account for preferences there is only cultural theory.[1]

At a second level of elaboration, community and self are reciprocal notions. The thesis is that the cultural project to make the city makes the selves at the same time. An endless dialogue about how to achieve the ideal community engages four kinds of culture, in each of which the self is required to play a different role. Each culture produces its own biases in knowledge as a result of the adversarial engagement between centre and peripheries. There will be four distinctive theories about how knowledge is legitimated. Four types of theory about the self also emerge, concerning the rightness of risk-taking and when it is right to be risk-averse. The crux is the attitude to knowledge. These topics recall the arguments about beliefs and values begun twenty years ago in *Natural Symbols* (Douglas 1970). The illustration will be the question of the acceptability of the medical profession's advice on how to be protected against a deadly virus.

Cultural theory shows the citizens reinforcing their theories of the body and of infection in face of a severe crisis, in this case the invasion of AIDS. This grave threat to the community generates a debate about the body's vulnerability, and about the sources of infection, and about the status of professional advice. The debate reveals three or four types of body, and as many responses to official medical information. It will become clear that the cultural project to form the city is no gentle, academic game, but a desperate struggle, a life and death struggle. Let us be careful not to idealize the community. It does not always deal kindly with its members.

## THE TYPOLOGY OF CULTURAL THEORY

### The city core or the central community

This is an ordered and to some extent centralized group. It may have one or two mutually co-ordinated centres, or even more. It is a symbolic system, attracting solidarity, capable of being mobilized in its own defence, holding strong views on correct norms of behaviour. Consequently it has a complementary view of what constitutes unacceptable deviance, and its members are generally in the habit of backing the agreed norms of behaviour with a list of natural dangers that will blot out the whole community if deviance is allowed. It is a complex group, it has developed consensus for a common pattern of order, and for dealing with the boundary against the outside. It has agreed methods of proper representation, and of protest. Usually an established community institutes some countervailing power within itself. For example, the Church and State contested and shared legitimacy in fifteeth-century Europe, Pope and Emperor in Byzantium, Rajah and Brahmin in India, royal dynasty against the instituted representation of commoners in many African kingdoms. By means of these countervailing institutions some formal protest is centrally incorporated into the community process. (But this is not the only protest engendered in the cultural project, most of it is in segments of the community unattached to the centre.)

This is a hierarchical structure in which a large part of the energies of members have been devoted to intellectualizing their commitment to its forms and to politicizing the forces of nature so that they are seen to uphold the right way of life and to penalize the wrong. When the epidemic comes, we would expect this part of the city to tighten its defences, to become more punishing and more controlling. Since the epidemic is held to be caused by deviant sexual practices, it is certain that the tension between the centre and the dissidents will be focused on the idea of the conjugal couple as the norm.

## Dissenting enclaves

Dissenting minorities are always present in the city, though often unrecognized or refused the recognition they demand. They do not have internally structured complementary and countervailing sections, nor do they organize by ranked, separate compartments.[2] Christian Church history gives many examples of the non-conformist religions, but there are many secular examples. Their cultural attitudes are coloured by their ongoing protest against the centre community which has pushed them into an enclave by rejecting their principles. Because the centre is seen to be structured, hierarchical, and oppressive to the dissident enclaves, the latter espouse equality, absence of structure, and unmediated directness of address.[3] They need to achieve consensus without being able to impose structure, and therefore, since the consensus that is achieved cannot be handed over to routine institutions, it has to be perpetually renewed. In these enclaves where formal institutions for leadership and decision are weak, charisma tends to rule.

In what follows we shall only be considering enclaves whose sexual norms are held to be highly risk-bearing in the medical opinion of the centre community, and who for that reason are segregated.

## Individualist

This is the culture of entrepreneurial professions, often in the market place, in entertainment business, in brokerage. It is also found on the entrepreneurial edge of any profession or business. The individualist by definition does not belong to any exclusive group, though he may aim to lead one if his dealings give him economies of scale which a following can realize for him.

In our European history the entrepreneur has traditionally been useful to both groups above, more especially to the central community. But communities value loyalty and just because his loyalty is not to be vouched for, he tends to be suspect or despised.

## Isolate

From any of the three other corners of the cultural map the isolates appear as a residual category. They have not been drawn into the structure as active subjects but find their own activities restricted by structures imposed by others. They are people whose autonomy has been withdrawn from them by the predatory expansions of the other cultural types. Gerald Mars (1984) identifies these people as occupationally in the most victimized part of the social structure, and Thompson (1984) in respect of their attitudes to major risks and to their own options, calls them 'ineffectuals' or 'fatalists'. It is easy for them to become victims, isolated and to some extent disorganized as they are, but they can often find ways of exploiting the rest of the system, for creativity and even financial gain.

These four types of culture are present in any city. They correspond to the four boxes in a 2 by 2 matrix:

*Grid*, a vertical dimension indicating degrees of autonomy; complete at zero where structure is minimal, and restricted at the top by structures imposed by various forms of organization.

*Group*, a horizontal dimension, indicating degrees of incorporation, minimal at zero, complete at the far right.

Figure 6.1 shows the four cultures of the city as four corners of the square. They are of course relative positions, not places. The two right-hand boxes show different forms of community consensus, not just different, but each defined in opposition to the other, and defined in the course of a struggle. The two left-

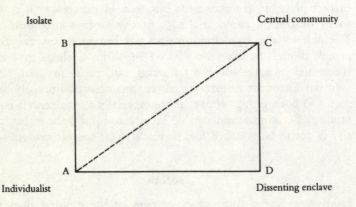

*Figure 6.1*

hand boxes show individuals whose membership of groups is not a constraint on their behaviour.

Running from top right to bottom left, between C and A, lies what is known as the positive diagonal. The line connects two modes of exerting power and influence. It represents the potential and often actual alliance of the centre community with its entrepreneur individualists, who bring in much needed information and supplies. The other diagonal, the negative, represents the two cultural categories who are either self-withdrawn, because they dislike the norms of the centre community, or expelled to the margins by the centre community.

There is tension between the two diagonals.

## THE STATUS OF KNOWLEDGE

The first source of difference in each type of culture is the attitude to the knowledge professions. The analysis will be similar to and compatible with Pierre Bourdieu's theory of *habitus* (1979), a quartering of the social field according to individual endowments of symbolic and economic capital. But comparison of how much economic capital and what kind of symbolic capital raises the question of thresholds and commensurability. In our own times, we could take as a basis for comparison a small town community, the local leaders in the liberal professions, law, statecraft, and medicine, and third generations of wealthy families. The centre community, because it has ways of controlling access to wealth and influence, corresponds to Bourdieu's category of persons well-endowed with symbolic and economic capital.

### The centre community

Here the authority of the established professions is accepted, and also the ranking generated from within them. Of course the community respects them, it set them up in the first place. The centre faithfully models its knowledge of safety in hygiene and diet on what it understands to be their considered position. The pressures to conformity come from the continual exchange between members of that category of advice in sickness, child care, shared meals at each others' hospitable tables, marriages, expenditures of time and social support. The social claims they make on each other are also cultural demands to conform. The favoured theory of where reliable knowledge is to be found upholds the established professions. These people would consider knowledge to be the product of slow, patient, accumulated, collective work. They would expect theory to be highly complex and difficult to transmit except by long apprenticeship to technical competence. They demand central establishment accreditation from all practitioners, and so would reject fringe medicine, alternative medicine, folk medicine, and popular 'panaceas'. This is going to be a regular source of friction between centre and periphery, and a point of frantic disagreement in time of epidemic.

## The enclave culture of dissenting minorities

This culture rejects the knowledge base of the central community, along with its authority (Shilts 1987). The learned professions are suspect. The minorities' social withdrawal from the centre frees them from the pressures of commensality and other social exchanges. They accept or create a social division between themselves and the centre. At the same time, having chosen to be or finding themselves peripheralized, they accept also the affinity this gives them (a negative community of interest) with other enclaves who may have very different reasons for dissent or exclusion. The enclave can hang loose, unimpressed by the prestige of established medicine, and open to alternative health advice. But since the enclave tends to be a strong and charismatic group, its members are subject to group pressures. Hence a tendency to develop its own favoured theories. For example, there was a fashion among some California gay communities to believe that healthy eating and macrobiotic foods could prevent HIV infection. These ideas do not stand up to the tests of complexity that the theoretical expectations of the central community would require. Practice can be quickly learned; accreditation depends on show of loyalty to charismatic teachers. Claims to innate personal talent weigh more than precise testing of technical knowledge. Authority is largely personal, in medicine as in politics.

A characteristic enclave style of knowledge emerged in the 1900s with the growth among artists, architects, and intellectuals of the Arts and Crafts movement. The enclave introduced healthy fashions in taking exercise, clothing, eating; it emphasized natural products, raw foods, and consistently placed itself against the fashions in the positive diagonal of the time, which it dubbed artificial. Modern 'enclave medicine' is a protest against the power-hungry, worldly elitist professions, particularly against surgeons and the pharmaceutical industry, and a government that does not care for its people:

> Some died while Reagan administration officials ignored pleas from government scientists and did not allow adequate funding for AIDS research until the epidemic had already spread throughout the country. People died while scientists did not at first devote appropriate attention to the epidemic because they perceived little prestige to be gained in studying a homosexual affliction . . . (Shilts 1987: xxii)

With all the energy that is always stimulated by conspiracy theory the enclave counsels against adulterated foods, against stimulants and sedatives, and artificial additives. Its stylistic preference is for homespun, folkloristic remedies. It is inevitably against the industrial mass production of fast foods.

Just as the social intercourse of the central community reinforces its knowledge base, so does enclave medicine respond to and reinforce an enclaved style of living. The status of knowledge reinforces group boundaries and internal social exchanges within the group (Mars and Mars forthcoming).

## Cultural frontiersmen and cosmopolitans

At every level of education or income the individualist is a trend-setter, in a community of trend-setters. They are the shibboleth breakers, the iconoclasts, the scoffers, the pioneers in taste and fashion. Likewise in knowledge, they are highly idiosyncratic in response to demands of safety in health and diet. Generally they are risk-takers: their lifestyle involves them in risk of heart failure and risk of high blood pressure from the ardours of competitive feasting. When they fall ill they regard their personal luck as having come to an end. As to therapy, always hopeful, the sick entrepreneur chooses an entrepreneurial therapist, the latest in surgical techniques, the newest whizzkid surgeon, but they also expect their doctors to carry proper accreditation as for the central community. Their sickness gives them one more forum for displaying their individuality.

### Eccentric culture of isolates

Without any regular social reinforcement for one theory over another, without support from others for their chosen cultural style, the isolates have no special respect for the attitudes to knowledge in any of the other three cultures. They tend to be very eccentric. Their eccentricity reinforces their isolation. They are fatalists. They expect conspiracy, but it does not shock or surprise them as it does the enclave dwellers. Whereas the fellow inhabitants on the negative diagonal, the dissenting minorities, believe in a conspiracy on a human scale which pits the wealth-hungry industrialists and power-hungry government against the innocent, the isolates extend the idea of mysterious conspiracy beyond the human sphere. Some demonic cause of ill fortune is just as plausible for them as a conspiracy of financial magnates and armaments manufacturers. Isolated means there is no one to argue with, no one to make claims on the continuity and coherence of their ideas. What they think does not matter to anyone else, so there, in the sphere of thought, they exercise autonomy. Where everyone else's freedom is restricted by the exigencies of cultural warfare, isolates are made free by their isolation. Not enlisted to any side, they make sense of the world as *francs tireurs* on their own behalf.

## IDEAS ABOUT THE BODY

If scientific information does not diffuse smoothly and quickly, it is because of its value in the cultural struggle. The status of knowledge in the four cultures of the city is more a battlefield than a classroom situation. In no other topic does the cultural contest reach so deep into the consciousness of the citizen as it does in regard to health and hygiene and risks of infection, as Foucault has pointed out. First consider the body's inherent powers of resistance to the HIV virus. Some consider their own body to be highly vulnerable to the virus, liable to attack from all directions; others regard their own body as immune. In the course of fieldwork in Brittany four popular attitudes to the risk of infection from HIV emerged.

1 The body is a porous thing, completely open to every danger-ous invasion; it can be brought low by virus or bacteria at any time, and in addition it has to carry its own tally of inhering

weaknesses. On this view the body is basically unprotectable. The person to whom it belongs lives in constant awareness of the possibility of death. When death does come, there is no need of any explanation.

2 The body is very strong; it is an effective immune system; it has power to cope with infection, its resources produce a self-restoring equilibrium. The owner of this body usually takes care to perform hygienic routines to allow it to function; but often he believes that it is so strong that there is no need of special precautions, or to change behaviour in any way.

3 The body is strong because it has two protective layers. One is its own physical skin, with specific points of entry and egress; the other protective skin is the community, which makes a social clarification of boundaries, controls points of entry and egress, and codifies acceptable sexual behaviour. The best immune system is the community; the body has not enough resources on its own. But the outside skin, the community, must be kept whole. It can be destroyed by wrong behaviour. Most of the efforts at prevention have to be focused on protecting this last protective layer.

4 The body is a machine that has its own protective envelope: if pierced it admits invasive principles which interfere with its functioning and expose it to infection. On this theory of the body, medical precautions are justified as part of normal regulation of the body. The owner of the body takes hygienic precautions, uses prophylaxis. Consistently he believes that contamination by AIDS will have been due to a mistake, a moment's carelessness, a failure to control sex or food. If a victim of AIDS had behaved with proper care he would not have succumbed.

These four beliefs are not described as such by the persons involved in the community dialogue about AIDS infection. They are abstractions distilled by the social workers and researchers from the responses to advice. The most baffling thing about the pattern is that a large number of the community at risk are impervious to information; either they know unshakeably that they themselves are immune, or recognizing that death is normal they draw the conclusion that to live trying to avoid it is abhorrent.

In short, among those who accept the teaching of science some also believe in an extra source of immunity, their community.

They turn a lot of their attention to protecting it instead of caring for their own bodies. Before unravelling these different views of the self as part of the cultural project to make a city, I should consider first the other side, the attitudes to infection.

## CREDIBILITY OF SCIENCE

The problem for medicine is that its teachings are always resisted. The response to medicine is a four-fold dialogue about the claims of the city. When it comes to a particular disease, the existing attempts on the part of the central community to segregate itself and control its borders have their effect on others. The establishment theory has to do battle with alternative theories developed to prevent the community from tightening its control over its periphery. The cultural project on which all citizens are engaged defines bodies and dangers and uses both as instruments in the contest.

Establishment medicine teaches that the AIDS virus is a lethal contagious disease. The transmission is through very specific bodily contacts. The life of the virus is fragile; left outside of the bloodstream it dies quickly. It lives in one body and enters another by entering the bloodstream, either by sexual penetration or by contact with blood through open cuts, such as infected hypodermic needles. It is definitely not conveyed by breathing the same air. It is contagious, not infectious. Within this official consensus there is room for a great deal of controversy, for example on the issue of transmission by saliva. It is agreed that droplets in the breath, using the same lavatory seat, breathing into the same telephone, and other indirect contacts caused by sheer proximity do not convey the disease.

The usual explanation of failure to accept the establishment theory on medical and other risks is lack of education among the public. Inevitably, the centre information comes from the centre culture. Part of its process of self-constitution as a community is for the centre to perceive itself as superior to those on the fringe. If the latter do not agree about hygiene and epidemic risks, it is because they are ignorant, they are irrational and prey to their emotions. The centre tries to turn the problem of disagreement into its own processes of incorporation and stratification. The process of misjudgement is analogous to colonial misperception of native superstition. Or rather, as we might borrow from Brian

Wynne's metaphor, the irrationally superstitious boot belongs on the other foot:

> The nuclear industry seems to show more social identity with primitive societies rather than with the modern science whose imagery it has appropriated. . . Through ritual declamations of rationality, nuclear thinking, like primitive thinking, expresses an underlying political authoritarianism and socio-psychological insecurity. (Wynne 1982)

The assumptions that the centre makes about the causes of disagreement lead to recommendations to educate the benighted, but the educational effort keeps failing. It fails not because the public is ignorant or irrational; citizens have their reasons for resisting information of certain kinds.

One favourite popular alternative to this view starts by refusing authority to science, usually by pointing to its lack of consensus. The defence of ignorance is that science does not really know; it does not speak with one voice, there is massive uncertainty underlying its pronouncements. Another dissident view is a confident belief that miasma conveys infection. Modern science to the contrary, the popular theory holds that there exist, in the surrounding air and on the surfaces we touch, hidden powers to transmit disease from any infected person who breathes the same air, shares a toothbrush, handles the same food utensils, cups, plates, glasses: proximity is dangerous. If there were no miasmic theory why would the television have to be disinfected after being gazed at by HIV positive patients? A nurse explained: 'I took the test, because I was expecting a child . . . there was a patient who often used our telephone, that was really why' (Calvez 1989: 80). The mother of an HIV positive child said: 'I don't see any special risk of contamination, except supposing he were to dribble, or if his brothers were to eat after him' (Calvez 1989: 80). A homosexual said that he was well aware of the look in his friends' faces as they wondered if it was safe to go on the lavatory after him.

Miasma is not a scientific theory, it is not alternative science, but it works like a causal theory about transmission of infection, a basis for prediction and explanation, a guide for action. Such possibilities of differing from the establishment medicine have always been available as instruments in the cultural contest.

The centre community is not homogeneous. Its view is fractured into the same four sides, contesting with one another for control and for avoiding control. In its own internal contest there are the four cultures in embryo, the same positive diagonal. For the bottom left of the diagonal find the liberal advocates of an open community, who want to make it into a tolerant place, a community that will include and generously extend its protection to its minorities, without forcing them into conformity. They find themselves in rhetorical alliance with the brokers and entrepreneurs who also demand tolerance. At the top right of the inner councils of the centre community are the stern advocates of rectitude, who see virtue as the only sure foundation of authority and peace. In this contest internal to the centre community the social workers are aligned on the side of liberal tolerance. A strict interpretation of the established medical scientific theory would be congenial and appropriate for clinics working with homosexuals and drug addicts. It is part of the role of the social worker to encourage the latter to control their own situation; the social worker tries to shield unfortunates against the attempts of the central community to put them under irksome control. The strict view enables the clinic doctor to say that there is not too much need to worry about the healthy population mingling with HIV positives, so long as everyone (without discrimination) takes the necessary hygienic measures. At the same time, the other view, that the infection is miasmic, serves the cause of those at the centre who want to reject outsiders and deviants, push them further into the periphery. The product of science, its knowledge, is made into a resource for claims and counter claims about how citizenship is to be defined. The debate goes on in consulting rooms, hospitals, at the hustings, in science research conferences. There is always plenty of scope for doubting authoritative pronouncements.

The argument against the centre makes strange allies. For example, consultants are responsible to their patients and tend to take a conservative view. If science says that with careful hygienic precautions the world can be made safe for the HIV positive and the rest of the population to live in proximity, it may not be wise to give this cheering news to patients. So they tend to be ultra cautious, emphasizing the uncertainty and controversy surrounding the subject. Unwittingly they find themselves lined up with those who reject science, and thus lending support to miasmic theories of infection. Miasma is an instrument of total rejection. The mere physical presence of the unwanted Other is

dangerous. Their use of the same space and times and their breathing the common air is a menace to the rest of the community.
The miasmic danger of AIDS is a reason for expelling foreign
workers, restricting immigration, prohibiting sexually deviant
practices, and, of course, drugs. In their minds the consultants
are not rejecting science, not at all. Where consensus is weak they
read uncertainty, and consequently advise maximum precautions.
Their professional responsibility to their clients requires no less
(Masters, Johnson and Kolodny 1988). The consultants are not
subscribing to a miasmic theory of transmission, but they can be
cited in defence of it by extreme right-wing political movements
whose platform rhetoric already appeals to xenophobia and conformism. The expectation that foreign workers are more likely
to be HIV positive, and that homosexuals, prostitutes, and intra-
venous drug addicts are populations at risk inflames their
exclusionary rhetoric.

## THE VIEW FROM COMMUNITY

Return to Figure 6.1 and consider the problem that faces the city.
Try to see the fragile cultural project from the community's
point of view. Their idea of the body includes a weak immunity
conferred by the double envelope, the body's own skin, and the
community's skin. The theory of infection is miasmic. Within
the community a person can be safe, so long as entry to the body
and entry to the community is controlled. The most appropriate
action to take in face of the epidemic is consolidation of the
community, exclusion of outsiders, and repression of deviants.
The first duty is to call home the wanderers, the true members
of the community who have gone abroad or whose work takes
them regularly to dangerous places abroad. Then the categories
at risk have to be defined, and isolated. Homosexuals are told to
organize themselves into segregated mini-communities of their
own, thus providing the centre community with a sexual cordon
sanitaire. All of this organizing effort is supported by blaming
procedures: the population at risk is divided into those needing
care and protection, and those needing forcible detention. Intellectual dilemmas which arise in the process are not easy to solve
honestly. For example, sending drug addicts and young homosexuals to prison is a default recourse; it pretends to be a form
of segregation, but it is a pretence which would only be true if

there were no sex in prison. French authorities are in a dilemma.
How can they make an official distribution of condoms to pris-
oners when officially prison is a place without sex?

The combined notions of territory and community form a
protective layer round the body. A farm worker from Marcel
Calvez's own Breton village, on hearing that he was working for
AIDS victims, replied: 'Ah, you really shouldn't have too much
to do on that . . . anyway, if they had stayed at home, it wouldn't
have happened to them' (Calvez 1989:44). The words 'at home'
refer to a set of relations in a stable group, rooted in the neighbourhood, where good comportment guarantees good health. A
psychiatric nurse described the danger to the community from
commuters:

> At first AIDS had nothing to do with us. The same with
> drugs. That was just for the rich children in Paris. But I
> don't really see why AIDS should be at Paris, but not at
> Rennes. There is a train between Paris and Rennes. People
> in Rennes work in Paris, who come back to Rennes every
> weekend. They can bring it back to Rennes. Now, with
> more transport, trains, cars, planes, that problem spreads
> like oil. So to imagine that because you are in the country,
> you are safe, that is a big mistake. (Calvez 1989:44)

Summer tourism drains a population of drug addicts into the safe
community area. The conviction that the home territory is pure
and safe is undisturbed by the knowledge that it is the normal
home of pockets of homosexuals. The possible contradiction is
surmounted by the idea that the homosexuals travel more than
other people, so they can be contaminated abroad and come back
to contaminate their home territory. A doctor in charge of a
blood transfusion centre answered people who claimed that their
town had nothing to fear:

> But you have compatriots who work continually in
> America. New York, it is very polluted, and the hotels,
> they are risky places. Lots of you work in America and you
> come back by charter flights for short trips. If it is one of
> the family, you know him, you don't have to worry, it is
> a cousin, or a neighbour – you know them. But going to
> America, there is a gap of a year, or two years. Sailors

come back every two months . . . the more you live in a big town, the more contaminated it is. (Calvez 1989:45–6)

So, like the body, the community itself is porous, vulnerable because too open. The simple and quite correct idea that a new infection has external origins is transmuted in the course of the cultural project into a complex weapon of control. If townsfolk could really believe it is a problem caused by transients: good, then it does not concern them, so long as they can cordon off the town. The middle class believe it is a problem of 'inner city', urban poverty: good, it does not concern them, so long as there is a cordon sanitaire. Stable citizens believe it is a problem of itinerancy, beggars, strangers, and travellers. So long as the class at risk can be kept in the margins, the public concern to pay for the research and the welfare of the victims will be the weaker. The comparison is with the savage measures to segregate the poor of London during the Plague years.

Whatever way they think about it, the central community is risk-averse, very much so. Its risk-aversion is part of its political defence against its own margins.

## VIEW FROM THE ENCLAVES

The homosexual citizens, after being categorized as 'groups at risk', develop solidarity in shared adversity. Pressed to give up promiscuous sex, told to form exclusive, stable sexual relationships, the persons at risk ask the central community to accord to them the supports that reinforce other citizens' personal contracts, that is, wedding bells, married status, and legal protection for the couple's rights as a couple. But the community generally refuses this. So they remain a 'muted category', not able to articulate their relations with one another as others do. This entails severe difficulties of organization, weakness of authority, absence of decision; the group in this situation is inherently fissile.[4]

Just as with the centre community, the homosexual enclave also develops the idea of the two skins, the double protective envelope. It believes that the body itself needs to be protected from infection, that hygienic precautions are necessary. It also believes that the community has to guard itself from invasion by outsiders who may contaminate it, and by expelling insiders who are 'at risk'.

However, the general mood is one of hostility to the central community. Rejection meets rejection. They say they have always known that they are persecuted; death and disease have always been their lot. Their community is inherently defined by death and disease. They are like a doomed concentration camp whose sinister future is organized by the society at large. This valuation, common to the negative diagonal, modifies their expectation that any careful hygiene will prevent the diffusion of AIDS among their members. Fatalism, sometimes dull, sometimes heroic, sometimes in the form of a religious conversion, makes the information from the clinics seem very irrelevant. As to being a population at risk, the definition meets an ethos that glorifies risk. Many in such a community would deride the cult of safety. Death comes to all in the end. Who would rightly want to live a safe life if that means no passion, no ecstasy, no abandon? The idea of a high-risk lifestyle is an accepted norm.

## THE EXCEPTIONAL DESTINY

Among homosexuals there are many individualists who do not belong in any community. They resist admonitions to be organized in groups and minimize the danger to themselves. This cultural type does not look for a protective skin from his own community. He is a citizen of the world, neither trying to make a community nor trying to enter one. Paradoxically, because it is implicitly a risk-taking attitude, the strict version of medical theory about transmission of the disease is acceptable in this culture. The idea of miasma is rejected. What the individualist wants from the cultural project is to be left free to pursue his own activities, uncriticized and uncontrolled by others. The theory that contagion enters by very specific routes gives him the cue for saying that he is in control of his own life. He argues rationally that he is in control of those routes, at least as much as he wants to be.

Ask them how they live with risk, and some express an extraordinary faith in their own personal destiny. One of these said in an interview:

No, I don't think so. I have always had the feeling, since I was a child, that I would live to be old; that is why. Some one who thinks, on the other hand, that he is going to die

young and who discovers that he is HIV positive, perhaps
that would frighten him more than me . . . so that is why
I have never worried about it all that much. (Calvez 1989:71)

A final recourse to reject interference is the claim to prefer high
risk. Death will come in the end; life without risk is not worth
living. Love is the greatest risk of all.

## CONCLUSION

In sum, the dialogue about infection follows the dialogue about
the community's cultural project. The centre community and the
homosexual enclaves both develop faith in an immunity conferred
by a territorial community envelope. Both are indeed tempted to
pay more attention to protecting the community envelope than
to protect the vulnerable points of access in the body itself. The
centre community uses this confidence combined with a profession of risk-aversion to control its periphery. The enclave uses
it to justify a risk-taking attitude towards dealing with fellow
members of the community. The individualists are risk-takers,
often explicitly. The top left corner of the cultural diagram (Figure
6.1) represents the drug addicts, the prostitutes and other loners
at risk. Because they are so isolated that they do not have to
develop a justification in the eyes of their fellows, their opinions
are less stable; they are neither risk-averse nor risk-taking, but
idiosyncratic.

The way that the citizen who is a member of the central
community responds to the epidemic is very threatening for the
other citizens. Before the epidemic, they never thought that their
loyalty was particularly in doubt. *In Time of Plague* brings this
out with shocking clarity. In the great plague London barred
itself against its own poor, for fear of infection (Slack 1988:378).
Muslims took the fatalist view, and did not cordon off the
infected. We have the choice.

A general predictive principle emerges. The bigger the gap
between rich and poor in income distribution and wealth, the less
contact between them and the more the poor appear to be an
alien sub-culture. The more unequal the ratio of numbers of
wealthy to numbers of poor, the more the poor will seem a
threat. When the poor are perceived as a distinctive sub-culture
the central community will be more likely to respond punitively,

attacking its dissidents and deviants in the name of stemming the spread of infection. The best protection for the victims of plague will be a community that already has taken social justice to heart. As the San Francisco gay organizations have shown, a community can have enough solidarity to protect its members. Research on the citizens' responses to epidemic needs to take systematic account of the kinds of culture in which victims are outlawed and those in which they are treated like citizens.

Finally, the central community's attitude to expenditure on research and health and medical treatment for the sick is conditioned for each disease by its expectation of getting the disease. If it is cancer or heart disease, enormous sums will be forthcoming. If the disease is categorized as something outsiders are prone to, along with their outsidership and their reprehensible behaviour, the same outlay will be sanctioned less readily. So the fears of those working with AIDS victims that they will be segregated, marginalized and discriminated against, are not unreasonable. The conscience of the central community is not essentially compassionate to all the citizenry.

## ACKNOWLEDGEMENT

This paper was originally given at the invitation of Dr Mercedes Fernandez-Martorell at the Barcelona Institute of Humanities, Conference on 'The City as Cultural Project', 20 February 1990 and, rewritten with Marcel Calvez (IRTS, Brittany), appeared in *The Sociological Review* 38,3:445–64.

## NOTES

1 See Mary Douglas, *Risk Acceptability* (California University Press, 1986), for the readiness of psychologists researching on risk perception to resort to this explanation to account for divergences of opinion between the public and the experts in matters of life-endangering risks.
2 A considerable literature on sects in cultural theory can be provided, starting with Douglas and Wildavsky (1982).
3 Not only for that reason: as argued in Douglas, *How Institutions Think* (Syracuse University Press, 1987), the situation of an enclave, peripheral and often hostile to the main community may make it extremely difficult to organize.
4 Mary Douglas and Aaron Wildavsky, *Risk and Culture* (California University Press, 1982). Mary Douglas, *How Institutions Think* (Syracuse University Press, 1987).

# REFERENCES

Bourdieu, Pierre (1979) *La Distinction, Critique Social du Jugement*, Paris, Minuit.

Calvez, Marcel (1989) *Composer avec un Danger, approche des reponses sociales a l'infection au VIH au SIDA*, Rennes, IRTS de Bretagne.

Douglas, Mary (1970) *Natural Symbols, Explorations in Cosmology*, Penguin.

Douglas, Mary (1986) *Risk Acceptability*, University of California Press.

Douglas, Mary (1987) *How Institutions Think*, Syracuse University Press.

Douglas, Mary and Wildavsky, Aaron (1982) *Risk and Culture*, University of California Press.

Mars, Gerald (1984) *Cheats at Work*, Allen & Unwin.

Mars, Gerald and Mars, Valerie (forthcoming) *The Cultural Theory of the Household*.

Masters, William H., Johnson, Virginia E. and Kolodny, Robert C. (1988) *Crisis: Heterosexual Behaviour in the Age of Aids*, Grove Press, NY, and Grafton Books.

Shilts, R. (1987) *And the Band Played on, Politics, People and the AIDS Epidemic*, St Martin's Press, New York, and Penguin.

Slack, Paul (1988) 'Responses to Plague', *In Time of Plague: the History and Social Consequences of Epidemic Disease*, edited Arien Mack, *Social Research*, 55, 3.

Thompson, Michael (1984) 'Among the Energy Tribes, A Cultural Framework for the Analysis and Design of Energy Policy', *Policy Sciences* 17, 3.

Wynne, Brian (1982) *Rationality and Ritual, The Windscale Inquiry and Nuclear Decisions in Britain*, The British Society for the History of Science.

# Part II

# WANTS AND INSTITUTIONS

# 7

# THE NORMATIVE DEBATE
# AND THE ORIGINS OF
# CULTURE

Culture is nothing if not a collective product. The very idea of collective action bristles with difficulties in economics. This chapter is an attempt to have a theory of culture that complements the theory of rational choice. There is no intention of supplanting the latter – indeed, some sort of rational choice should enter cultural analysis. The concept of culture is here developed to illuminate some of the dark areas in economics concerning the idea of the individual.

Economic theory does not pretend to offer an account of the place of the individual in society. Yet nowhere else in social theory is there anything like such a rigorous or elaborately developed account of interaction between individuals. Even psychology is not a close runner-up because its argument is so dispersed; it has too little disciplinary cohesion for formal axioms to be generally accepted. Economic theory can be as cohesive as it is because of the professional intensity of its discourse and because Western thought is impregnated with the Western experience of market. Louis Dumont has aptly said, 'The economic mode of thought naturally enjoys an ideological supremacy over the political in the liberal or capitalist world thanks to its embodying a purer or more perfect form of individualism' (Dumont 1985:259–60). In the market the focus is upon individuals exchanging privately owned goods; the individual and the rights that accrue to him from ownership are the given of the economic mode of thought, the rarely questioned starting point of the analysis. As Armen Alchian (1967) puts it, 'the question of economics, or of how prices should be determined, is the question of how property rights should be defined and exchanged and on what terms'.

125

Economic theory, like most disciplines, comes in a variety of forms. The form with which I am here concerned has as its basic assumption that individual behaviour is motivated entirely by self-regarding preferences. There is a certain implausibility about this, in that we know from experience that individuals often do not even try to pursue their self-interest consistently. Moreover, this assumption makes it difficult for economics to allow for moral feelings such as altruism or commitment. As a result economists from the earliest times have sought means of extending their field to encompass other motivations. Adam Smith, for example, used material gain as the basis for his theory of economic behaviour and sympathy as the basis for his theory of moral behaviour.

It is of course, possible to extend the notion of self-interest to include 'sympathy', 'psychic reward', 'social approval', or virtually any kind of emotion or moral sentiment which may be supposed to influence behaviour. Some economists have indeed endeavoured to do just this. The trouble is that by doing so we lose much of the predictive power of economics, and economics becomes what Amartya Sen calls 'a remarkably mute theory. Behavior, it appears, is to be explained in terms of preferences, which are in turn defined by behavior' (Sen 1977:325).

The technique which Steven Jones (1984) has called 'calculating avarice' is an extremely powerful methodology which has provided economics with many of its classic findings. When an economist 'proves', for example, that under conditions of perfect competition, prices will equal marginal costs, he is not making an empirical observation; he is, in effect, deducing this proposition from the assumption that each individual supplier in the market will seek the maximum material return for his effort. Any solution other than the equation of price with marginal cost can be shown to lead to lesser material reward for every individual under conditions of perfect competition. A market in which the supplier were motivated by some other passion than the pursuit of 'his own gain' would have a different equilibrium point. Amartya Sen argues that it would be possible to develop a range of 'meta-economics' assuming different dominant motivations.

Gary Becker is one economist who finds the economic approach not at all constraining. He claims that the three assumptions – maximizing behaviour, stable preferences, and equilibrium – which are used for understanding markets, also illuminate all types of decisions. Even within the family, usually regarded as a stronghold impregnable to economic analysis, he shows that allocations of time and money income can be interpreted on economic principles, although preference schedules may sometimes need to be enlarged to include more than conventionally defined material gain. For example, he claims that he can 'justify the popular belief that more beautiful, charming, and talented women tend to marry wealthier and more successful men' (1981:75). Any woman who has ever felt that she could be much more beautiful and more charming if she could only first marry a really successful man will resent the circularity here. His account of altruism in the family has the quality of total irrefutability: either the utility function of a person, say the husband, depends positively on the well-being of his spouse or children, so what passes as altruism is included in self-interest, or else the effects of envy within the family constrain what the egoist would like to do. After the event, apparently altruistic behaviour turns out to be in the narrower rational interests of the so-called altruist (1981:178–201). Thus he falls into the trap of circularity, explaining behaviour in terms of preferences.

A market presupposes a society of people with preferences, and how there can be a society at all is the question that economists cannot broach from their chosen platform. In analysing the market for private goods, classical economics jumps from individual self-interest to community interest, the interest of the society, by invoking the magic of an invisible hand. It is not difficult to see through something invisible. Behind it lies the community engaged in its normative debate and the laws, conventions, and social values to which the normative debate gives rise. Humans speak, they use rhetoric and scrutinize one another's speech. Their individual conflicts of interest surface and are overruled as they try to persuade one another to compromise or to stand firm. Faced with conflict, contestants have to resort to the rhetoric of the common good to support their private claims. De Tocqueville, writing of public associations, identified the basic mechanism of the normative debate that sets the ground rules for any form of social structure, whether that of a market, the state, or the voluntary associations with which he was primarily concerned. Citizens, he argued, 'converse, they listen to one another and they are mutually stimulated to all sorts of undertakings' (1966:124). As a result they may even 'learn to surrender their own will to that of all the rest and to make their exertions subordinate to the common impulse' (p. 127). Once engaged, the normative debate about how the common good should be achieved puts the rhetoric through local tests of non-contradiction. Anthropologists find that certain priorities, once agreed, rule out others. Listening to the debate is their way to approach the non-market behaviour which is so difficult to make sense of within economic theory.

## MARKET FAILURE

Economists recognize that market transactions do not include all rational transactions concerning goods. They have developed various ways of thinking about rational non-market transactions, generally designated by the term 'market failure'. Measuring the spill-over to the community from individual market transactions is one approach to the non-market used by economists. Externalities are a powerful tool for analysing certain problems in a market society (for example, the damage done by pollution, a 'negative externality', or the benefits of an educated citizenry, a 'positive externality'). To the anthropologist's eye the theory of externalities (and market failure generally) seems an elaborately backhanded way of studying the collective interest. Moreover the concept of externalities can both include too much and, at the same time, fail to explain some quite common forms of non-market behaviour.

Almost any action can be shown to have some externalities (whether positive or negative) and, as Richard Nelson points out (1986), literally everything has externalities once we grant that one individual derives satisfaction from the happiness of another. (Or, indeed, contrariwise! We are all members one of another, whether the bonds that link us are mutual envy or mutual charity.)

At the same time, the concept of externalities has little if any explanatory power in the case of several common forms of non-market society, those in which production is not for market and in which almost all legitimate transfers of property are made on grounds of kinship or friendship, as war booty, or as feudal dues. At first sight, another concept, that of public goods, seems more promising than externalities. It does not treat the collective good as a side-effect of individual market transactions, and it clearly distinguishes the private goods of market from the public goods of the community.

## PUBLIC GOODS

Public goods are defined by Samuelson (1954) as goods which are freely available and from the enjoyment of which no one can be excluded. The first characteristic, joint supply, postulates a good the consumption of which by one consumer does not reduce the amount available for others: if I consume a loaf of bread that same loaf is not thereafter available for anybody else; if I watch a circus or theatrical production, my enjoyment of that performance does not eliminate the possibility of someone else enjoying the same performance at the same time. Clearly the consumption of bread-eaters and the consumption of theatre-goers differ – indeed it is difficult to think of a theatrical performance being 'consumed' by the audience even though the demand for theatre clearly comes within the consumption pattern of the audience. Even so, the number of 'consumers' who can enjoy a theatrical performance is not literally infinite. Crowding soon introduces similarities between the two forms of 'supply' – the theatre has a limited capacity, and too large an audience will reduce the enjoying of all (Buchanan 1965). Markets, as the circus and theatre examples show, can cope with joint supply so long as access to the good can be controlled.

The second characteristic, non-excludability, is necessary to put the good into the public category. However, it is as rare to find goods that are necessarily non-excludable as it is to find goods that are in absolutely joint supply. In its origin the idea of public goods assumed superabundant supply, such as air or land in a sparsely populated country. But we have less and less reason to think of these as being in plentiful supply. Moreover, as Russell Hardin says, it is 'not easy to think of pure cases of goods characterized by the impossibility of exclusion . . . large bodies of law have as their purpose to erect exclusionary barriers where the naive might have thought exclusion impossible' (1982:18).

Olson's 1965 analysis of collective goods does not emphasize free availability so much as non-excludability. He seems to be right in avoiding, despite its obvious attraction, a definition that rests on the technical or material properties of the thing itself. National defence is a favourite example of a non-excludable public good: whether you pay your taxes or not, the defensive arm of the nation will cover you as well as your tax-paying neighbour. But even in this often cited case, military history records protection being withdrawn from border regions, according to the exigencies of defence. Samuelson (1955) admitted that public education, defence and highway programmes, the courts, police, and fire services do not fit well into the rigid category of public goods available to all. He defended his theoretical model of pure public goods as a polar extreme to contrast with the competitive equilibrium model of the pure private economy, each on an equally high level of abstraction. Essentially his concept of public goods divides individual transactions in the market which depend on private property from some polar opposite which depends on public or no ownership. Between pure public goods and purely private goods lies a whole spectrum of intermediate positions to which the very concept of ownership is ill adapted. Where the market is not highly developed most resources are not claimed by individuals, and so, by default, they are assumed to be held in common. As Richard Nelson (1986) says, 'it is a commonplace . . . to remark that pure public goods are rare. That is true but so also are pure private goods'. This is enough to show that the economist's conception of the non-market bristles with difficulties.

We can face this issue much more directly when positions on the scale between private and public goods are seen to rest on a collective decision. Public availability is conferred by the collectivity itself. What enters the list of public goods and the list of private goods and positions in between depends on community fiat and varies from one community to another. In England postwar governments tried to treat health care as essentially a non-excludable public good (although obviously not in joint supply) while in America it is largely treated as a private good. In many societies food and water are treated as non-excludable.

Recent developments in England give point to Peter Steiner's emphasis on 'non-excludability' as the main criterion, at the expense of 'joint supply'. Unlike Samuelson's definition, Steiner's says that 'any publicly induced or provided collective good is a public good' (1974:247). As Steiner points out, under this definition, a public good is not necessarily in joint supply (a collective consumption good). Instead, it is a good that differs 'appreciably in either quantity or quality [from] the alternative the private market would produce and [there is] a viable demand for the difference' (1974:247). Steiner's definition allows for health care to be provided simultaneously in the same community as a collective good and also as a good provided by the private market, with some differences of quantity or quality. Under Samuelson's definition, the fact that health care is clearly not in joint supply would, strictly speaking, preclude its ever being treated as a public good. Unlike Samuelson, Steiner fastens not on some inherent characteristic of the good itself but on the public's reaction to the good. For him, clearly, 'demand' has a political even more than an economic connotation. The economist is, to some extent, passing the buck to the politician; as the doctor said to the priest on the patient's deathbed: '*À votre tour, cher collègue* [It's your turn, my friend].'

Absolutely anything can be a public good in this sense. The concept can break out of the ethnocentric bounds to which contrast with markets had confined it. Three conditions need to hold: one is the decision to make something freely available; another is the will to make the public decision effective. The third is for the anthropologist or economist to set the analysis sufficiently far back from the individual transfer. For example, at too close range a transfer seen in isolation may appear to be a purely private benefit. When a trade union has negotiated a higher wage for a particular kind of job, each worker who takes his share has evidently a private benefit. But at the level of the ruling that all workers in that category now receive the higher wage, the ruling has made a true collective good – obviously non-excludable and, in some sense, in joint supply in that no one worker's receipt of the higher wage reduces the rate available to the others. Of course, the total number of workers in receipt of a wage may be reduced in consequence but this is not essentially different to the crowding that limits the applicability of the concept of joint supply in other cases.

Among many people who live by hunting, complex rules ensure that meat is distributed through the whole camp. Sometimes the rule is negative in form, such as that no one should go without. In this case, the product of the hunt is treated as a collective good very much in the way Olson suggests. In other cases, the rules prescribe the precise categories entitled to a particular cut, as for example, a haunch for the father of the hunter, one for the village chief, another part for the mother, another for the paternal aunt, and so on. In addition to observing distributive rules of this kind, the Lele hunter was also required to give a generous piece to anyone who saw him kill or bring home the game, 'because of the eyes'. This referred to the practical infeasibility of excluding anyone who had seen the meat. The effect is to make the whole kill into common property, out of which the hunter himself gets a modest allocation.

In constructing such distributive patterns all the various beneficiaries seem to have colluded. Such patterns are not merely the result of a number of individual voluntary transactions. The individual has no choice in the matter. It is true that if the rules have proved viable, in some statistical sense most individuals on balance are likely to benefit more than they lose from the maintenance of the rules, but the individual is entirely bound by the rule. A collective effort has established and sanctioned the rules of distribution. The result is a social order in which nearly every transfer lies in the domain defined as public. (Anthropologists somewhat confusingly term this a 'gift economy'.)

Putting gift economies into the theory of public goods does not help us to go much further, because economic theory is not very well developed on the subject. Another route is to go back to the idea of the normative debate and trace the institutional options confronting individuals deciding what shall be put into the public domain. For this we need to revise the economist's concept of the rational individual.

## THE NORMATIVE DEBATE

The rational individual is not a solipsist, but rather a *zoon politikon*: a being whose needs are not determined in isolation, but only in society. Accountability is written into his make-up. The rational individual has to be conceived as one who expects to be held accountable, who therefore seeks approval, and who gives out praise and blame to others. This individual has to be redefined as incorporated in a community of one sort or another. The change is not to deny the individual self-regarding preference but to point out that it can operate only within a context of accountability determined by the community. Capitalism is the system which probably gives the most scope for the exercise of the self-regarding preference (except, perhaps, for Hobbes's 'state of nature'). Yet even within capitalist society, the way the individual can pursue his own gain is determined by the society, its laws and conventions.

As to collective action, we can assume either that it is fraught

132

with difficulty or that there is no problem about it. We can assume that the social bond is inherently fragile or inherently tough. The choice depends on the model of the individual with which we start. If we take the benign view, there is no need for a theory to explain collective action; the initial assumption about human nature does duty in place of enquiry. Economists do not take that line; their initial assumption that self-regarding motives are dominant implies that the social fabric is vulnerable to private depredations. Experience backs the economists' assumption. When keeping the streets clear of litter is left to individual house-holders, some sweep their doorsteps, and some do not. In social theory inertia is still a power to be reckoned with, whatever reservations may be held about the concept of the individual fired only by self-regarding passions.

There may be a misleading natural bias towards thinking that the norm is for collectivities to be viable. To justify that bias we would need to ignore all the attempts at organizing that we ourselves have made and been forced to abandon for lack of sustained support. Our eyes get drawn to the enduring insti-tutions, and we tend to forget the attempts at revolution or reform that have failed. The records of anthropologists, on the other hand, keep track of communities that have split in acrimony or died out. An interest in failed collectivities, without being cynical, sharpens the spirit of enquiry. So the first assumption is that collective action is difficult.

The next assumption for cultural analysis is that in the course of judging one another's accountability individuals use their reasoning powers to scrutinize their social arrangements. They need to do so as they excuse themselves and monitor each other. From the first they involve one another in a primitive form of constitution making. Each individual who enters a social relation is drawn at the same time into a debate about what the relation is and how it ought to be conducted. This is the normative debate on which cultural analysis fastens attention.

At any time individuals may be heard reasoning with one another about how to achieve the goals they share. In the course of the debate they construct conceptual categories appropriate for their exchanges. Their shared experience, shaped in metaphor and fixed in ritual and history, is a collective good that they have made together. The object of their debate is to legitimize the form of their society.

One practitioner of cultural analysis addresses the point of interchange at which the individual choice distinguishes itself from the cultural pattern. Morris Freilich uses the term 'proper' to indicate the outcome of the public debate on what ought to be. Proper are shared techniques, agreed standards, stereotyped modes of behaviour, all that is recognized as correct and formal. In contrast, he uses 'smart' for individual skills, private ends, unpredicted and ingenious solutions (Freilich 1980). This usefully captures the difference between the idea of culture and the concept of the individual exercising his rational choice within cultural constraints. Freilich then proceeds to concentrate on their point of convergence. In contrast, I want to consider in detail how the proper category gets its content and the main varieties of proper ways of doing things.

Pierre Bourdieu practises another form of cultural analysis using the concept of *habitus*. This describes the social field in which individuals compete for legitimacy. The struggle is waged largely in the form of contested aesthetic and moral judgements (1979:171–83). This analysis illuminates the form that the contest takes and the strategies open to the contenders. It is not concerned with the form given to the society itself nor with how the social structure guides the progress of the debates. The cultural analysis I will present is like a prolegomenon to Bourdieu's analysis of *habitus*. The typology of cultural forms displays the internal debates between members of different kinds of social unit. It reveals the attitude to authority and the concept of the individual that make sense to those who have combined to form a social group of a particular type. It is an account of the prior debate that individuals will be having among themselves, whether they ever enter the larger political scene or not.

In the public debate the future form of the society is at stake; the contenders define the options. This is where individuals are heard threatening to defect, threatening to coerce or promising to bribe, promising to resist coercion or bribery, and mobilizing support for the common good. Their dilemma of whether to co-operate or to defect is very much on the surface of their talk. Even if individual self-interest were their only motivation, the debate must necessarily be conducted in terms of the collective interest, since the forum in which collective support is mustered is public.

## CULTURAL THEORY

From these preliminary assumptions cultural theory proceeds to develop an argument. The first step is to argue that out of the infinite number of distinct forms that human society can take, not all attempted combinations will be viable. Many different causes may destroy a human society. War or famine or vast migration may leave a land empty. These dangers are constantly invoked as members of the community put pressure on one another. Such risks may indeed cause the destruction of the community, but cultural analysis is concerned with only one cause of breakdown, the collapse of the normative debate. The speakers in the normative debate hear one another criticize contradiction and rebuke nonsense. Ultimately there is always a touchstone of practicability. A person cannot be in two places at once. One injunction cannot be accepted if it countermands established principle. One person cannot belong to two mutually exclusive groups. Redistribution and saving are at odds. Some kinds of institutions just cannot be added to other kinds because they will be indefensible by any common test. The debate will be in continual danger of falling into uproar or silence because the accepted categories of discourse make no sense.

## THE CONSTRAINED DIALOGUE

The idea of the normative debate is very close to Bruce Ackerman's notion that liberalism is based on a constrained dialogue. In a brilliant exercise aimed at analysing and justifying liberal philosophical principles, Ackerman examines the conditions for a liberal debate. He regards liberalism as 'a way of talking about power, a form of political culture' (1980:6). He finds that it can be defined within three constraints: rationality, consistency, and neutrality. Rationality means the requirement that any claim be supported by reasons. Consistency safeguards the intelligibility of the dialogue demanded by rationality. Neutrality protects the continuance of the dialogue against assertions of intrinsic superiority.

> No reason is a good reason if it requires the power holder to assert: a) that his conception of the good is better than that asserted by any of his fellow citizens, or b) that regard-

less of his conception of the good, he is intrinsically superior to one or more of his fellow citizens. (p. 11)

It is worth distinguishing the use made here of the idea of constrained dialogue. Ackerman's essay is in political philosophy. His initial assumption is that the elementary political contest is a struggle for power, so the dialogue has rules that set constraints on the struggle. Our concern is not with the struggle for power but with the viability of a form of society. However, he maintains that the constraints he argues on behalf of liberal philosophy are sufficiently general to be applied to any of the several forms of political structure identified by cultural analysis.

At this point we need to deal with an objection. Anyone who has attended a town meeting or a board meeting knows that the normative debate is a fumbling, half-coherent process. One proposition is made, only to be challenged by a contrary one. Decisions are difficult to reach. They rest on tacit assumptions, not on argued syllogisms. The stability and distinctiveness of a logical pattern is just as improbable as the stability of social forms. It is not plausible to argue that shaky institutions are shored up by equally shaky logical forms: both forms of collective action are so fragile that they are more likely to collapse together. In reply to this, cultural theory will need to save its analysis by recourse to system-sustaining effects that follow from initial decisions in favour of one type of organization rather than another. This is the nub of the argument: institutions stand on different forking paths of decision trees. Once embarked on one path, it is difficult to get back to the choice that would have led another way.

This is the central argument of cultural theory: culture itself is constrained. It cannot make any number of combinations and permutations. Inclusion is logically different from hierarchy; inclusion and hierarchy are different from equivalent exchange. Any human group will be drawn to use one or another of these principles to legitimize its collective action; in doing so it will encounter a specific set of organizational problems. Each initial choice will lead, by the logic of the normative debate, to radically different solutions. Each resultant type of culture will be legitimated upon a different logical base.

By following this argument we can broach the question of stable types from another direction. Assuming that flux and disorder are more probable in social life than order, cultural theory should explain how any type of collectivity can resist pressures to transform. Hierarchy, market, and sect are very different. Given the greater likeliness of disorder, this typological stability is itself curious. Half of the explanation comes from the distinctive legitimizing processes released in the course of the normative debate. The other half follows from the institutional consequences of responding to the logic.

## THE TYPOLOGY

The ability of individuals to legitimize coercion is the very question at issue. The list below of initial problems, successful solutions, and institutional reinforcements assumes no illegitimate use of coercion. We assume that the self-sustaining powers of each distinctive system are drawn originally from the legitimating process but will not endure without some system-sustaining reinforcements, in other words, a functional argument. Jon Elster's criticism of the way that functional analysis is often used in explaining social behaviour leads him to conclude that in the social sciences good functional aruguments may not be quite impossible but they are exceedingly rare (Elster 1983; Douglas 1986). This is partly because they cannot be justified within any overarching theory such as provided for biology by the theory of evolution. However, in a modest way the lack of a major organizing theory can be supplemented by a good little typology of systematic interactions in which system-maintaining loops channel resources back to the collectivity.

The political rhetoric reveals a minimal three types of legitimation, each so distinctive that no speaker in one type can appeal to the justifying principles which uphold another type without landing in contradiction.

The first bases its whole system of relations on bonding insiders together against outsiders. The second upholds the trust necessary for exchange between individuals. The third legitimizes the up–down hierarchical bonding of individuals. Each of these is stabilized in a uniquely specialized normative order. The principles of one cannot be borrowed by either of the others without obvious and grave inconsistency. It makes a good starting place to indicate what problems of collective organization each of the three types is best able to meet and from there to consider the overflow of benefits to the collectivity that follow from each solution.

## Inside–outside

The logical principle of inclusion gives rise to the social type that focuses attention on the relations between insider and outsider. This is a type of organization evolved to solve problems caused by too-easy defection. Anyone who threatens to move out puts the wished-for collective good in jeopardy. Unlike the market, as described by Hirschman (1970), this is a community whose future is at the mercy of defectors. In such a case penalties for defection are not going to work. An attempt to impose penalties will merely make the membership melt away even faster. According to circumstances, and according to their objectives as a community, there are three strategies theoretically open. Two of them would have the effect of moving the community to a different point in this typology.

First, they could theoretically institute a more regulated regime in which each committed member signs an enforceable contract. For example, many communes require that goods be held in common. Then defection is effectively stopped by the heavy loss and disadvantages suffered by a would-be defector who can take no property with him. When the commune adopts this solution, it makes a radical change in the tone of the normative debate. Defection having become difficult, the community generally starts to accumulate centralized authority. It can become a hierarchy. This appears to be what happened with the Mormons. This solution is theoretically feasible. If the normative debate goes in this direction, it escapes what I have called the 'sectarian trap' (Douglas 1986). But this means overcoming individual resistance to collective action. It tends not to be a practical proposition if the objects for coming together in a community are rather restricted and if the members have no wish to give up their scope for seceding; by definition in this argument, no one can force them to accept regulation.

Another theoretically possible solution would be to institute trade. Then the community is turned into the second type, based on exchange. But that is not always possible. Market requires certain conditions, as we will see below. It is not so easy to move out of the first position as defined.

138

The third solution, in order to avoid the threatened defections, is to find a way of staying together without either exerting authority or giving special enticements to stay. A community without authority tends to be harried by charges of arbitrary behaviour. It needs a rule acceptable to all, and only a rule that is demonstrably fair will do. To meet this requirement of fairness the community is drawn to institute equality. If all power and all goods are held equally and in common, no one can complain of arbitrariness. Once the community has founded itself upon the principle of equality, the normative debate has taken a decisive turn. The community has made itself attractive to all: it does not countenance the despoiling of some members by others. But now it has another problem. Equality as a principle of distribution can be monitored in the public debate, but it is not so easy to ensure equal productive effort. Unless it can persuade its members each to 'surrender his own will to that of the rest', this kind of community tends to be a prey to free-riding and the inertia that Olson sums up as the principle of 'Let George do it.' The equality rule has not solved the defection problem nor the free-rider problem, though it is adopted as a response to both. Something more has to happen if the commune is to be stabilized, even at a low level of co-ordination.

In itself the rule of equality has the unintended effect of impeding decision-taking and leadership. It has the further unintended effect of exposing the fragile fund of mutual trust to the strains of ambiguity. For the one defence the community has devised against the charge of unfairness is to refuse to define any one member as distinct from any other, to refuse to institutionalize differences of office or differences of reward. This follows from deciding to take seriously the threat of defection (and rightly, since it would have destroyed the community if it had been ignored).

Now, labouring under ambiguity and lack of leadership and lack of authority, this community is going to be riven by factions. At an early stage in its life the normative debate starts to focus on the theme of betrayal. Members of one faction will seek to clarify by accusing the others of betraying the founding principles. The community would be destabilized early in its career if such accusations did not have unintended positive effects. Axiomatically, this is a society without authority and so one in which delinquents cannot be penalized directly – even if it were possible to agree, in the midst of such ambiguity, on what constitutes delinquency. Accusations of grave treachery against the community have the effect of summoning up enough anger and fear to produce effective collective action. Accusations and threats of expulsion result in greatly clarifying the boundary between virtuous insiders who accept the community norms and all outsiders. A commune (as I shall call it here, in default of a better technical term) generally defines two kinds of individuals, those who truly belong, the insiders, called, saved, elect to salvation, or purer, and the others, the outsiders who, in the light of accusations made against those who have truck with them, are morally inadequate human beings. The measures to institute equality and a normative debate focused on preventing defection finally can combine to make a strong protective constraint.

Defection, which everyone was initially tempted to threaten, now shows in a culpable light: it must be wicked to leave the good and join the bad. So by the moral judgement, which was inherent in the direction the debate was carried, the weakness of the outer boundary is shored up. The normative debate has created a viable institutional form for very difficult conditions, probably the only institutional form which can persist in the face of easy defection.

It is also worth mentioning, in reply to Bruce Ackerman's assumption, that the main concern for many societies is not always the struggle for power and scarce resources. In this common type everyone is worried by fear of losing members.

## EXCHANGE

A collectivity based on exchange, such as a market system, rests just as heavily upon the support of its normative debate. When individuals start to exchange and when prices begin to emerge, the embryonic market can be subverted by lack of trust. Without trust transactions are severely limited. One way in which trust can be created is to let the exchanges flow down the lines of preexisting relationships, reinforcing ties of kinship, friendship, or patronage, thus developing a network of obligatory giving. Then the emergent market system will give way to the gift system, either within a hierarchy or within a commune, and in either case a regime in which free bargaining of private goods is virtually absent.

But let us assume the emergent market overcomes this first hurdle. Essentially the market system depends on open markets, free bargaining, private property, and some protection for contract. These requirements do not combine into a harmonious whole. Markets are built over the tension between the requirement of private property and the requirement of an open market. Private property is basic to a market economy since a market is a method of exchanging property rights. But property rights are by their nature restrictive and the tension within the market is between the restrictions that can be allowed and those that cannot: patents legitimately protect private information; insider trading illegitimately exploits private information. The normative debate has to paper over the cracks in the logic so that a sufficiently strong consensus can emerge to protect the market from subversion. The dialogue has to be something on the lines worked out by Bruce Ackerman for liberalism, a philosophy whose substantive values are essentially techniques for keeping the debate itself going.

One threat faced by the market, once established, is monopoly, which will let the most successful trader use the rule of private property to block the rule of free access to the market and so turn his own family into a privileged dynasty or a mafia. How is this avoided? The normative debate pronounces its anathemas against greedy mergers threatening to restrict trade and take over the community. But the normative debate might not be powerful enough by itself, were it not for chains of consequences which it indirectly establishes, consequences which recreate market-sustaining conditions. For example, many informal redistributive mechanisms may prevent the sons of very successful traders from starting with excessive advantage over their rivals. Among the Chimbu in New Guinea, every trader is forced to borrow to the limit of his credit; when he dies his children will be lucky if they can use his estate to pay all his creditors (Brown 1961). Consequently every rich man's son starts from scratch; even if his father did not leave an estate encumbered by debt, what he has to spend by way of a suitably lavish funeral will reduce his circumstances as much as if he had paid an enormous inheritance tax.

A market system needs freedom to expand, to find new outlets, and to justify increased scale of production. Consequently it cannot depend on the exclusiveness which upholds the insider-outsider type of society. Private property protects it from would-be free-riders so it does not need to worry about defectors from the community (unless they try to abscond without settling their private debts, and against such clear delinquency the community will have legitimated sanctions). Nor will the market type be tempted to appeal to the hierarchical principles which uphold the third type, because such principles obviously operate in restraint of trade.

Before we consider the third type, hierarchy, some comparisons of the normative debate in the first two are in order. Commune and market differ in how they work, in where they can flourish, and in the principles on which they can be grounded. As we have seen, the logical problem of the communitarian normative debate is ambiguity; the logical problem in the market is contradiction. The internal arguments of market and commune also generate different conceptions of the individual.

The individual who is most likely to operate successfully in a market society conforms closely to the model of the rational agent to which Herbert Simon brought his famous objection – someone with a mind like a calculating machine, sovereign in control of his own choices, decisive and consistent enough to give clear signals to partners. It is very difficult for such an individual to operate successfully in a commune. The communard needs to be like the saint that the normative debate in the commune upholds as a model, self-effacing and committed, prepared to bow out, quite unlike the ruthless free-rider supposed by rational choice theory to exploit the regime when public goods are freely available.

## Up–down, down–up

This is the third type, which we have been calling hierarchy, in which authority flows between the top and bottom. A group might start in the midst of a crisis when quick and clear decisions will save the day. This does not necessarily mean that the group will support a strong leader or even stay in existence for long. If the opportunities for defection are plentiful, the group once formed might easily try to stop members from leaving by turning itself into the insider–outsider type of community, but on the other hand, if trade is rewarding it might dissolve its group boundaries and develop into an individualist system of market exchange. In whichever direction the community starts itself off, it is not going to be able to maintain the pattern without effort. For a hierarchy to try to keep centralized leadership with a clear line of authority is probably as difficult a challenge as developing either of the other two forms of organization. If the community were to start a centralized command, privilege would accrue to the power holders, which in itself would help to keep them in power. But unless they divest themselves punctiliously of hereditary advantages, their leadership becomes vulnerable to subversion from below as well as from rival factions in the elite group. The normative debate has to work very hard at monitoring a hierarchy; the whole system depends on the trustful compliance of the people it advantages least. One way of getting this compliance is to create a circular principle of responsibility, by the following stages.

The debate will assert that someone has to be first (thus safeguarding the principle of strong decision), but then it will also declare that the first shall be last, that the chief is the servant of his people, and that the pope is the servant of the servants of God. This is what Dumont describes as the holism which legitimates a hierarchical system (Dumont 1983). Saying is not enough, ritualizing is not enough. It is not enough to keep saying that what is done is for the good of the whole. Putting the principle of mutual dependence into the normative debate allows it to be publicly challenged. The demands of consistency require words to match deeds. Those in command must be seen *not* to be lining their private pockets. The robber baron who abuses the power which has been created for the common good must be seen to be chastised. The powerful lord must be seen to provide the protection to his liegemen that the system implies. Without this self-correcting power from the normative debate, hierarchy will not last. No more than the market can be sustained without support for contract, or the commune without accepting the principle of equality, the hierarchy cannot be sustained without commitment to the circle of responsibility.

Like the other two types, the hierarchy's future can be saved by chains of consequences that follow once it has been set up in the first place. Hierarchical principles easily ensure that material wealth flows toward the centre; accumulating there it constitutes a reserve of power that can be used to maintain the system and a store of value that can be redistributed in patronage.

The rhetoric of service which maintains the hierarchy is not going to be acceptable or plausible in either of the others. It may well be easier to live at peace with one's neighbours in a hierarchy than in a commune or market society. First, there are so many good reasons given for the way things are. Contradiction does not so obviously underlie the hierarchy as it does the market, and ambiguity is reduced in a way it can never be in a commune. But it has its special weaknesses. Hierarchy needs information to flow from bottom up as well as top down. The channels of information being organized vertically and authority being centralized, it is a truism of organization theory that sending commands down is easier than receiving news from below, as a truly collegial hierarchy would require. The subversion of the hierarchy into a tyranny is easy. This kind of society works well in situations needing strong, centralized command. To work efficiently it needs good intelligence. But because the system depends on the consent of the majority who benefit only as a collectivity, reasons must be given for explaining why some (only a few) are in the command positions. The value of the reasons depends on the value of the system as a whole to those it privileges least. They need to perceive an overspill from the powerful individuals' transactions to themselves as a collectivity.

Inevitably the command fears its chain of reasoning is not strong enough to be convincing and is tempted to exclude the voices of the followers. When the normative debate becomes an affair of the elite, there is a tendency to reinforce good reasons with censorship. Censorship spells the end of the flow of information on which hierarchy depends, and digs its trap.

Now we have identified three forms of normative debate, or three forms of culture. Each is composed of a mixture of sensible strategies and mutual exhortation, both submitted to the best available logic. Each has its own theory of what the individual human is like. The model of the individual is adapted to the model of the social system in which the individual is expected to operate. The individual in the market system is the only one which is held to be driven by self-interest.

As Albert Hirschman has pointed out, the idea that greed is the dominant human motive only came to be generally accepted after the sixteenth century when market itself became dominant and was expected to be a motive force that would curb the passion for power (1977). It is not too fanciful to point out that each of the three cultural types described above has its own specific temptation in the list of deadly sins: if greed is written into the account of the individual operating in the exchange system, envy can be written into the account of the unbuffered individual trying to lead the good life amid the stressful ambiguity of the commune. As for the individual in the hierarchy, pride is the motive underlying his characteristic lust for domination. Only the first, greed, has been incorporated into an axiomatized theory of social forces. But there is no intrinsic reason why the conditions for a society composed of envious or prideful individuals could not be formalized.

My friends will recognize in this typology the familiar outline of grid-group analysis of which there are now several variants used for different kinds of problems. James Hampton originally helped me to develop a two-by-two matrix to capture the features of four distinctive social environments (1982). Michael Thompson turned it into an ecological model driven by the competition between different forms of social organization, each seeking to absorb or eliminate the others (1982). Jonathan Gross and Steve Rayner have provided a formal basis for measuring and comparing these different social environments (1985). Gerald Mars has used the four social environments for identifying kinds of occupational crime (1982). Why then have I only studied three types in this chapter, when colleagues have done so well with four? The answer is the same as it is for Aaron Wildavsky, who has applied this method of analysis to political cultures (1984). By definition the fourth type is politically mute: it is a social environment which separates individuals, cuts down their communication with one another, and limits their options. Such a social environment with a high degree of regimentation and no clear group affiliation is quite common in complex societies. On the fringe of markets are individuals who have little scope for trading; on the fringe of hierarchies are other individuals who are very weakly enfranchised. They may indeed speculate, but it is hardly realistic for such individuals, whose autonomy is severely limited, to be conducting a normative debate about how their society should be constituted. Their best option is to band together to start a group of their own. Otherwise, they can only try to put in disconnected remonstrances to the debates going on around them.

## THE DEBATE ABOUT PUBLIC GOODS

We ought now to be in a stronger position to confront the vexed question of public goods. According to the principles we have explored, the question of public goods arises in different forms in each kind of community, and the different definitions proffered reflect the different social forms which frame the debate. Economists naturally try to focus on relations between persons and things, since that, as Dumont has said, is a distinctive market way of thinking. From the point of view of a community based on market relations, public goods can only be envisaged as a residual class, a set of goods which inherently escape from market conditions, products which cannot be appropriated or costs which cannot be reclaimed. From the standpoint of such a society, the fact that transactions in these goods have to be external to the market will appear as the crucial characteristic, and Samuelson's definition of pure public goods is based on an ideal form of perfect externality. Being without bounds or centre, the market type of society is not well placed to think of collective goods except as residual to all the private goods.

On the other hand, this definition hardly would work in a commune of the extreme polar type in which all goods are held in common. Here the private goods are residual. The Hutterite community, for example, allows each member a small box in which to keep personal mementoes, but these private goods do not enter into exchanges. The equivalent of public goods in a commune are collective goods. This is where the focus on non-excludability (characteristic of Olson's definition and of some others wrestling with the problem of collective action) has its full force.

Neither of these definitions works well to describe the non-market sphere in a hierarchy. In the extreme polar case of hierarchy most goods would be compulsorily allocated according to status, as part of the definition and requirement for holding a status within the community. This is the so-called gift economy we have mentioned, exemplified by feudal dues. Steiner's definition – any publicly induced or provided collective good – is broad enough to embrace it.

In sum, the effort to find one good definition of public goods is probably doomed. What counts as public does not depend on kinds of goods or kinds of transactions but on kinds of communities.

## ACKNOWLEDGEMENT

I am particularly grateful for help in the writing of this article to John Ikenberry, Richard Nelson, Steven Jones, and James Douglas. This article first appeared as 'Culture and Collective Action', in Morris Freilich (ed.), *The Relevance of Culture* (New York, Bergin & Garvey, 1989):1–26.

## REFERENCES

Ackerman, Bruce (1980) *Social Justice in the Liberal State*, New Haven, Yale University Press.

Alchian, A.A. (1967) *Pricing and Society*, London, Institute of Economic Affairs.

Becker, Gary (1981) *A Treatise on the Family*, Cambridge, Harvard University Press.

Bourdieu, Pierre (1979) *La Distinction: Critique Social du Jugement*, Paris, Editions de Minuit.

Brown, Paula (1961) 'Chimbu Death Payments', *Journal of the Royal Anthropological Institute* 91, 1:77–96.

Buchanan, J.M. (1965) 'An Economic Theory of Clubs', *Economica* 32, 2:1–14.

Douglas, Mary (1986) *How Institutions Think*, New York, Syracuse University Press.

Dumont, Louis (1983) *Essais sur l'Individualisme, une Perspective Anthropologique sur l'Ideologie Moderne*, Paris, Seuil.

Dumont, Louis (1985) 'The Economic Mode of Thought in an Anthropological Perspective', in Peter Koslowski (ed.), *Economics and Philosophy*, Tübingen, J.C.B. Mohr.

Elster, Jon (1983) *Explaining Technical Change: A Case Study in the Philosophy of Science*, Cambridge, Cambridge University Press.

Freilich, Morris (1980) 'Smart-Sex and Proper-Sex: A Paradigm Found', *Central Issues in Anthropology* 2, 2:37–51.

Gross, Jonathan and Rayner, Steve (1985) *Measuring Culture*, New York, Columbia University Press.

Hampton, James (1982) 'Giving Grid and Group Dimensions an Operational Definition', in Mary Douglas (ed.) *Essays in the Sociology of Perception*, London, Routledge & Kegan Paul.

Hardin, Russell (1982) *Collective Action. Resources for the Future*, Baltimore, Johns Hopkins University Press.

Hirschman, A.O. (1970) *Exit, Voice and Loyalty: Responses to Decline in Firms, Organizations and States*, Cambridge, Harvard University Press.

Hirschman, A.O. (1977) *The Passions and the Interests*, Princeton, N.J., Princeton University Press.

Jones, Steven (1984) *The Economics of Conformism*, Oxford, Blackwell.

Mars, Gerald (1982) *Cheats at Work, A Study of Occupational Crime*, London, Allen & Unwin.

Nelson, Richard (1986) 'The Role of Government in a Mixed Economy', paper for Conference on Privatization of the Public Sector, Wharton School, University of Pennsylvania.

Olson, Mancur (1965) *The Logic of Collective Action*, Cambridge, Harvard University Press.

Samuelson, Paul A. (1954) 'The Pure Theory of Public Expenditure', *Review of Economics and Statistics* 37, 1:387–9.

Samuelson, Paul A. (1955) 'Diagrammatic Exposition of a Theory of Public Expenditure', *Review of Economics and Statistics* 37, 1:350–6.

Sen, Amartya K. (1977) 'Rational Fools: A Critique of the Behavioral Foundations of Economic Theory', *Philosophy and Public Affairs* 6, 4:317–44.

Simon, Herbert (1955) 'A Behavioral Model of Rational Choices', *Quarterly Journal of Economics* 69:99–118.

Steiner, Peter O. (1974) 'Public Expenditure Budgeting', in A.S. Blinder (ed.) *The Economics of Public Finance*, Washingon, D.C., Brookings.

Tocqueville, Alexis de (1966) *Democracy in America*, vol. 2, J.P. Mayer and L. Lerner (eds), New York, Harper & Row.

Thompson, Michael (1980) 'Postscript: A Cultural Basis for Comparison', in H. Kunreuther and J. Linnerooth (eds), *Risk Analysis and Decision Processes*, Berlin, Springer Verlag.

Thompson, Michael (1982) *Among the Energy Tribes*, Working paper 82–59, Laxenburg, Austria, International Institute for Applied Systems Analysis.

Wildavsky, Aaron (1984) *Moses, The Nursing Father*, Montgomery, AL, Alabama University Press.

Wildavsky, Aaron, and Douglas, Mary (1982) *Risk and Culture*, Berkeley, California University Press.

# 8

# WANTS

To be in want is not to have. The obverse of want is satisfaction or having the wherewithal for happiness. Much Eastern philosophy recommends happiness based on few wants, just as much of Western philosophical comment condemns excessive wants. The economists' view is different. They tend to worry when an economy comes to rest at a low level of wants and to feel more sanguine when the demand for new possessions goes up, even if they become worried again if demand is inflationary. They are clearly interested in wants. Yet the way that demand for goods is treated within economic theory blocks their curiosity about how wants are generated. This is not to say that distinguished economists have not seriously pondered the subject. Many have produced catalogues of wants, sometimes contrasting material with spiritual satisfactions, sometimes comparing long-term with short-term wants, or psychic joys (such as music or affection) with physical requirements (such as food and warmth). Such lists tend to dangle free of theoretical constraints. They remain mere lists whose parts do not mesh into any theory.

Anthropology is in no state to supplement this missing element in economics. Both disciplines have an explicit theory about the circulation of goods but only an implicit theory of wants. In economics the implicit assumption is that the origin of wants is to be found inside the individual's physical and psychic constitution. In anthropology, the implicit assumption is that wants are defined and standardized in social interaction. This latter view makes a better start for thinking about wants because it integrates the choices of the individual agent within a model of the whole economy, whereas economics leaves the choices unexplained except in regard to price. To get into such a starting position

149

economics would need to modify the concept of the consumer as an independent rational agent choosing to satisfy personal needs. It would also need to take an interest in what happens to goods after purchase. The word consumption implies that the goods are destined to be used up in the purchaser's home. Once in the shopping basket they hold little interest for economic theory, but that is the point at which the anthropologist's interest begins. Most goods are likely to be widely shared or passed from hand to hand over a certain span of time. Instead of someone who buys for private purposes the consumer would have to be seen as someone engaged in long-term interactions with other social beings and using goods to promote the particular social patterns that he values.

For the anthropologist, wants are primarily generated in social life; if this is so, when the pace of social interaction slackens, demand for possessions will go down. This approach began with Malinowski's account (1922) of Trobriand Islanders going in canoes to exchange shell ornaments and other products through vast reaches of the Pacific. These people made a clear distinction between trade and gift, and used both to build up partnerships which were not only profitable but supported their intentions within their local political systems. Marcel Mauss (1925) extended these insights to a general theory of solidarity based on reciprocal obligation. From these beginnings, succeeding generations of anthropologists came to study all kinds of transfers of rights and property as flows marking the important channels of social obligation. The focus on types of reciprocity as the basis of solidarity was formalized by Claude Lévi-Strauss in a general theory of kinship. One kind of repeated marriage pattern can produce long lines of exchange embracing everyone in the community and all generations in a generalized system of transfers; another has more restricted effects, linking only two or three descent lines; endogamy is the limit case of marrying-in at the expense of a wider solidarity. Such variations have direct implications for the political system and for the economy. Marrying or procreating appear as part of the total system of reproduction. It has generally been assumed that this kind of analysis applies only to societies in which market organization is weakly developed. However, it can be argued that the sharp disjunction between market and non-market is an artefact of economic theory and one which makes theorizing about demand peculiarly difficult.

The implicit assumption in anthroplogy is that individual wants are standardized by the same processes that establish social solidarity. Put crudely, the reason anyone wants anything (physical needs apart) is for sharing with or showing or giving to someone else in recognition of similar gestures, gifts or services received in the past. On this assumption, being severely in want means being unable to take part in the major reciprocal exchanges by which future entitlements are conferred. This is no trivial matter. Lacking entitlement is equivalent to becoming a third-class citizen or even to losing civic status. Anyone who exerts no claims on the rest of society finds that his sons and daughters are not sought in marriage; he wants for protection and can expect an indigent old age. Such a theory of wants is capable of being made explicit and generalized beyond the range of societies the anthropologists usually study. It would enable economic theory to integrate social life, family structure, demography, and the labour market into the rest of the economy. The obstacle lies in the way that the theory of demand has been formulated.

The original utilitarian philosophy presupposed that wants are in some sense commensurable. Mathematical treatments of wants based on this assumption were already being applied to economic analysis when the theory of diminishing marginal utility was worked out independently in 1871 by Carl Menger and W.S. Jevons; Walras also arrived at it in the same year and independently, though he published a little later. Such a simultaneous convergence upon an intricate idea would be quite impossible if the common infrastructure of theory was not already in place. The relevant point for an article on wants is that the problem to which they all found the same answer was not how to formulate a theory of wants, not at all. The problem was how to formulate the concept of demand so as to harmonize this part of economic theory with the rest of the theory of supply and demand. Diminishing marginal utility means that an individual purchaser gets marginally less satisfaction from each additional increment of a commodity. The underlying metaphor is physical: more and more bread or beer or beef gives less benefit to the eater and bigger and bigger doses of a medicine may actually harm instead of curing the patient. By incorporating diminishing marginal satisfaction for the consumer, demand theory matches the theory of supply according to which marginal costs increase with increase in the volume of production. Beyond a certain point, rising costs mean that the price must rise to encourage extra output. As the marginal utility to the consumer falls, he becomes less willing to spend his income on it. The rising supply curve cuts the falling demand curve and the see-saw comes to rest.

Whereas the theories of production, exchange, and capital formation drawn up on this model only had to face technical criticism, when the model was applied to wants, philosophical and political objections appeared. How can human wants be given numerical expression (Edgeworth 1881)? How can one person's wants be compared with another's? How can such comparisons not carry a load of political prejudice (Mackenzie 1981)?

In the history of science it often happens that a theory does not apply well to the behaviour it is supposed to explain, because its coherence within a larger theory prevents the bad fit with data being taken seriously. In this case the theory of demand cannot give an account of wants simply because this is not what it was designed for. The very completeness of its embedding in the larger, unified theory makes it incapable of focusing on its nominal subject matter. It gives a gravely misleading account of wants for the following reasons.

First, violence is done to the concept of the individual consumer by making it parallel to the concept of the individual firm. The consumer's wants do not correspond to the profit maximizing objectives of the firm. This is essentially because the consumer is not an individual among other consumers as the firm is an individual in the market. In order to live in a society the individual consumer has to develop categories of thought and tastes conformable with those of his fellows. The processes of standardization which should be at the centre of a theory of wants are ignored by economic theory. In default of a theory of how wants are collectively generated, it falls back on hidden assumptions about the priority of physical needs. As a result of this heavy disadvantage in thinking about wants, the threat of famine tends to be perceived as a physical failure of the supply of physical necessities, not as a failure of demand. It is true that in a famine the would-be buyers have nothing to offer in exchange for the food they need. But to know how they got into that situation is to see how demand is generated by a variety of reciprocal exchanges which guarantee future entitlements. A.K. Sen (1981) has argued that the misdiagnosis of the causes of major famines is due to inability to see how individuals enter the economic system and stay in it. Without what he calls exchange entitlements, individuals and their dependents are vulnerable to shocks in the economic system. Such a systemic view of the way that wants enter the economy and are shaped by social and legal processes is necessary if the anthropological approach is to be joined with economics in a general theory of wants. In this perspective the pattern of wants is the surface appearance of a pattern of social relations and social opportunities. Goods are needed as aids to interaction and as clues for constructing intelligible worlds. The consumer is engaged in a continual task of grading goods and occasions and matching them appropriately, as every market researcher knows. It should be useful for a theory of demand to take the social pressures into account. The more isolation and segregation, the more is demand dampened, the more the interaction, the more the need for a symbolic system articulated by finely graded patterns of consumption.

Third, the theory makes one connection (price) between consumption and production but misses another. It treats tastes as personal and subjective and so uninfluenced by the organization of work. But tastes depend upon shared consumption, so the timing of work, the location of homes, the lifecycle expectations which are engendered by different occupations, all these and other aspects of the labour market influence the standardization of wants.

To correct these weaknesses in the only theory that claims to be a theory of wants would involve taking much more interest in shared cultural categories that characterize a community. Economists expect to apply their theories to public policy. But whenever they are tempted to speak of what is good for a community, their theory leads to contradiction. As Arrow's theorem proves, the ranked preferences of several individuals cannot necessarily be aggregated into a single ordered set for them all unless, of course, they happen to have the same preferences. In respect of material things they very frequently do. But there is no theory about how this comes to pass. So the theory is at a loss when it comes to thinking about community welfare. Starting from incommensurable, subjective, individual preferences it cannot proceed to theorize about what a community wants. Yet, there seems to be no inherent reason why a theory of wants, which gives credit to their social origins and their social definition and to their community-imposed character, should not serve the needs of economic theory as well as, better than, the one which has historically developed from the concept of the individual as a surrogate for the firm.

## ACKNOWLEDGEMENT

This article first appeared in *The New Palgrave Dictionary of Economic Theory*, 1987.

## REFERENCES

Douglas, M. and Isherwood, B.C. (1979) *The World of Goods*, New York, Basic Books.

Edgeworth, F.Y. (1881) *Mathematical Psychics. An Essay on the Application of Mathematics to the Moral Sciences*, London, Kegan Paul.

Lévi-Strauss, C. (1949) *Les structures élémentaires de la parenté*, Paris, Presses Universitaires.

Mackenzie, D. (1981) *Statistics in Britain, 1865–1930*, Edinburgh, Edinburgh University Press.

Malinowski, B. (1922) *Argonauts of the Western Pacific*, London, Routledge & Kegan Paul.

Mauss, M. (1925) 'Essai sur le don', *L'année sociologique*, 2nd series, Vol. 1, 23–4. Trans. as *The Gift*, London, Cohen and West.

Sen, A.K. (1981) *Poverty and Famines: An Essay on Entitlement and Deprivation*, Oxford, Clarendon Press.

# 9

# NO FREE GIFTS
## Introduction to Mauss's essay on
### *The Gift*

Charity is meant to be a free gift, a voluntary, unrequited surrender of resources. Though we laud charity as a Christian virtue we know that it wounds. I worked for some years in a charitable foundation which annually was required to give away large sums as the condition of tax exemption. Newcomers to the office quickly learnt that the recipient does not like the giver, however cheerful he be. Mauss's essay *The Gift* explains the lack of gratitude by saying that the foundations should not confuse their donations with gifts. It is not merely that there are no free gifts in a particular place, Melanesia or Chicago for instance: it is that the whole idea of a free gift is based on a misunderstanding. There should not be any free gifts. What is wrong with the so-called free gift is the donor's intention to be exempt from return gifts coming from the recipient. Refusing requital puts the act of giving outside any mutual ties. Once given, the free gift entails no further claims from the recipient. The public is not deceived by free gift vouchers. For all the ongoing commitment the free gift gesture has created, it might just as well never have happened. According to Marcel Mauss, that is what is wrong with the free gift. A gift that does nothing to enhance solidarity is a contradiction.

Mauss says as much in reply to Bronislaw Malinowski who was surprised to find such precisely calculated return gifts in Melanesia. He evidently took with him to his fieldwork the idea that commerce and gift are two separate kinds of activity, the first based on exact recompense, the second spontaneous, pure of ulterior motive. Because the valuable things that circulated in the Trobriand Islands and a vast surrounding region were not in commercial exchange, he expected the transfers to fall into the category of gifts in his own culture. So he expended a lot of care in classifying gifts by the purity of the motives of the giver and concluded that practically nothing was given freely in this sense, only the small gift that a Trobriand husband regularly gave his wife could count. Pure gift? Nonsense! declares Mauss: the Trobriand husband is actually recompensing his wife for sexual services. He would have said Nonsense! just as heartily to Titmus's idea that the archetypal pure gift relationship is the anonymous gift of blood,[1] as if there could be an anonymous relationship. Even the idea of a pure gift is a contradiction. By ignoring the universal custom of compulsory gifts we make our own record incomprehensible to ourselves: right across the globe and as far back as we can go in the history of human civilization, the major transfer of goods has been by cycles of obligatory returns of gifts.

Though this insight was taken up by archaeologists and historians for reinterpreting antique systems of tax, revenues, and trade[2] a fancy archaeological insight was not Mauss's objective. The essay on *The Gift* was a part of an organized onslaught on contemporary political theory, a plank in the platform against utilitarianism. This intention is fully recognized in the new journal, *MAUSS*.[3] Mauss himself wrote very little about political philosophy but *The Gift* does not spring from nowhere: references to Emile Durkheim make quite clear where to look for the rest of the programme. And nor does Durkheim come from nowhere. First I will explain the plan of the book, then I will place it in its context. Finally I will indicate some of the work that has stemmed from it, and suggest what is still to be done to implement the original programme.

In his book Mauss produced an idea that he had probably been mulling over for a long time. Indeed, the idea is profoundly original. We have seen how it runs against our established idea of gift. The book starts by describing the North American potlatch as an extreme form of an institution that is found in every region of the world. The potlatch is an example of a total system of giving. Read this too fast and you miss the meaning. Spelled out it means that each gift is part of a system of reciprocity in which the honour of giver and recipient are engaged. It is a total system in that every item of status or of spiritual or material possession is implicated for everyone in the whole community. The system is quite simple: just the rule that every gift has to be returned in some specified way sets up a perpetual cycle of exchanges within and between generations. In some cases the specified return is of equal value, producing a stable system of statuses; in others it must exceed the value of the earlier gift, producing an escalating contest for honour. The whole society can be described by the catalogue of transfers which map all the obligations between its members. The cycling gift system is the society.

*The Gift* is a grand exercise in positivist research, combining ethnology, history, and sociology. First Mauss presents the system as found in working order. This takes him to the ethnography of North America. What is striking about the potlatch among the Haida and Tlingit of the Northwest coast is the extreme rivalry expressed by the rule always to return more than was received: failure to return means losing the competition for honour. There comes a point when there are just not enough valuable things to express the highest degrees of honour, so conspicuous consumption is succeeded by conspicuous destruction. Then he turns to Melanesia where, in a less extreme form, there are the essentials of potlatch, that is, totalized competitive giving which incorporates in its cycles all things and services and all persons. He treats Polynesia as a variant, because there the totalized giving does not presume rivalry between donor and recipient. When the paths of Polynesian gifts are traced a stable, hierarchical structure is revealed. It is not the competitive potlatch, but it is still a total system of gift. Where does the system get its energy? In each case from individuals who are due to lose from default drawing obloquy on defaulters and from beliefs that the spirits would punish them. The system would not be total if it did not include personal emotions and religion.

After presenting the system of gift functioning among American Indians and in Oceania, and among Eskimo and Australian hunters, Mauss then turns to records of ancient legal systems. Roman, Germanic, and other Indo-European laws all show signs of the basic principles. There are no free gifts; gift cycles engage persons in permanent commitments which articulate the dominant institutions. Only after the full tour of ethnographic and legal evidence do we finally reach the chapter on the theory of the gift in classical Hindu law. Now we have definitely moved away from working social systems to myths, legends, and fragments of laws: not the system of gift but, as the chapter heading says, the theory of gift. Mauss's early essay (1889), with Henri Hubert, on sacrifice[4] took for its central theme a Vedic principle that sacrifice is a gift which compels the deity to make a return: Do ut des; I give so that you may give. Given the centrality of India in Max Muller's philological speculations on mythology, any book at that time on religion would need to study Hindu law and epic deeply. It strikes me as likely that Mauss did get the idea of a morally sanctioned gift cycle upholding the social cycle from the Vedic literature which he studied in that first major research. I am inclined to think that he harboured and developed the great idea all those years. Certainly there is a close connection of matter and treatment between the two books.

In some histories of anthropology the main difference between old-fashioned folklore and modern ethnography has been identified as the replacement of library research by fieldwork. But I would suggest that the more important change came from a new criterion of sound analysis. The Gift was like an injunction to record the entire credit structure of a community. What a change that involved from current ideas about how to do ethnology can be seen by reading any of the earlier books cited in the voluminous footnotes whose unsystematic accounts of beliefs and ceremonies provided the bare bones of the gift system.

Because it starts from Northwest Coast American Indians and Melanesians, and goes on to Polynesia, and then to ancient texts, the book would seem to spring from the fusty debates of library researchers on comparative religion. Yet it is not about religion. It is about politics and economics. After the survey of evidence come the political and moral implications. Following Durkheim, Mauss also considered that every serious philosophical work should bear on public policy. The theory of the gift is a theory of human solidarity. Consequently a brief reference to contemporary debates on health and unemployment insurance is in place, with the argument deduced from the preceding pages that the wage does not cover society's obligation to the worker. No obligations are ever completely covered. Though Mauss here refers approvingly to some English proposals on social policy, he is writing in a tradition strongly opposed to English liberal thought. At this point the Durkheimian context needs to be filled in.

The main strands in Durkheim's opposition to the English Utilitarians were already formulated by French political philosophers.[5] As Larry Siedentrop summarizes a tradition that stemmed from the eighteenth century, from Rousseau and de

Tocqueville, it made three criticisms of English liberalism: first, that it was based on an impoverished concept of the person seen as an independent individual instead of as a social being; second, that it neglected how social relations change with changes in the mode of production; and third, that it had too negative a concept of liberty and so failed to appreciate the moral role of political participation. Furthermore, early English empiricist philosophy did not explain the role of social norms in shaping individual intentions and in making social action possible; their sensationalist model of the mind allowed no scope for explaining rule-governed action. Individualism is the essence of the French critique of utilitarianism. This is exactly where Durkheim's life work starts, as would appear from the following paragraph by his biographer, Stephen Lukes:[6]

> Benjamin Constant believed that 'when all are isolated by egoism, there is nothing but dust, and at the advent of a storm, nothing but mire',[7] while it was Alexis de Tocqueville who gave *individualisme* its most distinctive and influential liberal meaning in France. For Tocqueville it meant the apathetic withdrawal of individuals from public life into a private sphere and their isolation from one another, with a consequent and dangerous weakening of social bonds: individualism was 'a deliberate and peaceful sentiment which disposes each citizen to isolate himself from the mass of his fellows . . . [which] at first saps only the virtues of public life, but, in the long run . . . attacks and destroys all others and is eventually absorbed into pure egoism'.[8]

Among French socialists individualism was a bad word, referring to laissez-faire, anarchy, social atomization and exploitation of the poor under a regime of industrial capitalism. However, Durkheim's position was more complex. He believed that the success of a political system would depend on the extent to which it allowed individual self-awareness to flourish. He tried to keep a delicate balance between reproaching utilitarianism for overlooking that humans are social beings and reproaching socialism for overlooking the demands of the individual.

If one were to be forgetful of this traditional hostility to English utilitarianism it would be easy to misunderstand Durkheim's language and to fall into the trap of thinking that he really believed that society is a kind of separate intelligence, which determines the thoughts and actions of its members as the mind does those of the body it is lodged in. Arguing against the nineteenth-century forms of utilitarianism, especially against the political philosophy of Herbert Spencer, it would have seemed hard for the anti-utilitarians to over-estimate the importance of shared norms. And as for those whom he attacked, especially those across the Channel or across the Atlantic, it was evidently easier to misrepresent him than to disagree with what he was actually saying. Bartlett refers to Durkheim's idea of the collective memory as a quasi-mystic soul: Herbert Simon dissociates himself from Durkheimian 'group mind' implications; Alfred Schutz disdainfully dismisses Halb-wachs' theories on the 'Collective Memory of Musicians' (which are very much the same as his own) because they are tainted by Durkheim's alleged theory of a unitary group consciousness; see also Bruno Latour on Durkheim's 'big animal'.[9] All these and many others forget that Durkheim's work was actually part of an ongoing research project with close collaborators who quite clearly did not give it this interpretation. So the counter-attack has travestied versions of 'group mind', 'mystical unit', 'group psyche' which his language occasionally justifies but which his precepts as to method certainly do not. This is why positivism was such an important plank in his programme. Positivism represented an attempt at objectivity. This is why it was necessary for Mauss to set out the plan of his book by beginning with the survey of functioning social systems, ending with Hindu texts about a vanished system or one that had perhaps never existed in that form.

Today the same political debate is still engaged, between the contemporary utilitarians and those who, like Durkheim, deplore the effects of unfettered individualism. Some of those working in learned communities that embrace methodological individual-ism may be right to feel threatened by his teaching. Personally I think it would be better for them to take it seriously. Hostility and a sense of threat are a sign that collective representations are at work. Our problem is how to take our own and other people's collective representations into account. Durkheim expected to do so by setting up sociology as a science, using positivist methods and looking for social facts. Science was to be a way of escaping bondage to past and to present loyalties. It is easy to mock his scientific pretensions, but who would deny that we really do need to seek for objectivity and to establish a responsible sociological discourse free of subjective hunches and concealed political pressure?

From this point of view *The Gift* rendered an extraordinary service to Durkheim's central project by producing a theory that could be validated by observation. For anthropologists the book has provided a basic requirement for modern fieldwork. It quickly became axiomatic that a field report would be below standard unless a complete account could be given of all transfers, that is of all dues, gifts, fines, inheritances and successions, tributes, fees and payments; when this information is in place one also knows who gets left at the end of the day without honour or citizenship and who benefits from the cumulative transfers. With such a chart in hand the interpreter might be capable of sensing the meanings of ballads, calypsos, dirges, and litanies; without it, one guess will do as well as any other.

Mauss rendered other inestimable services to Durkheim's project of a science of sociology. One is to have demonstrated that when the members of the Durkheimian school talked of society they did not mean an undecomposable unity, as many of their critics have supposed. If they had thought of society as an unanalysable, unchanging, sacralized entity the researches of Durkheim's best pupils would never have been undertaken. *The Elementary Forms of the Religious Life*[10] gives snapshot pictures of Australian aborigines and American Indians worshipping spirits who sustain the social forms. It all seems very cut and dried. Durkheim and Mauss, in *Primitive Classification*,[11] write as if categories are never negotiated but always come ready tailored to fit the institutions. Their argument at that point was not about change. They did in fact have a theory of change, that is that changes in the organization of production radically transform the system of categories and beliefs.[12] If their theory had really been about a static social system, there would not have been any point in Maurice Halbwachs considering how public memory changes when part of the population goes away, taking its memories with it, or when a new influx comes bringing memories of their own past to the common pool.[13] Nor would Georges Davy have been so interested in the conditions under which oath breaking is thought to be punished by God and those in which the sacredness of the oath diminishes.[14] It is an ignorant reading which supposes that Durkheim and his colleagues were looking for static correlations. The modern economy with its increasing specialization of functions is the backdrop to all these comparisons, and particularly to the gift system yielding place to the industrial system.

Another of Mauss's contributions to this collaborative effort is to have introduced a realistic idea of individuals in the pre-market social system where, according to Durkheim's formulations, one might expect only a community of humans mechanically connected to one another by their unquestioning use of the same ideas. Durkheim shared the common belief of his day in a gradual enriching and unfolding of the personality as the collective representations loosened their grip. However Mauss manages to incorporate individuals acting in their own interests, even in the kinds of societies in which Durkheim had thought that there was no scope for individual self-interest. On this Mauss rightly remarks that the concept of interest is itself modern.[15] He introduces psychology into the new sociology with essays on collective representations about death, about the body, and about the person.[16] In these he takes off from Durkheim's ideas and develops extended innovations upon them.

He also discovered a mechanism by which individual interests combine to make a social system, without engaging in market exchange. This is an enormous development beyond Durkheim's ideas of solidarity based on collective representations. The gift cycle echoes Adam Smith's invisible hand: gift complements market in so far as it operates where the latter is absent. Like the market it supplies each individual with personal incentives for collaborating in the pattern of exchanges. Gifts are given in a context of public drama, with nothing secret about them. In being more directly cued to public esteem, the distribution of honour and the sanctions of religion, the gift economy is more visible than market. Just by being visible, the resultant distribution of goods and services is more readily subject to public scrutiny and judgements of fairness than are the results of market exchange. In operating a gift system a people are more aware of what they are doing, as shown by the sacralization of their institutions of giving. Mauss's fertile idea was to present the gift cycle as a theoretical counterpart to the invisible hand. When anthropologists search around for a telling distinction between societies based on primitive and modern technologies, they try out various terms such as pre-literate, simple, traditional. Each has limitations that unfit it for general use. But increasingly we are finding that the idea of the gift economy comprises all the associations, symbolic and interpersonal and economic, that we need for comparing with market economy.

When I try to consider what would be needed now to implement Mauss's original programme I wonder which current ideas would be replaced if *The Gift* were to be as significant as he could have hoped. Where anthropology is concerned he would surely be more than satisfied. Nothing has been the same since. The big developments stem from this work. Before we had *The Gift*'s message unfolded for us, we anthropologists, if we thought of the economy at all, treated it almost as a separate aspect of society, and kinship as separate again, and religion as a final chapter at the end. Evans-Pritchard, who promoted the original English translation and wrote a Foreword to the edition which this one replaces, had Mauss's teaching very much at heart when he described the marriage dues of the Nuer as a strand in the total circulation of cattle and wives and children and men; every single relationship had its substantiation in a gift.[17] This was a beginning, but there is no doubt that Claude Lévi-Strauss is the most indebted, which means of course that he gave counter gifts as magnificent as he received. After *The Elementary Forms of Kinship*[18] we had to count transfers of men and women as the most important among the gifts in total symbolic systems. Numerous very fine comparative studies stand as testimony to the transformation of our outlook. However, it is not so easy to carry forward these analyses and apply them to ourselves.

The problem now is the same as it was for Mauss when it comes to applying his insights to contemporary industrial society. Yet this is what he wanted to see done. As the last chapter in *The Gift* shows, his own attempt to use the theory of the gift to underpin social democracy is very weak. Social security and health insurance are an expression of solidarity, to be sure, but so are a lot of other things, and there the likeness ends. Social democracy's redistributions are legislated for in elected bodies and the sums are drawn from tax revenues. They utterly lack any power to involve persons in a contest of honour. Taking the theory straight from its context in full-blown gift economies to a modern political issue was really jumping the gun. His own positivist method would require a great deal more patient spade-work, both on theory and in collecting new kinds of data. I myself made an attempt to apply the theory of the gift to our consumption behaviour, arguing that it is much more about giving than the economists realize. Class structure would be clearly revealed in information about giving and exclusion from reciprocal voluntary cycles of exchange. Much of the kind of information I needed about what happens in our society was missing from census and survey records.[19] It was information that could have been collected if Mauss's theory was recognized. If we persist in thinking that gifts ought to be free and pure, we will always fail to recognize our own grand cycles of exchanges, what categories get to be included and which are excluded from our hospitality.[20] More profound insights into the nature of solidarity and trust can be expected from applying the theory of the gift to ourselves. Though giving is the basis for huge industries, we cannot know whether it is the foundation of a circulating fund of stable esteem and trust, or of individualist competition as Thorstein Veblen thought.[21] We cannot know because the information is not collected in such a way as to relate to the issues.

I conclude by asking why this profound and original book had its impact mainly among small professional bodies of archaeologists, classicists, and anthropologists. The answer might be that the debate with the Utilitarians which Mauss was ready to enter before the First World War had lost its excitement by the time he published this volume. One of the most fascinating topics in Lukes's biography is the relation of Durkheim's school to Marxism. Before the war the real enemy, the open enemy of French political philosophy was Anglo-Saxon utilitarianism. After the war utilitarianism became the narrow province of a specialized discipline of economics. The political enemies of social democracy became communism and fascism. I have remarked how they traced a counterpoint to Marx's central ideas, neutralizing them as it were from communist taint and making something like Marxism safe for French democracy by diluting the revolutionary component.[22] The political mood of the inter-war years was dominated by concern for the erosion of civil liberties and excessive corporatist claims on the individual.

Now however the fashion has changed again. Utilitarianism is not just a technique of econometrics, nor a faded philosophy of the eighteenth century. Solidarity has again become a central topic in political philosophy. Social Darwinism walks again and the survival of the fittest is openly invoked. Philosophically creaking but technically shining, unified and powerful, utility theory is the main analytical tool for policy decisions. However, its intellectual assumptions are under attack. The French debate with the Anglo-Saxons can start again. This time round the sparks from Mauss's grand idea might well light a fuse to threaten methodological individualism and the idea of a free gift.

## ACKNOWLEDGEMENT

This article first appeared as the 'Introduction' to the new translation of *The Gift*, by Marcel Mauss, published by Routledge in 1989.

## NOTES

1 R. Titmus, *The Gift Relationship* (New York, Pantheon, 1970).

2 Karl Polanyi, C.M. Arensberg and H.W. Pearson, *Trade and Market in Early Empires* (Glencoe, The Free Press, 1957).

3 An acronym for Mouvement Anti-utilitariste dans les Sciences Sociales (*New Series, Vol. 1, 1988, La Decouverte, Paris*).

4 Henri Hubert and M. Mauss (1899) 'Essai sur la nature et la fonction du sacrifice', *Annee Sociologique* 2:29–138.

5 Larry Siedentrop, 'Two Liberal Traditions', pp. 153–74 in Alan Ryan (ed.), *The Idea of Freedom* (Oxford, Clarendon, 1979). Starting from Rousseau in the eighteenth century, and with Bonald Condillac and Larry Maistre. Siedentrop names as the nineteenth-century protagonists of this criticism Madame de Stael, Benjamin Constant and Les Doctrinaires. The latter group included Guizot and de Tocqueville who took the critique of political theory as an urgent post-revolutionary reform. There was more than a touch of political reaction in the movement. The Doctrinaire theorists were strongly committed to the idea of hierarchy and the Doctrinaire government (1815–20 and 1820–27) tried to restore the conditions of the *ancien regime*.

6 Stephen Lukes, *Emile Durkheim, His Life and Work* (London, Allen Lane, 1973), pp. 197–8.

7 Benjamin Constant quoted in Lukes, himself quoting H. Marion 'Individualisme', in *La Grande Encyclopédie* (Paris, n.d.) Vol. xx.

8 A. de Tocqueville, *De la démocratie en Amerique*, ii,2, ch. 11 in J.P. Mayer (ed.) *Oeuvres Completes*, (Paris, 1951), t.1. pt. 2:105.

9 F.C. Bartlett, *Remembering: A Study in Experimental and Social Psychology* (Cambridge, Cambridge University Press, 1932). Herbert Simon, *Administrative Behavior. A Study of Decision-making Processes in Administrative Organisation* (New York Free Press, 1945). Alfred Schutz, 'Making Music Together', in *Collected Papers*, 1–3, (The Hague, Martinus Nyhoff, 1951). Bruno Latour, (1988) in a review of Mary Douglas, *How Institutions Think*, in *Contemporary Sociology, An International Journal of Reviews*, pp. 383–5.

10 Emile Durkheim, *Les Formes Elémentaires de la Vie Religieuse* (Paris, Alcan, 1912).
11 E. Durkheim and M. Mauss (1903) 'De quelques formes primitives de classification: contribution à l'étude des réprésentations collectives', *L'Année Sociologique*, Vol. 6.
12 Emile Durkheim *De la Division du Travail Social: étude sur l'organisation des sociétés supérieures* (Paris, Alcan, 1893).
13 Maurice Halbwachs, *Les Cadres Sociaux de la Mémoire* (Paris, Alcan, 1925).
14 Georges Davy (1922) 'La Foi Jurée', *Etude Sociologique du Problème du Contrat, la formation du lien contractuel*, (Paris, 1922).
15 See Albert Hirschman, *The Passions and the Interests* (New Jersey, Princeton University Press, 1973).
16 M. Mauss, (1926) 'L'Idée de la Mort', *Journal de Psychologie Normale et Pathologique*; 1936 'Les Techniques du Corps', *Journal de Psychologie* 3–4.
17 E.E. Evans-Pritchard, *The Nuer: The Political Institutions of a Nilotic People* (Oxford, Clarendon, 1940); *Kinship and Marriage among the Nuer* (Oxford, Clarendon, 1951).
18 Claude Lévi-Strauss, *Les Structures Elémentaires de la Parenté* (Paris, Presses Universitaires de France, 1949).
19 Mary Douglas, *The World of Goods* (New York, Basic Books and Penguin, 1978).
20 Mary Douglas (ed.) *Food in the Social Order* (New York, Russell Sage Foundation, 1984).
21 Thorstein Veblen, *The Theory of the Leisure Class* (New York, Vanguard Press, 1928).
22 Mary Douglas 'Introduction: Maurice Halbwachs (1877–1945)', in Maurice Halbwachs *The Collective Memory* (New York, Harper & Row, 1980).

# 10

# INSTITUTIONS OF THE THIRD KIND
## British and Swedish labour markets compared

## CULTURE AS EXPLANATION

In social theory the word 'culture' becomes an extra resource to be wheeled in after other explanations are defeated. It is the flexible, powerful residual factor where other reason fails. It works because of what it can say implicitly, drawing upon the reserves of understanding created by discourse in the regular culture. However, because it remains implicit it is the weakness at the core of the so-called social sciences.

You can recognize culture being misused in sociological explanation when you hear behaviour being explained by reference to a cultural value cherished by the actors. Enthusiasm for work (or its absence) is explained by saying that the workers subscribe or do not subscribe to the work ethic. Authority being successfully exerted is explained by a deferential culture. A difficulty in establishing consensus is explained by the value placed on individualism or independence. The submission that we make here is that any explanation by appeal to a dominant value is tautologous. It just says again the thing that is being wondered at. Furthermore the values have not been analysed. There is no hint about where values come from or about how to explain them. These questions fall outside the common discourse but they should not fall outside sociological inquiry which needs to link a careful analysis of the values to the institutional forms.

For example, both the Swedish and the British labour movements put a high value on freedom. But the institutional forms are very different. The fragmented and competitive British workers' unions and employers confront one another in an adversarial way very different from the way the co-ordinated collectives of workers and employers confront each other in Scandinavia. The British unions express aversion to external regulation of any kind, even an antipathy to law and legal enforcement of union rules or collective agreements. And this does not only apply to the workers. The employers too are reluctant to co-operate among themselves if this means sacrificing competitive advantage. They are almost as uncomfortable as the labour unions with the notion of compulsory arbitration. The Swedish system of industrial relations with heavy sanctions on breach of collective agreements is just as alien to them as it is to their employees.

Foreigners ask why anyone would prefer conflict to peaceful co-ordination? Why prefer an adversary system to a collegial one, and still prefer it when the evidence shows that prosperity is one of the bonuses of choosing co-operation? The answer from the workers' side is that they might think more about the co-operative option if they could really believe that any new prosperity would reach down to the workers as a result of their agreeing to legal interference. But there is too much mistrust.

Cultural values seem to come in packages: a high value placed on freedom usually complements a low value placed on trust. We should be able to find a way of explaining how the package gets put together and established.

## NEGATIVE AND POSITIVE FREEDOM

In a famous essay Isaiah Berlin[1] reflected upon two concepts of liberty. One is expressed negatively as freedom from control, freedom from interference, freedom from exploitation. This is the primary sense of freedom. Problems arise with freedom in this sense as soon as we try to put it into a political context. Our freedom from control is likely to impinge on someone else's freedom not to be exploited. A solution to this problem is to create private spheres, for example a system where we have freedom to express our own views or to observe our own religion while at the same time legislation prescribes behaviour in a delineated public sphere.

By contrast, there is the other idea of freedom, a positive freedom to be in control of our lives, which ultimately leads to our taking a share in public responsibilities. This idea has been interpreted as something like the notion of self-determination, freedom from control by one's own disorderly desires, the freedom of self-control, the freedom of not being a slave to our baser passions. But who is going to say which are our baser passions? If the concept is about our rational control of ourselves, then surely, Berlin argues, we are not talking about freedom. On the other hand, if someone else is going to legislate for our good so that we can achieve their idea of our full potential as a human being, then obviously we are going to be enslaved. Isaiah Berlin refused to be led to the paradox that freedom is to be gained by submission to control either by others or by reason. He regarded this positive sense of freedom as a misuse of language.

The two concepts of freedom have been elaborated. Rousseau is associated with the idea of negative freedom, freedom from chains, freedom to resist intrusion; Marx, with the idea of positive freedom, self-determination, the freedom to be involved in determining the community good, even if this does paradoxically imply being a slave to the public service. It has been argued that positive freedom is a more viable idea than Berlin allowed. Various ways in which the two ideas can be reconciled or combined have been proposed.[2]

We plan to use these two contrasted ideas as pegs on which to hang an account of the differences between the British and the Swedish labour market cultures. We will present the Swedes as having embraced the idea of positive freedom and the British the idea of negative freedom. The analysis will connect the value preferences with two distinct institutional structures. The philosophers have devoted thought to reconciling the two senses of the idea of freedom. Yet in practice when one is entrenched, it tends to exclude the other.

The logic which is used in institutionalizing the one contradicts the logic needed to institutionalize the other. As a philosopher Isaiah Berlin insisted that: 'Everything is what it is. Liberty is liberty: not equality or fairness or justice or culture or human happiness or a quiet conscience' (p. 127). And he added that there is no necessary connection between individual liberty and democratic rule: 'The answer to the question "Who governs me?" is logically distinct from the question "How far does government interfere with me?" ' (p. 130). The demand that when someone says one thing he should not be saying something else at the same time is a political force to be reckoned with. With this we are alerted to the role that logic plays in stabilizing cultural forms.

If we listen to the Trade Union Congress debates we keep

hearing the words freedom, basic rights, autonomy, and independence. This body of people has a strong commitment to freedom. They tend to be rough on unions that allow themselves to be used as flunkeys of capitalism, that truckle to authority, or submit to paternalism or exploitative interference. The TUC and its constituent members usually reject both external controls and external support. The usual misuse of culture would leave the explanation at this point. It would say: we have found the answer – it is the love of freedom and love of independence which are at the back of the difference in institutions.

But wait a minute! Does this mean that the Scandinavians love freedom less? Or that the Scandinavians are less committed to their independence? Can their democratic procedures be said to be less inspired by love of freedom and independence? There must be some misunderstanding here. Does love of liberty have to mean conflict? Does it necessarily militate against trust and cooperation?

## LABOUR MARKETS

We will use this paradox to illustrate a way of thinking about culture. First we will show that this question is not purely abstract or remote. It has practical consequences. If it is true that the British labour market has entrenched a culture which is antipathetic to collaboration and regulation, the social sciences seem at first sight to present only two solutions. One is to break the unions' power, keep them at arm's length, and reduce their power. (Arguably this is what the British government, under Margaret Thatcher, tried to do.) The other is to suggest that we wait in the hope that the culture will change over time. Both approaches strike us as wrong. The first is wrong because the unions have played a central role in British national life and because capitalism cannot operate fairly without the countervailing power of collectivized labour. In every locality and every trade an employer is bound in practice to have some monopolistic advantage in the labour market that can only be corrected by a measure of organization in the labour he purchases. It would diminish us all if the strengths that the labour unions represent were to be dispersed. The second is wrong because it is based on a mistaken view of the effects of time on culture. Some cultures are very stable: with these waiting will not help, since time only fortifies them.

Before we get to that part of the argument we need to look at the history of the British labour market to be convinced of the extraordinary stability of its cultural bias.

## DOES CATASTROPHE LEAD TO COLLABORATION?

Some modern industrial countries have managed to move swiftly from devastating industrial strife to negotiations at the national level between representatives of workers, employers, and government. One popular theory holds that it was precisely because things got so bad in Switzerland and Sweden that everyone was forced to realize that co-operation was better than industrial conflict.

Take a bit of the Swiss chronology to see how bad things were before the modern phase of industrial co-operation. In 1907 the Swiss army threatened the women workers in a chocolate factory with canon; in 1918, there was a revolutionary general strike followed through the 1920s with violent industrial action; in 1932, workers were fired upon by the army in Geneva, leading to a communist government between 1933–6; then suddenly in 1937 the so-called 'Peace Treaty' was signed between the Swiss Watch and Metal Workers' Union and the employers by which unions got recognition; and so was inaugurated partnership and prosperity.

Over the same period in Sweden the unions got the basic recognition and right to organize in 1906, but strife did not cease at that point; in 1909, the Labour Organization (LO) called a general strike, which was defeated; industrial conflict deepened and threatened to ruin the economy, until the Saltsjobaden Agreement of 1938 between the employers' federation and the LO. This opened the period in which 'Swedish society gained and – at least until recently – retained the reputation as a model of reformed capitalism, democratic socialism or both'.[3]

The theory cannot really be maintained that if only a catastrophe is devastating enough a better state of affairs is bound to follow. Total collapse can easily follow catastrophe. The contemporary world scene provides plenty of examples. The theory has at least the merit of conflicting with another popular theory, the real anger or real betrayal theory. On this, British workers have had such good cause for embitterment that they could not possibly trust employers or government. On this view, the worse things get, the more insoluble. (This, incidentally, does not explain why the unions do not trust one another to the same extent as their Scandinavian or German parallels.) The cases just cited of extremely violent industrial conflict suggest that labour forces with as good reasons as the British for feeling embittered can collaborate.

## THE INFLUENCE OF THE CLASS SYSTEM

A third kind of popular cultural theory is based on the uniquely oppressive British class system. This is also unconvincing. It says: the British worker does not feel that Jack is as good as his master, as does the American worker, and so he is driven to protest rather than to co-operation. But the American worker too is driven to protest. And we still do not understand why this should stop labour unions from combining with each other more effectively. Neither does the heavy hand of the class system explain the successful organization of collectivized labour markets in other class-ridden societies such as Germany and Austria. It can also be argued that an effective labour movement could have changed the class structure of Britain over a hundred years, as it did in Sweden. So the argument from social class leads back to values: why is the demand to be in control of one's fate weaker in the English labour market than the desire not to be interfered with, why this emphasis on negative freedom?

The results of not organizing are much to our disadvantage as a nation. The problems of our labour market are far from the only cause of stagflation in this country and a national incomes policy is only one aspect of the success of the economies that weathered the oil shocks of the 1970s better than we did. However, the connection between unemployment, inflation, and the organization of the labour market is worth examining.

## UNEMPLOYMENT AND INFLATION

Richard Layard[4] suggests that the rate of unemployment compatible with non-accelerating inflation (NAIRU) will depend on the institutional structure including the structure of the institutions of the labour market.

Colin Crouch[5] summarizes a now well-substantiated view:

> Once a union movement represents enough of the workforce to have macro-economic effects, its contribution to restraining or exacerbating inflation will depend on the extent to which it is capable of centralised strategic action in relation to the economy as a whole.

The institutions which permit such centralized strategic action he calls 'neo-corporatist', (following Philippe Schmitter).[6] They consist of labour and employers' unions each co-ordinated by an effective peak organization capable of bargaining with the other and with government. Crouch shows that, in relation to the percentage of the workforce in union membership, the economies with collectivized labour markets have (a) significantly less industrial conflict, (b) lower inflation rates, and (c) less unemployment associated with inflation. The UK takes a middle position in the degree of collectivization. The USA is at one extreme, illustrating the most competitive type, with a relatively low proportion of the workforce in unions and peak organizations with little authority over member unions. At the other extreme is Sweden, highly collectivized, with a large proportion of the workforce unionized and the labour and employers' unions incorporated in peak organizations which have a high degree of authority over members. Here in the UK the combination is a high proportion of the workforce unionized and peak organizations with little authority. But the middle position for the typology is the worst from the standpoint of economic performance.

It seems that those economies in which the distribution of the wealth created by economic growth and the costs of economic shocks are subject to centralized negotiation between representatives of labour, management, and government perform better than those in which these matters are left to decentralized market forces.

Figures 10.1 and 10.2 have been drawn to a common scale. Each year takes the line to a new percentage point for inflation measured as the increase on the Consumer Price Index and a new percentage for unemployment. Successful performance is shown by movement close to the point of origin. As the line moves out to the right of the chart the NAIRU rises or, in the older lan-

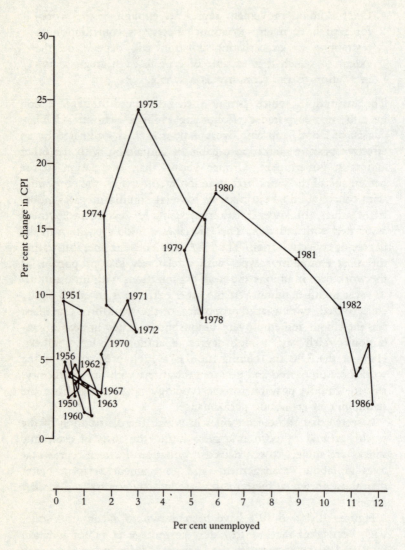

*Figure 10.1* United Kingdom: plot of per cent change in CPI by per cent unemployed (1950–1986).
Source: OECD Statistical Year Books

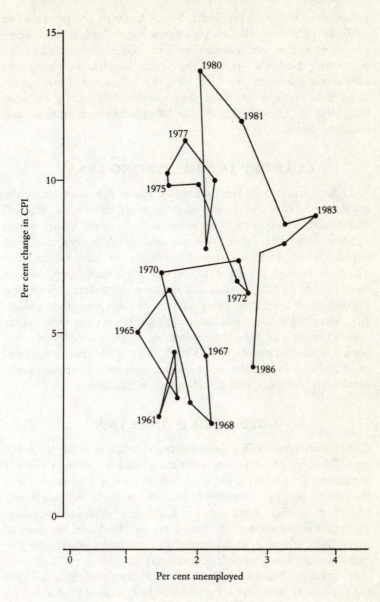

*Figure 10.2* Sweden: plot of per cent change in CPI by per cent
unemployed (1960–1986).
*Source*: OECD Statistical Year Books

175

guage, the Phillips Curve drifts. Sweden, during the period from 1950, keeps to a small area corresponding to both lower unemployment and lower inflation than the USA. Britain starts the post-war period with one of the lowest NAIRU but soon zigzags across the chart, and even now that inflation and unemployment have come down from their peaks is still among the least successful on the criterion of the balance between inflation and unemployment.

## CULTURE IN THE STRONG SENSE

We take culture to be the package of values that are cited in the regular normative discussions that shape an institution. We will first examine institutions that prove stable and the values which uphold them. We cannot assume that stability does not need explanation. Nor do we assume that the cherishing of the right values is enough by itself to sustain the organization, so we have to assume that a stable institution needs external favouring conditions to keep it in being as well as the appropriate values. And since there is no guarantee that either of these will appear spontaneously and regularly enough to account for stability, we are led to another assumption. This is that a stable type of organization includes in its own make-up some capacity to stimulate the reinforcing conditions that will enable it to survive.

## GRID–GROUP ANALYSIS

Those of us who work in cultural analysis find that we can make sense of a lot of otherwise inscrutable data by using three (or sometimes four or five) kinds of stable types of institutions. For the present purpose we will use three: 'hierarchy', 'individualism', and 'sect' – each term having a rather specialized meaning. Hierarchical institutions are based on the up-down bonding of individuals within a social group (for example, bureaucracies). Individualist institutions (e.g. markets) are based on quid-pro-quo exchanges between individuals. Institutions of the third kind (such as sects and communes) base their relations on bonding insiders together against outsiders. Inclusion is logically different from hierarchy. Inclusion and hierarchy are different from equivalent exchange. Each cultural type is founded on its distinctive logical premise.

Our friends will recognize in this typology the familiar outline of grid–group analysis of which there are now several variants used for different kinds of problems. James Hampton[7] originally developed a two-by-two matrix to capture the features of four distinctive social environments. Michael Thompson[8] turned it into an ecological model dynamized by the competition between different forms of social organization, each assumed to be actively seeking to absorb or eliminate the others. Jonathan Gross and Steve Rayner[9] have provided a formal basis for measuring and comparing these different social environments. Gerald Mars[10] has used the four social environments for identifying kinds of occupational crime. Why then have we only studied three types in this essay, when colleagues have done so well with four? The answer is the same as it is for Aaron Wildavsky[11] who has applied this method of analysis to political cultures. By definition the fourth type is politically mute: it is a social environment which separates individuals, and so cuts down their communication with one another. (See Figure 10.3.)

In Figure 10.3 the great bureaucratic hierarchies of government and civil service would appear in the upper right-hand sector. The individual politicians who form governments, on the other hand, would appear in the competitive individualistic bottom left-hand sector. The diagonal linking these two is where a great deal of power in society is located. It is here that government-to-industry relations take place. It is along this line that the bureaucracies of the large firms recruit their managerial superstars, employ their consultants, lawyers and accountants. Two points need to be borne in mind about Figure 10.3. First, the positions are not absolute: there is no absolute hierarchy – organizations are merely more or less hierarchical. Second, the position of a given organization in Figure 10.3 may differ according to the level of organization that is being examined. For example, a fairly large firm which we are seeing as an independent supplier in a competitive market for its product will appear in the bottom left-hand sector but if we are looking at its internal structure, it might very well appear as a hierarchy in the upper right-hand sector. Note, incidentally, that as an industry concentrates, it tends to move up the 'diagonal' with entry becoming more difficult and individual firms' policies more regulated.

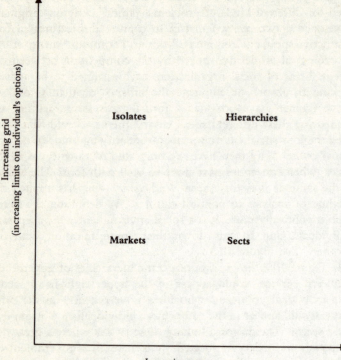

*Figure 10.3* Cultural analysis by grid–group dimensions.

## BRITISH UNIONS AS SECTS

The Swedish labour market organizations correspond to hierarchies. The TUC and the British Employers' Confederation are not hierarchies by any test; their members are individualists all right, but the constitution of the institutions themselves is collective. Such collectivities of essentially autonomous individuals approximate to the structure of the sect or commune. Some employers and some workers stay outside any collective organization and obviously count as individualists (i.e. on the low-group left-hand side of Figure 10.3).

Using the model as a guide to organizational strengths and

weaknesses, there is no mystery about why the British unions act as they do. The TUC is not a weaker version of the Swedish Labour Organization; a defective hierarchy. The familiar questions about why it does not do what other labour movements do are beside the point; it is a quite different kind of culture. The question of how it could change itself becomes a matter of practical means instead of a pious hope.

Though we do not wish to underestimate them, we give less weight to physical environmental factors making for stability than to institutional ones, as the neglected topic is cultural analysis. Sometimes it is useful to talk of three elements, the culture, the institution, and the physical factors. But a reference to the latter alone is hardly any more convincing as an explanation of why an institution is what it is than the simple reference to cherished values. As an institution entrenches its values in the minds of its members it cumulatively transforms its environment.

## SOCIAL MODELS

How does a new institution establish itself in one or other of these cultural types? First, as the institution comes into being, there is a limited choice of social models. Only certain alternative slots are available according to the group's expected place in society, its objectives and relations with the law.

When the union movement started at the end of the eighteenth century its enemies assimilated it to the conspiracies which preceded the French Revolution. They were seen as secret societies as subversive as the Jacobins. While successive legal reforms gave them immunity from the charges of conspiracy, restraint of trade, tort, etc., they had from the start been placed in the position of requiring freedom from interference and to this day 'the abstention of the law', as Clegg calls it, remains a unique characteristic of British industrial relations.

By the turn of the century, when the Swedish union movement got under way, the conspiratorial model had been superseded. While the Swedish employers originally resisted and fought the growth of trade unions, by 1906 unionism had achieved recognition thanks to an agreement made by their peak organization, the LO, with the employers' peak organization, the SAF. Under this agreement the employers undertook to recognize the unions' rights to organize and negotiate wages and conditions while the unions undertook to respect the employers' prerogatives to direct work in all other respects. The LO had been established in 1898 on the initiative of the Social Democratic party who were seeking an industrial wing to their political movement. Thus from the outset the Swedish labour organization was not placed in an enclave on its own but derived power from its ability to negotiate nationally. Its position on the grid–group diagram was therefore on the 'diagonal of power' linking the powerful bureaucracies in the high grid/high group corner with the entrepreneurial business-men in the low group/low grid corner.

These, for cultural analysis, are initial orientations that lay the trail for the development of hierarchical institutions in the one case and institutions of the third kind in the other.

## INSTITUTIONS OF THE THIRD KIND

Most economic and sociological analysis concentrates on hier-archies or markets. The third kind, which we argue represents a distinctive and viable form of organization, has been studied (almost exclusively) in the special context of religious sects, yet this pattern, we believe, is in reality quite common in the secular world. Apart from industrial relations, it is the basis of those international organizations that consist of states unwilling to sacri-fice their sovereignty. Interestingly, British trade union leaders often compare industrial relations to international relations.

Institutions of the third kind have certain specific problems requiring specific solutions which, in turn, lead to the adoption of particular values.

Any group that is regarded as beyond the pale of the law, or that perceives itself as unable to use the law to retain its members has to settle for a voluntary membership and will tend to make a virtue of it. Thus voluntarism becomes a basic value. This creates problems for the leadership, as we have tried to describe elsewhere.[12] The leadership constantly fears that its following is about to melt away. With weak leadership there is little authority and rival factions make the group highly fissile. The Children of Israel heard what Moses said to Pharaoh about their right not to be exploited, and then they complained unceasingly about his use of authority over them. How can a leader declare: we have the right to withdraw and to withdraw completely if need be, and then refuse to let his people withdraw from his leadership if need be?[13]

## FLOURISHING ON OPPOSITION

To meet such problems, those committed most deeply to the group adopt the strategy of building up a strong moral condemnation of the whole of the outside world and a fear of infiltration. This form of cultural dialogue results in the sectarian trap; it becomes politically impossible for anyone in the group to deal with outsiders except in a directly confrontational way; having truck with the enemy attracts abuse as cat's paw, running dog, toady, or whelp of Satan.

As the community establishes itself in a stable form, it proceeds to redesign its environment. The sect does not call forth sects that match itself, but it flourishes on opposition.

This analysis, based on religious sects, does not apply in its entirety to the TUC. For example, unlike religious sects, the TUC has not had to deal with the problem of rival groups setting up in opposition to the parent body. The problem has been rather to establish any central organization for the trade union movement. We do not pretend that the TUC is as sectarian as a dissenting religion; merely that the analogy with sectarian religions helps us to understand some of its distinctive characteristics as a peak organization of the British trade union movement.

In the case of the labour market, the employers and the government can be faction ridden, or individualist, or hierarchical. The only thing a sect needs to do to improve its viability is to accept the adversarial role. In labour markets around the world there is a remarkable affinity between the organization on both sides of the bargaining table. If the workers are not organized, the employers do not see the need to organize themselves; either side being organized forces organization on the other side. The Swedish Employers Confederation (SAF) was formed in 1902 to present a co-ordinated front to the workers' organization founded four years before. Each time one side tightened up its organization, the other reciprocated. Thus the highly centralized structure adopted by the SAF from the start is credited by Tom Burns[14] with forcing the LO in its turn to adopt a degree of centralization that precluded any member union from taking industrial action without the LO's sanction. Perhaps the TUC would have climbed out of the sectarian trap if the employers had been as strongly combined as those in Sweden and Germany, but the British employers are, as they have always been, fragmented and competitive. In particular industries where the exception holds, it holds for both sides, more organized employers talking to more organized unions.

Furthermore, the oratorical forms are reciprocated. It makes sense to use the vocabulary of your opponent if you do not want to be talking past each other; so rhetoric chooses the same metaphors and makes the same sort of claims.

## A DILEMMA FOR LEADERSHIP

A system, once embarked, entrenches itself with cumulative force by a kind of ripple effect. The same pattern spreads itself more and more widely. We can see it at work at the purely rhetorical level, and in internal strategy. A leader cannot invoke a sacred principle for all mankind to get justice from the opponents and deny the same principle to his followers. Least of all can he use obvious double talk in a voluntarist community in which the members are liable to drift away. A leader who has successfully used the threat to withdraw labour from the employer has not got a plausible answer to followers who want to withdraw from his control. So it is that many of the British unions in their own structure echo the form of the fight with the employers. Anyone has the right to withdraw and join another union. Difficult to refuse, this is a disastrous concession for the union organizers. Immediately their attention is turned on to the competitive survival of their union against other unions. Eyes riveted on recruitment and membership ensure a sectarian outlook and a black and white sectarian cosmology.[15, 16]

The same ripple goes on to give its shape to the relation between unions. There must be no coercion and no seduction, poaching, pinching, or other interference. They must also be free to withdraw from the TUC and the TUC's authority must be limited. It is arguable that the 1982 miners' strike could have been ended more satisfactorily for the miners if the NUM had been prepared to accept the authority of the TUC.

## THE RIGHT TO EXIT

Markets are based on the right of individuals to exit[17] and groups on the right to exclude individuals from entering. When a group cannot control the exit of its members, its culture faces certain contradictions.

A community whose members are all free to leave at any time has some secondary problems which flow from the initial weakness. The line of least effort will suggest some standard solutions which, once adopted enable the system to function in a certain way. The solutions become entrenched and a culture of the third kind instituted. Some typical solutions to the typical problems of organization concern classification, co-ordination, sanctions, history, and the use of the concept of the outsider.

Administration requires control over classification. The idea that classification could be devised legalistically by an administrative authority is not only repugnant but absurd to institutions of the third kind. When other countries were setting up a union structure based on a classification of industry, the TUC (Edinburgh 1927) declared that 'there is no way of defining industrial boundaries' and hence a 'rational scheme of integration' is impossible. An attempt to by-pass or supersede the rights of individual union's conference or collective machinery is always resisted. As human authority is at a bare minimum in this kind of community, the principles of classification have to be treated as natural phenomena – arising spontaneously or as a result of history. To prevent the spontaneous groupings from coming into conflict, first arrival is made the basis of adjudication, in the Bridlington codes as in many simple communities around the world. The history of the different unions is made to do duty as an ultimate justification for the scope of their jurisdiction without reference to human authority. Hence the relative weakness of the Bridlington rules.

The haphazard result of relying on voluntary mergers is made a virtue, a sign of the naturalness of the process, compared favourably with the central regulation of industry in iron-curtain countries. However, since the essence of the system is that it is unguided, power does inevitably accumulate randomly during the historical process. To balance it the TUC has to hold the ropes between the old craft unions, the big industrial unions, the small unions, the big general unions, the moderates, and the extremists

– all the potentially divisive forces within the movement. This corrective role could easily become its main function, turning its attention inwards as with other sects. The LO, on the other hand, identifies its role so closely with the economic welfare of Sweden that, in the late 1960s and early 1970s, it began to lose credibility with its own rank and file.

## A SEPARATE POLITICAL ENCLAVE

Since the sect is a community of unranked natural groupings of people inspired by a common objective and communitarian principles, it is neither necessary (nor possible) to spell out commitments. In the internal history of any sect ambiguous promises of support lead to inexplicable and unforgivable betrayals. A lot of the bitterness which workers feel against exploitative employers becomes directed inward and against each other by the sectarian structure.

The most inclusive natural spontaneous class for this self-renewing system is the TUC itself. Outside the limits of the community are other people. Sects in general tend to draw the line rather sharply between insiders and outsiders. The strong classification of the employer as outsider is another result of the system. It is not surprising that in industrial strife credibility gaps at the negotiating table block communication.

The TUC never felt confident of its political role or comfortable with the Labour radicals. As Walter Citrine said, the intellectuals never really understood the movement:

They assigned to it a militant outlook which most of its members did not possess and they were irritated at the reluctance of the trade union leaders to respond to their flights of idealism in a world of sterner realities.

He was referring to Tawney, Postgate, Kingsley Martin, Laski, Attlee, and G.D.H. Cole. He added significantly: 'Bevin had little time for them . . . he resented their intrusion into trade union affairs.'[18]

Though it collaborated with Labour and coalition governments, the TUC never saw itself as an arm of economic government or even as a very active collaborator of Labour governments transforming the nation or defending its economy. It had a better sense than the government in 1931 that deflation would be disastrous, but unlike the LO in Sweden it was in no position to make its good advice effective. This is the workers' movement that had no entanglements with communists, that disliked compulsory arbitration, resisted incomes policy, and preferred conflict to co-operation. It still (until recently) presents itself as a separate enclave in the political system, a place beyond the law. Once we know the kind of institution it is, there is no point in saying that the TUC should make the labour unions do this or do that. It is not a hierarchy. This kind of institution is organized for negative freedom.

The institution of this type can only mobilize consensus to support its own internal, egalitarian structure against outsiders. It cannot easily mobilize support to sanction collective agreements between its members and employers or penalize unofficial strikes as hierarchies such as the LO can do.

History plays a distinctive role in the shaping of institutions of the third kind. It is always used against authority whereas in a hierarchy history works the other way, on authority's behalf.

## CONCLUSION

The practical incompatibility between the two kinds of freedom results from one being entrenched upon the sovereignty of members and the other upon authority over them. For the former the central question is 'Who interferes?' and for the latter it is 'Who governs?' Isaiah Berlin pointed out that they mean quite different things. In the 1880s the TUC seemed to have a choice before it. As Hugh Clegg put it: the new socialists wanted a radical pro-gramme; skilled and unskilled workers should unite to get politi-cal representation, reduce unemployment, eliminate the trade cycle, redistribute wealth. This was substantially the programme adopted and still being carried through in Sweden by the LO. In Britain the old guard was 'bound to doctrines of non-inter-ference',[19] and the old guard won. The movement consistently unfolded as one of resistance to interference and refusal of outside support.

## ACKNOWLEDGEMENT

This paper was given as the Charles Carter Lecture at the Univer-sity of Lancaster (1989) and first appeared in *The Journal of General Management* 14,4:34–52 (1989).

## NOTES

1 Isaiah Berlin, 'Two Concepts of Liberty', in *Four Essays on Liberty* (Oxford University Press, 1969).
2 Alan Ryan (ed.), *The Idea of Freedom* (Clarendon Press, 1979).
3 Bo Gustafsson, 'Conflict, Confrontation and Consensus in Modern Swedish History', in L. Arnedson (ed.), *Economics and Values* (Stockholm, 1986).
4 Richard Layard, *How to Beat Unemployment* (Oxford University Press, 1986).
5 Colin Crouch, 'Conditions for Trade Union Wage Restraint', in Leon N. Lindberg and Charles S. Maier (eds), *The Politics of Inflation and Economic Stagnation* (Brookings, 1985).
6 Philippe Schmitter, 'Interest Intermediation and Regime Governability in Contemporary Western Europe and North America', in Suzanne Berger (ed.) *Organizing Interests in Western Europe* (Cambridge University Press, 1981).
7 James Hampton, 'Giving Grid and Group dimensions an operational definition', in Mary Douglas (ed.), *Essays in the Sociology of Perception* (Routledge & Kegan Paul, 1982).
8 Michael Thompson, 'Postscript: A Cultural Basis for Comparison', Appendix to H. Kunreuther and J. Linnerooth (eds), *Risk Analysis and Decision Processes* (Springer-Verlag, 1983).
9 Jonathan Gross and Steve Rayner, *Measuring Culture* (Columbia University Press, 1984).
10 G. Mars, *Cheats at Work* (Allen & Unwin, 1982).
11 A. Wildavsky, *The Nursing Father: Moses as a Political Leader* (Alabama University Press, 1984).
12 Mary Douglas, *Risk Acceptability According to the Social Sciences* (Russell Sage Foundation, NY, 1986).
13 A. Wildavsky, *The Nursing Father: Moses as a Political Leader* (Alabama University Press, 1984).
14 Tom Burns and Anders Olsson, 'Collective Bargaining Rule Regimes and their Transformation', in Tom Burns and Helena Flam (eds), *The Shaping of Social Organization* (Sage Publications, 1987), pp. 176–212.
15 Mary Douglas and Aaron Wildavsky, *Risk and Culture* (University of California Press, 1983).
16 Mary Douglas, *How Institutions Think* (Syracuse University Press, 1986).
17 A.O. Hirschman, *Exit, Voice and Loyalty* (Harvard, 1970).
18 W. Citrine, *Men and Work: An Autobiography* (Hutchinson, 1964), p. 300.
19 H.A. Clegg, *The History of the British Trade Union Movement since 1899*, Vol. 1, (Oxford University Press, 1964), p. 54.

# 11

# AUTONOMY AND OPPORTUNISM

This chapter is concerned with a convergence of interest from two directions on the topic of individual autonomy. On the one hand, transaction costs theory focuses on the cost to the individual of preserving autonomy in the market place. It pays special attention to the causes of asymmetry among dealers, to classifying different kinds of asymmetry, and to assessing their respective effects on market structures. Its concern with individual reactions to constraints on autonomy has made it necessary to rewrite the economist's conception of the rational being.

On the other hand, the cultural theory, which has its roots in anthropology, classifies different types of cultures according to the amount of autonomy enjoyed by individuals. Taking patterns of autonomy as a key to cultural bias, cultural theory considers the different kinds of constraints and how to measure them. The way persons justify, to themselves and to others, the limitations that their society places on autonomy is central to the idea of cultural bias. The theory uses a typology that contrasts group membership (as one kind of restriction on autonomy) with restrictions on individual freedom to negotiate and choose among options. This produces something parallel to the contrast between markets and hierarchies which is prominent in transaction costs economics.

I use Chester Barnard's *The Functions of the Executive* (1938) to show the difficulties of making good organizational theory without a systematic approach to culture. This famous book is particularly apt for the exposition because Chester Barnard was trying to formulate a theory of the interaction of individuals with the organization they work in. Some of what he tried to do has been achieved. Some of the difficulties that he could not surmount

187

remain as stumbling blocks to this day. Reading a formative book fifty years after it was published is like entering an echoing cave backwards. Modern concepts bounce anachronistically off the pages of Barnard's book.

## CHESTER BARNARD

Barnard's theory depends on the connection between the purposes of members of organizations and the purposes of their organizations. The connection is still missing. There are gestures toward the relationship, good arm-waving, but in general the two kinds of purposes are treated separately: social psychology and personnel management attend to the individual person, and organization theory attends to the organization. The failure to co-ordinate the two parts of a single field is not trivial, as Barnard knew well. He assumed (plausibly) that an organization cannot succeed unless it satisfies the goals of its members. But to go any distance from that starting point he would need to know how their goals are formed. For this, I submit, he would need a cultural theory.

Barnard's thinking made liberal use of metaphors from economic theory. Most would agree that for any organization two levels of needs must be satisfied: the needs of the whole and those of its constituent parts. In his day, and since, this problem is often discussed with biological metaphors. Barnard's originality was to express it within utilitarian theory as a problem of rational choice. He tried to deal with it as an equilibrium problem. Borrowing the metaphor of international trade according to the theory of his day, he regarded any organization as the result of exchanges between various contributors; he expected that in a successful organization the exchanges would generate a surplus of satisfactions for all contributors; if not, the individuals would be contributing more than they were giving and would tend to withdraw their contributions, resulting in failure of the enterprise.

One can be impressed with the presence of this – written before exchange theory and game theory – a precursor of Mancur Olson's (1965) theory of collective action. Barnard's conception of an organization rendered ineffective by weak incentives corresponds to Mancur Olson's concept of a latent organization. But more than the prophetic vein in *The Functions of the Executive* of a man writing before his time, one catches echoes of eighteenth-century system-building on the idea of individual rationality, of

Ricardo, and of Bentham's greatest happiness principle and hedonic calculus.

There is an advantage in using Barnard's work to introduce cultural theory, because of the common interest in the relation between individuals and their social environment. The same methodological individualism that blocked his efforts in that direction seems to spoil the social theory of our day. It also provides a telling case against the argument that modern people autonomously choose their ideas, unlike culture-ridden primitives. Barnard exemplifies the opposite point, namely, that some modern individuals are very culture-ridden.

## PROBLEMS WITH METHODOLOGICAL INDIVIDUALISM

Methodological individualism starts with an ultimate unanalysable factor, the rational being sovereign over his own choices. This starting point gets in the way of any attempt to relate the structure of individual goals to the goals of an organized social environment. This is largely because it is not possible to say what the individual desires. The one interaction that seems to be theoretically acceptable (perhaps because it does not imply any sociological determinism) is the calculus of costs. Excessive costs for a particular choice will make a rational being change his mind about the ordering of his goals. This theorizing puts no intervening social influence between an individual and his preferences. The social environment is differentiated only by costs. Preferences arise mysteriously from within the individual (Wildavsky 1987). Theoretically costs are determined by individual preferences, but in practice economic analysis has to proceed on the basis that rational preferences are known.

Chester Barnard attempted to work out an equilibrium model to describe the balance achieved between the contributions of the members of an organization to its functioning and the return contributions made by the organization to the fulfilment of its members' private goals. As Herbert Simon says (1945) this is the start of a theory of public goods. Barnard allowed that the return to the individual would not only be in terms of remuneration and pension but also of various fringe benefits, esteem, and so forth. The attempt to work out this equilibrium theory foundered

189

(but in very good company) on the relation of the individual to the organization.

## FOUR PROBLEMS

Barnard confronted four problems in his attempt to link the rational choices of individuals to the survival of organizations.

First, he shirked making a theory-driven categorization of organizations. His classifications came from the world in which the organizations themselves function. This is using what anthropologists call actors' categories. In other words, he started with and stayed with the agents' own functioning classifications. These classifications impede theorizing: the anthropologist only ends up saying what the agents under study had been saying all along. At least it ensures that the people he is writing about will understand the book. From their comments on their own budgetary processes Barnard could make the distinction between failed and successful, complete and incomplete, and dependent and independent organizations; from their legal processes he could make the distinction between formal and informal, superordinate and subordinate organizations. In fact, he was not very concerned with making an independent classification of organizations. He certainly did not perceive the need for a categorization that would calibrate his own theory of authority, or even the need for a theory that might not be the same as that of a successful president of an organization. Sometimes he wrote as if the main objective was to distil the wisdom of successful directors.

Oliver Williamson (1975) helps Barnard's project on this first shortcoming. He, too, takes the usual administrative categories – markets and hierarchies – or the usual economists' categories – the extremes on the dimension between perfect and imperfect competition. But he defines these according to criteria that work in his theory – that is, in terms of contractual features, of which communication (one of Barnard's interests) is a major part.

Second, though Barnard talked about the environment of the organization and though he said a lot about mutual adjustment, he only described one blanket kind of environment. He shirked making a typology of the different external conditions to which the organization must adapt and which it is in a continual process of modifying. It is almost as though he chose not to typologize in order to keep to an appropriately vague level of generalization.

Williamson (1975) again helps to overcome this weakness. He identifies a set of critical dimensions for describing transactions, within which the ease of mutual adjustment varies systematically, and also the organizational structure within which a transaction is embedded. Thus, he has a theory-driven categorization of both the internal structure of firms and surrounding conditions, which enables him to develop a theory of the influence of transaction costs on market structures. (That he thinks about a dynamic interaction between kinds of organizations operating in different kinds of environments endears him to anthropologists.)

Third, Chester Barnard taught that satisfactions for the individual members need to be sufficient to compensate contributors for what they give. But he never showed any reason to expect this could happen. Far from having a theory about how firms ought to behave, he left firms crossing their fingers and just hoping that they have the right lines of communication, and that their leaders are competent (for what certainly sounds like an impossible job). This is not an equilibrium model; such a model must postulate some process that brings opposing forces into repose. Otherwise the mention of equilibrium is just interior decoration. Barnard needed something equivalent to the concept of diminishing marginal utility in economics. Without this concept in economic theory, demand and supply could never settle at a market price and the whole theory would collapse. I propose that the missing mechanism is described in cultural theory.

Williamson's model of the market is set in motion and comes to rest because he postulates that individuals rationally choose to shoulder transaction costs when they are small and move into hierarchies when the costs become too high to be borne profitably. He escapes my rebuke to Barnard by finding a mechanism to justify the oscillations and the equilibrium; here again he has helped to achieve what Barnard was aiming at.

However, on the fourth point, I do not think Williamson rescues Barnard from his dilemma. As is usual in rational choice analysis, Barnard treated individuals' objectives as independent of those of other people or the organization. He allowed that, after a minimum subsistence level is satisfied, their principal concern is for esteem. This was not original at the time, and it has been richly elaborated since. While the desire for esteem (a cultural concept) is the linchpin of the connection that Barnard made between the organization and the individual member, he did practically nothing with the idea. Esteem is a static and empty notion in his book. He had no sense of any ongoing dialectical transformation between the goals of the individual and those of the organization. He did not conceive of a process by which the purposes of the one might interpenetrate the purposes of the other, and still less of how they tend to drift apart. Yet an interaction affecting their private goals and generating common ones is the cultural mechanism that would have helped his theory.

Williamson also adopts methodological individualism. He has a theory of firms, but his theory of the relationship between individuals and firms could be better. He believes firms vary, but not individuals. He has the same representative rational individual marching into one kind of contract or refusing to renew it and entering another kind for the same set of reasons, namely, the cost of transactions in a given economic environment. He might claim, in rebuttal, that he does not need a less impoverished concept of the individual person, since his theory is not about the relationship of individuals to their organization.

My argument is precisely that it does matter to the economist that ideas of esteemed behaviour are generated collectively (see Chapter 8, this volume). Barnard would have been helped by a theory of how individuals negotiate with one another over what kinds of esteem their organization will provide (a gold watch at the end of a lifetime of service, a place at High Table, a medal, an obituary notice, a memorial plaque) and the sources of dis-esteem that they will not tolerate (South African investments, dirty washroom, no parking, insult from employers).

The anthropologists are interested in how standards of what counts as estimable vary. We find that the different standards come out of different kinds of organization. What the individual is going to want is not entirely his own idea, but consists largely of a set of desires that the social environment inspires in him. For example, in a commando unit or the fire brigade, opportunity for heroic deeds is the means of achieving esteem; elsewhere longevity rather than heroism may bring esteem; in some communities esteem is more directly connected to wealth than Barnard reckoned. In some, jealousy is under control while in others it cuts destructive swathes. A cultural theory of variation in ideas of esteem and variations in the scope for blaming and responsibility (Wildavsky 1987:283–93) would supply some of the mechanism that Barnard lacked for explaining the success of organizations.

## COMMUNICATION

What can we say about Barnard's theory of communication? It is a kind of primitive telegraph system; its elementary signals, like the morse code, need to be clear and unambiguous and their origin authenticated. The simplicity of Barnard's conception of communication becomes more painful when we see it amplified in Herbert Simon's *Administrative Behavior* (1945, Ch. 8). For both, the system of communication is always external to the communicators; the code is established independently; someone (at the centre?) thinks it up and the others use it as it comes. This discourse about communication allows no scope to consider how the communication categories are constructed, or how the members of an organization may adapt the categories. The communication is treated as one thing and the organization as quite another. The idea that organizations are kinds of message–coders is quite alien.

To an anthropologist in this day and age Herbert Simon's description of what he calls the presentation of a problem reads very strangely. He says that decision-making cannot begin until the right way to present the problem has been found. Finding how to present it is described as a deliberate cognitive effort. If only that were the case! Problems are presented according to the way that the institution's culture has set up the categories, and it is very difficult (though not impossible) for members to rethink them. All they can do in the way of radical rethinking is to revise the institution itself. The difficulty of explaining cultural bias to economists is a discomforting case in point.

Even in 1938 the continental insulation that rejected any notion of the shared construction of concepts is worth noting. Durkheim's *Primitive Classification* (with Marcel Mauss) came out in 1903, and his *Elementary Forms of the Religious Life* in 1912. But these books were not translated till later. Simon's footnotes in the 1945 edition (p. 24) show that he considered this teaching to partake of the fallacy of 'group mind'. The fallacy is to attribute organic unity to collective action. Because individuals can act together to produce a collective language and shared culture, this does not mean that they have mysteriously become welded into one thinking machine or 'group mind'. Durkheim's discussion of what he called collective representations has frequently been interpreted by Anglo-Saxon critics to mean that a society is one big thinking animal, a misrepresentation that allows them to dismiss the whole subject as absurd.

The heritage of ideas about collective construction of categories comes from Hegel and Marx. It is understandable that writing about the organization of capitalist industry would not put one in a milieu susceptible to Marxist ideas about categorization. Furthermore, the idea that clarity in coding messages may not be just a technical matter but involves shared second-order preferences is also incompatible with methodological individualism; each individual thinker is supposed to come freely to his own ideas. Nearly the whole effort of British social anthropology (without being under Marxist influence) was developed under the assumption that organization results from the process of adapting categories of thought. When I write that common categories are the basis of the social bond, reviewing anthropologists castigate me for stating the obvious. Considering the fact that Michel Foucault has lived, and written so effectively about the relation between power and knowledge (1977), and that he has died already, and that much water has gone under the bridge in the intervening fifty years since 1938, we can hope that ideas which were unacceptable before may be less threatening now.

## THE PERSON

Focusing on the relationship of the individual to the organization, Barnard faced a problem that many have pointed out to me. It is all very well for individuals in primitive tribes to think and act in unison; the simplicity and uniformity of their experience makes that understandable. But for us today, social experience is utterly heterogeneous. There is no reason to expect coherent forms of culture to emerge. As Barnard said, a person belongs to many organizations – a golf club, a rotary club, a church – but in each he experiences a different culture. In defining the individual in an organization Barnard decided to strip him of antecedent associations. His idea of the individual was bare of history and attachments. Hirschman (1982) has pointed out that this is usually the case in theories of rational behaviour. Barnard wrote only about the part of the individual's purposes that was related to the organization. Such a person as he postulated, whose identity could change from scene to scene and whose purposes were equally labile, might conceivably exist. But if you assume that such a person, far from being exceptional, is the best model for thinking about how human individuals behave in organizations, you have to accommodate an impossibly splintered and spineless creature within your general theory of society. This creature would be useless to a theory of rational choice because it is defined as incapable of choosing.

If you have written some capacity to choose into the make-up of your rational agent, you would want to allow him to choose which church, which sports club, which voluntary service he joins, and which kind of work he does. Even the most restricted circumstances usually offer some minor choices of workplace, work friends, religious worship, or not worshipping, and leisure time. In making these, as one choice affects another, we can perhaps be allowed the minimal assumption that the person is trying to arrive eventually at some manageable environment. From that assumption results a unitary person trying to fulfil a set of feasible purposes. On this assumption the various associations that constitute a person's social environment may well have some degree of homogeneity, resulting from personal proclivities. When we find an organization of a particular type rewarding behaviour of a certain kind and penalizing other kinds of behaviour, it is not unreasonable to assume that it is inhabited by persons of a certain type who have been attracted to it, and also that its environment has transformed others who did not choose it but found themselves in its ambit.

To sum up at this point, although Barnard does not fare very well under scrutiny, succeeding generations of economists and organization theorists have not done better on the problem he made his own. Most of his troubles come from his fidelity to the economist's conception of the ultimate rational being, which is inherently unanalysable. Since he wants to say something about how organizations relate to their contributors, Barnard's theory needs to consider further why different individuals desire different goals, how their goals change, or how these goals mesh with the purposes of an organization. He does not try to categorize organizations into their kinds, nor to divide the kinds of environments; so he does not have a model of organizations interacting with and adjusting to their environments. His idea of an equilibrium of contributions from the organization to the members and from the members to the organization is the kind of easy-going, optimistic functionalism that has attracted the derision of Jon Elster (1983). He can only say that the equilibrium works because and when the firm is seen to work. Post facto, he can indicate which organizations have evidently achieved the right balance, because their members stay with them and they stay in business, but he has no theory to explain why many organizations fail: all he can say is that they must have got the balance wrong or had faulty communications. His references to equilibrium are more a matter of exhortation (a sermon about caring for the interests of members) than a basis for analysis.

## INDIFFERENCE

Barnard's idea of equilibrium between contributions has been less fruitful than his idea about the zone of indifference within which authority is unquestioned. This is a significant enrichment of the concept of the individual, since it differentiates between preferences. Each person has some strong preferences, others more weakly adhered to, and a whole zone of not caring. Barnard taught that a leader is followed easily if his commands fall within the zone of indifference, where the members of the organization do not mind what he asks them to do. Naturally his problems arise when he asks them to follow him against their inclinations.

Where did Barnard get the idea of a zone of indifference? It is reasonable to see his usage as another metaphor borrowed from economic theory. It sounds like an adaptation of Edgeworth's technical solution to the problem of measuring utility, but Barnard's use of the term is very different from Edgeworth's. Barnard's idea may seem only a small step from saying that, for each item acquired, diminishing marginal utility produces a point at which the consumer is indifferent to the prospect of acquiring an additional increment. The step is, in fact, a big shift. The focus, which was originally on the relation of the individual to some desirable class of objects, has been shifted to a graduated nimbus of desires surrounding each individual. Desires for everything are graded into zones of intensity, the more intense fanning out gradually to a zone of indifference in which authority is easily acceptable. The idea is a prototype for the origin of conventions, as used by Thomas Schelling (1960) and David Lewis (1969). In their work some zone of indifference is the starting point of co-ordination; it indicates a limit to individual aims, a neutral area in which conflict is in abeyance because no one cares enough.

Herbert Simon took up the idea more exactly in Barnard's sense, in Chapter 7 of *Administrative Behavior* (1945), where he discusses the problem of achieving co-ordination. In this book he is a docile follower of Barnard, repeating the account of a zone of indifference as the area in which authority has no problems. However, when he (Simon 1955) writes about rational choices, what seems to be the same idea about a zone of indifference gets quite another twist. Here the question is about the grotesque optimizing calculus that economic theory expects the rational being to perform on all choices. Through a brilliant leap, the zone of indifference around each person's wishes has been transformed into the zone within which his desires can be satisfied without optimization, and therefore without the calculus. It introduces the new concept of satisficing and of bounded rationality.

In Simon's original version the boundedness of rationality appears to be a useful, necessary contrivance by which rational beings let decisions beyond a certain range of interest take care of themselves, or rather be taken care of by relying on organizational and environmental cues. The scope of the wording suggested that bounded rationality is an aid to competent decision, since without being bounded rationality cannot work at all. The discovery of this advantage to humans hinted at a new approach to thinking in general.

However, bounded rationality has come to mean merely the limits on cognitive competence. Whereas Simon treated it as a good thing because it is a form of economizing on cognitive energy, Williamson actually started to count the value of the saving. Considering that the limits on rationality take energy to overcome, Williamson regards institutional solutions to decision problems as savings in energy that would otherwise be dispersed because of boundedness (1985:46). He treats boundedness as a weakness, a source of incompetence.

## COGNITIVE INCOMPETENCE AND MORAL TURPITUDE

Williamson gives his own turn to the concepts of rational behaviour and opportunism:

By opportunism I mean self-seeking with guile. This includes but is scarcely limited to more blatant forms, such as lying, stealing, and cheating. Opportunism more often involves subtle forms of deceit. . . . More generally, opportunism refers to the incomplete or distorted disclosure of information, especially to calculated efforts to mislead, distort, disguise, obfuscate, or otherwise confuse . . .' (1985:47).

Williamson regards cognitive incompetence and opportunism as indispensable assumptions for correct analysis of asymmetries in economic relations. On both issues he is picking up and altering an idea espoused by Barnard. Bounded rationality (at least in Simon's first formulation and in Barnard's concept of a zone of indifference), was an unfocused area of ideas and purposes. For each individual it indicated a horizon, appropriate relief from vigilance, and respite from choosing, without implying anything about incompetence. As to opportunism, in Barnard's 1938 version, and in Simon's of 1945, the word has no moral implications whatever.

Transaction costs theory characterizes individuals in the market place as weakly rational and weakly moral. This is because it focuses on uncertainty and difficulties in getting parties to stand by their contracts. Corporations consisting of formerly autonomous individuals provide a system of governance. By monitoring, penalties, and rewards, the hierarchy can make assets flow that would otherwise be blocked.

This approach removes a large element of physical automatism that was implicit in the description of market behaviour. The classical idea of monopoly starts with the case of natural monopolies, advantages of location, or natural control of a physically locked-in resource; it then describes artificial monopolies made by collusion; in this view, collusion is exceptional. I have no grievance against the heavy dose of original sin in Williamson's account of human behaviour. It is a distinct improvement to have shifted attention away from a price and costs system that was thought to function automatically because of natural conditions of supply and demand. The shift to all too human interaction is a shift toward cultural factors. It opens the door for cultural analysis to enter the account of economic behaviour.

The first wedge to put into this welcome opening is the structuring of knowledge and morals. First, we should observe that opportunism is rarely unlimited. Nor is the boundedness of rationality random. The zone of indifference is not entirely a private matter. What one can safely ignore is largely contained within a boundary etched by a collective process. Regarding opportunism, what counts as responsible initiative is culturally defined. What looks to the outsider like resort to low cunning, lying, stealing, and cheating may be highly prescribed. Moral attributes are really irrelevant.

## AUTONOMY

The concept of autonomy will be plainer if I can illustrate the cultural structuring of opportunism. Fortunately a superb example is at hand in Gerald Mars's book on occupational crime (1984). This focuses on opportunism in the full sense. It starts with considering the scope for autonomous action in different types of organizations. It expects that wherever a chink of freedom appears for appropriating resources or for withholding information, it will be exploited. The industrial pattern of autonomy is the structure of the alternative economy.

The workplace provides asymmetries; complex arrays of advantages and disadvantages can be charted in terms of degrees and kinds of autonomy. Mars starts with a careful classification of occupations in modern industrial society. His angle on opportunism is congenial to Williamson's since he is interested in the forms of predation that each work system permits. The classification includes three types of predator, which Mars calls 'hawks', 'vultures', and 'wolves'.

Hawks are those lone operators who make their killing without needing any collaborators. They are employed taxicab drivers whose accounts the owner of the vehicle cannot check. They are the entrepreneurs who work in the interstices of Soviet bureaucracy, performing an invaluable task by knowing just where to lay their hands on a load of missing supplies, and who make a good unaccounted profit on every kind deed.

Vulture jobs are unranked, unspecialized, but some solidarity is enjoined. These jobs offer considerable autonomy and freedom to contract, but the freedom is subject to bureaucratic control. The workers are treated by the employer as a collectivity, which encourages some solidarity. 'Like vultures, they need the support of a group to exploit their terrain, but when they find their opportunity, they are on their own' (Mars 1984:33). They include sales representatives, travellers, and semi-skilled craftsmen. Each has his semi-autonomous field, his scam territory, or his 'fiddle-fief' as Mars calls it, which the individual exploits to the best of his or her ability. The bureaucracy cannot impose changes that disturb the 'fiddle earnings' of all members of a group. For example, if the organization starts to monitor and control all the sales representatives in a neighbourhood, it provokes a collective reaction: the reps will focus on some faked excuse for blocking the reorganization. If the managerial changes affect only one individual member, the group will not react on his behalf. But when the whole staff of a restaurant or a nursing home fleece a client, it will be no good complaining to the maître d' or the doctor.

Wolves hunt in packs. They are ranked and get their biggest spoils when they work in a stratified team or gang, keeping to their ranks and specialized work roles. Wolves attack any unguarded supply line. They might typically be miners, long-shoremen, long-distance truck drivers, garbage collection crews, airline crews. Every individual's skill is needed as much to organize pillage as to organize the legitimate work. And they have no place for the individual working on his own.

These are classes of workplace opportunists. Mars's system also includes one type of absolute victim in the workplace, the employee who has no autonomy whatever and so no option but to bear all the burdens assigned. These victims of opportunism he calls donkeys. Prototypical positions of minimum autonomy are the cashier in a cafeteria and the worker on the factory assembly line. Donkeys combine the extremes of powerlessness and power, because sabotage is always possible. When driven to the limits of endurance the donkey throws off his load: the cashier jams the cash register, the worker crashes the assembly line and walks away, but only to find another donkey job.

The animal names are not offensive since the writer's sympathies are with the opportunists. His informants have gleefully told him how they beat the system. Nobody recognizing themselves as running in a wolf pack, descending like vultures on a carcass, or profiting from the stupidity of others would be uncomfortable at reading how his autonomy has been asserted.

## CULTURAL ANALYSIS

Mars has used for his classification of organizational environments the two dimensions developed in cultural theory, which are designed to capture as much as possible of the social environment that affects persons' relations with one another. One is the dimension of structure; the other is the dimension of boundary. Structure and boundary represent two kinds of social restriction on autonomy.

In Figure 11.1 the horizontal (group) axis presents the insulating boundary around a group; the vertical (grid) axis presents the degree to which the individual is personally insulated from the rest of society. This is a map of possible social environments, varying in the degrees and kinds of autonomy permitted to individuals. Any one social environment can be compared with any other for its structuredness. The more structure it has (i.e., the further up the grid dimension), the narrower the scope for negotiating individual options. At the theoretical limit, a person can be in such a constricted social space (in corner B) that no options are available. The less the environment is structured, the more of life would seem to be open to negotiation.

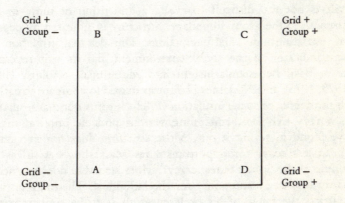

*Figure 11.1*

The criteria for group inclusiveness depend on the field of interaction. How does one become a member of the group? How much does it absorb its members' time and energies or give them their life support? The golf club may be an all-embracing circle of devotees whose lives revolve around its tournaments, or so might be a church, or a commune. Or these groups might only meet on weekends, monthly, or irregularly.

How does the group regulate its boundary against the outside world? What is involved in being admitted to the club or the fellowship, and what breaches will provoke blackballing or 'disfellowshipping'? We have given a lot of thought to how this concept of relative group strength can be made operational. (By 'we' I mean about twelve colleagues who are working together on developing a theory of cultural variation, and about thirty who have been applying it to various questions.) If the social unit is a firm or a college, the question is how to assess the relative strength of its group boundary compared with that of another firm or college. The investigator has to discover the relevant distinctions, say among permanent members on the payroll, *ad hoc* consultants, and boards of advisers or trustees. A pre-war Oxford college would score more for group than an American university because its trustees and the faculty were the same, and the inter-war Oxbridge college would score more than the post-war one because before the war its fellows normally expected to spend their whole lives there.

It is not too difficult to create a dimension of more or less strength in the group boundary. Structure is indicated by degrees of restricting individual interactions. The idea that insulation is a key indicator of the social environment and its culture comes from Basil Bernstein's insight into educational sociology (1970, 1973, 1975). In 1970 James Hampton started to compare variations in the degree of social insulation (1982). It turns out that insulation is a very rich idea, concealing various possible implications, as we found in trying it out. More structure does not necessarily mean less scope for opportunism (as Mars shows with his example of the Soviet bureaucracy). More structure does not necessarily imply less autonomy for the individual. The brahmin who restricts the range of his preferences so as to be content with a bowl of rice has increased his autonomy by reducing his options. Developing an all-purpose dimension of grid turns out to be more taxing than we expected. Various experiments are being made, in various contexts, to develop a model of the social environment that explains how cultural values cluster.

This background may help explain why Mars's classification of industrial opportunism does not always mesh with Williamson's account, though there is a fair amount of overlap. Mars has neatly mapped his zoo as in Figure 11.2. The line from A to B measures lessening degrees of autonomy. The donkeys are shown at B as the extreme case of reduced autonomy. Thus, he shows only one set of victims. He could easily make cells for victims of each type of predation, or otherwise enrich his model.

## OPPORTUNISM

To examine Mars's account side by side with Williamson's would be a rewarding exercise. Here I can only make a few points. First, both accounts focus on the asymmetries in exchanges, and both expect the rational agent to exploit whatever specificity his or her own resources possess. Mars's account of the unwary diner being fleeced by the colluding members of a restaurant staff exactly corresponds to Williamson's account of locked assets; once he has taken off coat and hat and looked at the menu it is too late; the diner is already locked into the exploitative situation (see Mars and Nicod 1984), and this applies even more to the patient who has undressed and got into bed in the nursing home; exit is practically impossible.

Transaction costs theory says little about opportunism within

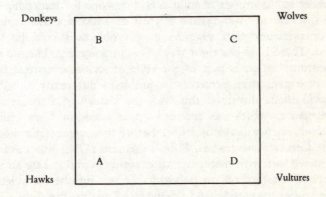

*Figure 11.2*

a centralized system partly because it assumes that centralizing is a way of bringing opportunism under control. Nor does Mars say much about it. he is more intent on describing the bonding process that commits each member of the wolf pack to the system, much as in Fagin's kitchen the child is enrolled after he has proved himself as a pickpocket. However, if we were to take Williamson's invitation to be systematically cynical, we would look at the diagram to see what kind of predation each place is best organized for. Then the opportunism of the lone operator, which is the type Williamson starts from, preys indiscriminately against any likely victim. The hierarchy is organized to exploit its own lowest orders, since the best pickings go to the top ranks, and the lowest have the least autonomy. The vultures are organized for sharing loot equally; the weakness of their team organization itself ensures that they can only make short forays for big loot and must content themselves most of the time with small regular pilferings.

## CATEGORIES

A brief glance at opportunism has shown the convergence on autonomy. With some idea of the technique of cultural analysis in hand, we can now return to Barnard's (and Simon's) ideas about communication. I maintained earlier that it is important to take into account the joint construction of categories, instead of treating them as neutral vehicles of things called messages, symbols, or meanings. Before any message is sent out by a would-be leader to his muster of followers, the scope for leadership has been determined by the shape of their organization. The style of the organization itself suggests how problems should be presented. There is no one right way of communicating. The method of communication is part of the style of its organization. Each type of organization perceives its problems differently.

David Bloor illustrates this with the history of a theorem in mathematics, which has received much attention from philosophers of science (Lakatos 1976). Before the bureaucratic reform of the German universities, Euler's theorem (1758) was carefully hammered out with mathematical experiment and debate so that it applied satisfactorily to polyhedra of any number of sides or edges, cubes, pyramids, and tetrahedra. Then, in the second half of the nineteenth century, the theorem was confronted with new shapes – cut out, flattened, and reformed – that still conformed to the theorem but were unlike anything that the theorem had been devised for. The reactions of mathematicians (as sketched by Lakatos) to these new attempts to stretch the concept were mapped by Bloor on the grid–group diagram as prototypical responses to anomaly. Departments that can, by their organization, be located in quadrant D (small, isolated groups, resistant to the larger outside world of maths) regarded the new shapes presented as polyhedra as abominable monsters, to be barred from the scope of the theorem. Larger, better established departments in larger, better established universities (i.e., hierarchical communities) merely created a separate compartment of theory within which the new shapes could be accommodated without disturbing Euler's theorem. This is what Bloor calls the monster-adjustment process. Smaller, more routinized, less autonomous institutions saw no need to adjust any theories or to make exceptions in the reigning theorem. He plots them as shown in Figure 11.3.

The explanation of the varieties of response is in the history of the organization of the German universities, following the Prussian defeat by Napoleon in 1806. The bureaucracy transformed cliquish, self-absorbed, and faction-ridden groups (D) and large, smugly entrenched, hierarchical citadels of privilege (C) into competitive fields working for international acclaim (A). By opening up the university system to foreign appraisal and making personal scholarly achievement a prime reason for advancement, they

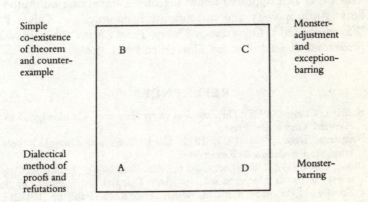

*Figure 11.3*

installed the kind of science institutions Robert Merton (1957) has described, in which only individual invention gives individual honour. The more the organization approaches A, the more it treats the apparent anomaly as a challenge and opportunity.

David Bloor shows that the changes in the institutional structure change the way problems appear to members. He makes the attitude toward anomaly a critical test of institutional style. In one case anomaly is a threatening abomination; in another the institution has enough autonomy to sweep the anomaly quietly under the carpet, leaving everything unchanged. In one case the scope for interaction is so restricted that the members of the institution hardly know what all the fuss was about. In the competitive case, in which individual autonomy is highest, discovering an anomaly is an opportunity for an individual to make his name by refuting an accepted theorem. In short, what the message is, and even whether there is a message at all, depends on the form of organization.

Two different disciplines converge on restrictions on individual autonomy. That this is a curious coincidence should not end the matter. This convergence enables a well-defined dimension of culture to be incorporated into the concept of the rational agent, and thus gives a clearer picture of organizations and of the functions of the executive.

## ACKNOWLEDGEMENT

This paper first appeared under the title 'Converging on Autonomy: Anthropology and Institutional Economics', in Oliver E. Williamson (ed.), *Organization Theory, From Chester Barnard to the Present and Beyond* (Oxford University Press, 1990).

## REFERENCES

Barnard, Chester (1938) *The Functions of the Executive*, Cambridge, MA, Harvard University Press.

Bernstein, Basil (1970, 1973, 1975) *Class, Codes and Control*, 3 vols, London, Routledge & Kegan Paul.

Bloor, David (1982) 'Polyhedra and the Abominations of Leviticus: Cognitive Styles in Mathematics', in Mary Douglas (ed.), *Essays in the Sociology of Perception*, London, Routledge & Kegan Paul, pp. 191–218.

Bloor, David (1984) *Wittgenstein: A Social Theory of Knowledge*, New York, Macmillan.

Douglas, Mary (ed.) (1982) *Essays in the Sociology of Perception*, London, Routledge & Kegan Paul.

Durkheim, Emile (1956) *The Elementary Forms of the Religious Life*, New York, Macmillan (Orig. published in French in 1912).

Durkheim, Emile and Mauss, M. (1963) *Primitive Classification* (ed. Rodney Needham), London, Cohen & West (Orig. published in French in 1903 in *L'Année Sociologique*).

Elster, Jon (1983) *Explaining Technological Change: A Case Study in the Philosophy of Science*, Cambridge, Cambridge University Press.

Foucault, Michel (1977) 'Knowledge and Power', in D.F. Bouchard (ed.), *Language, Counter-Memory and Practice*, Ithaca, NY, Cornell University Press.

Gouldner, Alvin (1970) *The Coming Crisis of Western Sociology*, London, Heinemann.

Hampton, James (1982) 'Making Grid and Group Operational', in Mary Douglas (ed.), *Essays in the Sociology of Perception*, London, Routledge & Kegan Paul, pp. 64–82.

Hirschman, A.O. (1982) *Shifting Involvements, Private Interest and Public Action*, Princeton, NJ, Princeton University Press.

Lakatos, Imre (1976) *Proofs and Refutations: The Logic of Mathematical Discovery*, Cambridge, Cambridge University Press.

Lewis, David (1969) *Convention: A Philosophical Study*, Cambridge, MA, Harvard University Press.

Mars, Gerald (1984) *Cheats at Work: An Anthropology of Occupational Crime*, London, Allen & Unwin.

Mars, Gerald and Nicod, Michael (1984) *The World of Waiters*, London, Allen & Unwin.

Merton, Robert (1957) 'Priorities in Scientific Discovery: A Chapter in the Sociology of Science', *American Sociological Review* 22, 6:635–59.

Olson, Mancur (1965) *The Logic of Collective Action*, Cambridge, MA, Harvard University Press.

Schelling, Thomas (1960) *The Strategy of Conflict*, New York, Oxford University Press.

Simon, Herbert (1945) *Administrative Behavior: A Study of Decision-Making Processes in Administrative Organization*, 3rd edn 1976, New York, The Free Press.

Simon, Herbert (1955) 'A Behavioral Model of Rational Choice', *Quarterly Journal of Economics* 69:99–118.

Wildavsky, Aaron (1987) 'A Cultural Theory of Responsibility', in Jan-Erik Lane (ed.), *Bureaucracy and Public Choice*, Beverly Hills, Sage Publications, pp. 283–93.

Williamson, O.E. (1975) *Markets and Hierarchies, Analysis and Anti-Trust Implications*, New York, The Free Press.

Williamson, O.E. (1985) *The Economic Institutions of Capitalism*, New York, The Free Press.

# Part III

# BELIEVING AND THINKING

# 12

# THOUGHT STYLE EXEMPLIFIED
## The idea of the self

## THE IDEA OF A THOUGHT STYLE

In West Africa each person is composed of multiple souls. In India selves migrate from one body to another. Widespread in the world is the idea that a human person can be transformed into an animal and back again. There is also the separate idea that every human person has an animal shape and that everyone doubles back and forth between the two bodies, human and animal. In the West all these theories about the self are rejected. For us it is a fact that a person inhabits one body between birth and death; normally the person in the body is a rational, responsible being, deviations from the norm have legal consequences. It is very simple and straightforward. Psychoanalysts, to be sure, have more complex ideas about the machinery inside the person: it is layered into areas of control, it may be an arena where different agencies contest, or segmented into independent cognitive and affective realms. Apart from psychologists' writings where something like homunculi can be supposed to operate the parts, there are tomes on subjectivity in literature and art, and whole libraries of counselling on how to achieve self-awareness in counselling. But this counts as speculation or therapy; when it comes to law or philosophy the central discussion focuses on the unitary, rational, once and for all embodied person. In this essay I will take this learned consensus about a fact as an illustration of a 'thought style'.

Ludwik Fleck argued that any community (which he called a thought-collective) developed its own thought style, a more or less disciplined, consensually agreed set of principles about how the world is, and what is a fact and what is speculation.[1] Fleck's

211

examples were drawn from scientific communities. In *How Institutions Think*[2] I have tried to extend the idea, which to an anthropologist seems quite straightforward and acceptable. Many philosophers of science find it controversial, and others repugnant. To help to present the anthropological approach it may be useful to give an illustration of a thought style outside of the history of science. I will use the example of the broad consensus about the nature of the self and the person. First I will say why it is so important to all our democratic institutions to be able to have an articulate conversation about why other people's ideas of the person seem bizarre to us.

## THE ENTERPRISE SELF

Setting up something called an enterprise culture is sometimes justified by the claim that it frees persons from constraints under which they should not be. The person in this context is said to be driven by self-interested motives. Community demands imposed by bureaucratic regulation inhibit the pursuit of freely chosen objectives, and so infringes essential liberties of the person. The utilitarian case for the free market is transferred from economics where it can be tested, to psychology where it cannot. If the market for ideas is important at all there would have to be important arguments about the nature of persons as well as about their interests. However, although there is forthright political argument about the interests, on the nature of the person there is much dodging of the topic, skirting around or avoiding it. Every culture protects some matters from questioning by declaring that enquiry about them is impossible. Such avoidance is known as taboo behaviour. It seems that in our Western industrial culture knowledge of the person and the self is deliberately sunk into one of those areas of protected public ignorance.

The case for maintaining that nothing can be argued about the self is that the idea of self is heavily locked into ideology. The Frankfurt philosophers taught unequivocally that the self is ideology, and irredeemably enmeshed in political myth.[3] Trying to become emancipated from myth by the light of reason is vain: reason is the instrument of oppression. To the ear of the anthropologist, to whom ideology is in some ways synonymous with culture, this is not the point to discard reasoning. On the contrary, by recognizing the ideological structure of the self Adorno and Horkheimer pointed to the right starting point for an investigation. The idea of the self driven by self-regarding motives is undoubtedly an ideological and cultural construct. This is well recognized, but the comparative programme it indicates has not been attempted. The process of investigation needs to identify other self concepts, responding to other ideological demands, within a typology of possible ideologies. The first task is to explain more fully why our learned conversations about the self are muffled, conflicting, and inconclusive compared with talk about the nature of the self in traditional African societies that anthropologists study. The second is to start a more anthropologically sophisticated conversation on the subject, and then to work back from considering a variety of culturally constructed selves to considering what the self has to be like to be able to operate in an enterprise culture.

The starting point is that claims to know about human persons are part of the rhetoric of political coercion. Westerners have taken to heart the idea that the self is an ideological construct. The blank space in our theoretical scheme has been constructed precisely to meet that understanding: better disallow anything that may be said in advance, rather than lend the notion of the person to political abuse. Confronted with Nazi theories about two kinds of human persons, Aryan and other races, Christianity had something to say, but its views rested on doctrine, not on knowledge that could be validated in the way of other disputed facts. A viable idea of the self cannot be entrenched by reference to religious doctrine, since the latter is not entrenched. Anyone who is ready to reject the authority of the Church can be free of its doctrine. There is no immediate automatic feedback as there would be from denying the principles of gravity.

In earlier European history Christian claims for orthodoxy invoked knowledge about persons being constituted with immortal souls; the claims to knowledge about the person justified forcible protection from the effects of sin and heresy. That this teaching allowed violent political coercion is one reason why the said doctrinal claims have lost their appeal: one doctrine confronting another doctrine needs more than loyalty in its defence. In Europe witchcraft ideas were used to inculpate persons with the wrong constituent elements in their souls; or two persons allegedly inside one body, one controlled by the devil; or to restrain a person alleged not to be a full human being at all, just a victim of demonic possession, whom it would be kinder to put out of the way. Ideas about persons as witches and sorcerers have been used in the past to justify torture of marginals and deviants, and there would be no way in which the accused could rationally defend themselves. Biological-determinist theories of gender differences are also used to oppress.[4] Likewise, we could be fooled by the theory that the self flourishes in an enterprise culture and is stifled in a culture of hierarchy. Unless we can submit it to reasoned enquiry this idea of the self could be just as coercive as any other. It matters a lot to be able to have a reasoned argument about the self's constitution and capabilities so as to be able to respond with reasons to arbitrary political coercion.

Isaiah Berlin was exercised by this very problem. His essay on two concepts of freedom distinguished one, which he regarded as legitimate, freedom from interference. The other concept, in his view illegitimate and nuisible, was the idea of freedom to become or be a certain kind of complete, fulfilled person. He argued that the second is a contradiction of the idea of liberty. Who is going to define the fulfilled person and the person's completeness? Anyone else's definition of a person is apt to become an instrument of coercion.[5] To prevent the concept of freedom being put to coercive uses he emptied it of content. At the same stroke he emptied the concept of the person. The liberal concern with freedom has put around this kind of knowledge a hedge of ineffability. The strategy is to insist that inside the person's physical appearance there is an inner self, the real person who is beyond knowledge. The strategy is to place the topic of personhood under taboo. A strong protective response (like taboo) prevents an articulated theory of the person.

However, it is not true that we live together without any exchange of ideas about what constitutes a person. In practical life, without being philosophers, we need to know what can legitimately be expected from other persons. Over the past three hundred years the self and the person have become separated in the discourse of our Western civilization. The category of self has been classified as the subject, inherently unknowable. The category of person has been filled by the need to meet the forensic requirements of a law-abiding society and an effective, rational judicial system. As pragmatically viable ideas, the self and the person are compatible and work. However, they are weak as logical aids for arguing against theories of personhood with uncongenial political implications. If someone wanted to oppose the idea underlying utilitarian philosophy that the human being is motivated primarily by self-interest, there is no logically powerful argument in its favour to amend.[6] The case for an alternative view of the motives and satisfactions of persons would only be as strong as the gut reaction it could provoke in its favour.

## THE INEFFABLE SELF

The problem in its modern form was posed by Hume who, like Locke, denied the existence of a 'self-substance', something underlying the episodic experiences we have of ourselves. The idea of a unitary, continuous, responsible self fell under the knife of his general philosophical scepticism. For lack of evidence, and for lack of reasoning to justify it, Hume concluded that the self's identity and unity are fictions. We are bundles of representations held together plausibly by the similarity of the experiences we have from moment to moment. There being no self-substance, our idea of our self arises out of the well-oiled grooves of mental associations; our remembered experiences, and the similarities between them, and other connections between them which we recognize, create relations between our ideas. These habits produce our idea of a continuous, rational, responsible self, which nothing else can justify. This is where he felt compelled to leave the problem, with much regret, and this is more or less where it still lies. Many distinguished philosophers have proposed alternative accounts of the self's existence, sometimes mystical, sometimes scholastic, sometimes idealist. The alternatives can serve well enough, for anyone who rejects Hume's empirical philosophy. But if you stay with the problem in the terms Hume set for it, the belief in the unitary self is objectively unjustifiable; necessary and true, but founded on a great leap of faith.

For example, Heidegger suggested that we could get round the problem by assuming the self to be transcendent to all experience, its necessary ground. Sartre made nonsense of this attractive solution by showing a logical flaw: if the transcendent self is the ground of experience it cannot itself inspect itself, so how can it be known? What we know of the self is based on what we see of its activity of knowing, and we have no grounds for postulating some intrinsically unknowable self behind that activity. Intuitively we want to side with Sartre in denying that the self is something intrinsically unknowable, forever inaccessible. What follows below is in sympathy with the project for knowing the self through its activities. In everyday encounters the knowability of the self is heavily engaged. We claim with confidence to know a lot about ourselves. But we cannot validate our knowledge of selves except by its reliability in prediction. As to persons, for public knowledge about personhood we are left without any agreed theory about when the person starts, or ends; we stand in moral dilemmas about transplant surgery, abortion, mercy killing, brain death. We disagree, while lacking a way of airing our disagreements coherently.

Knowledge of God comes under the same disabilities. The strategy of claiming ineffability did not work too well for the defence of the idea of God against the European tide of disbelief. But making God undefinable and unknowable might prevent members of a plural community from trying to impose their idea of God upon one another. Ineffability will do as much for the self. However, the claim that it is ineffable is weak as an intellectual defence. Ineffability blocks a certain kind of enquiry, but it will not protect the self from arbitrary dictators with brand new theoretical justifications for discriminating between us. The only supports for the idea of ineffability are goodwill and consensus. Suppose goodwill absent and consensus failed? Suppose we ourselves, fickle to our principles, should change our mind about the worthwhileness of those liberal values which the ineffability principle is devised to save? The idea of the ineffable self is just a blank space, a no-go area for logical discourse. It gives no entry for reasoning and no hold in rational debate against our own possible wishes to espouse arbitrary, coercive theories of selfhood and personhood. It is a peculiar cultural construct.

## THE BODY-MIND LINK

In Western culture whatever we say seriously about selfhood and persons needs to some extent to be compatible with what a jury in a court of law will accept. This demand imposes a non-negotiable link between the person and the person's living body. Because of embodiment, we cannot claim to be able to be in three places, or two, at the same time. For the jury the capacities of the self have to conform to the accepted constraints of space and time. This means that for us there are several philosophical problems about selfhood which other civilizations do not find problematical. First, the concept of the multiple self is absolutely objectionable. The jury room has no use for a concept of person with several constituent selves because responsibility must not be diffused. So there is no pleading for a criminal in the name of a theory of homunculi who take over different compartments of the self's choices and responsibilities. Second, the concept of the passive self is unacceptable. It is no good explaining in court that a person's actions are under the control of external agencies, such as furies, capricious gods, demons, personified emotions. It will not do to deny responsibility by saying that a sorcerer has turned the person into a zombie. For any of these versions of diminished responsibility to be accepted in the courts would entail a great deal of rewriting of the law-books. For any of them to be philosophically accepted would make utilitarian philosophy even more difficult to maintain than it is now. But though we may not like them at the level of gut response, we are in a weak position for saying that they are wrong, since we have put the topic of the internal constitution of the self out of bounds. We cannot either say how those theories are wrong or how they might be right.

Other people's ideas about the self are stacked on anthropologists' shelves, ethnographic oddities not worth bothering about for a technologically superior Western civilization. The argument here is that the idea of a unitary self, because it concords so well with our legal and economic institutions, exerts a stranglehold on public dialogue like that of primitive philosophies. Fit with legal and economic institutions controls the possibilities of discussion. Thank God for the stranglehold. In the history of Western jurisprudence this particular version of self, unitary and fully embodied, is the cornerstone of our civil liberties, a block against arbitrary defamation. We cannot accuse someone of doing harm by occult means in a distant place while there is good evidence that he was asleep in his bed. The impossibility of being in two places at once puts evidence based on visions and dreams out of court. On that impossibility, most verdicts of witchcraft would fail. It is not at all my intention to disallow our entrenched view of the person, only to show how and why it is entrenched, with a view to using the notion of thought style to develop an argument about community and culture.

Approaching the self pragmatically by this external route defuses the charge of political bias and gives us a way of comparing ideas of self with the legal institutions they uphold. The forensic uses of the self accord with the idea of the self as an ideological construct. The idea of the forensic self was proposed by John Locke to solve the philosophical problem of justifying the notion of a continuously conscious and responsible self. He tried to defend the idea on grounds of theological necessity. When we stand before the Judgement Seat of God at the end of our lives, he asked, how could we be expected to answer for our deeds if we have multiple or fragmented personalities? Therefore there must be a unitary responsible self.

> Person, as I take it, is the name for this self. Wherever a man finds what he calls himself, there, I think, another may say is the same person. It is a forensic term, appropriating actions and their merit; and so belongs only to intelligent agents capable of a law, and happiness, and misery. This personality extends itself beyond present existence to what is past, only by consciousness, whereby it becomes concerned and accountable, owns and imputes to itself past actions, just upon the same ground and for the same reason that it does the present. . . And therefore, conformable to this, the apostle tells us, that, at the great day, when everyone shall 'receive according to his doings, the secrets of his heart shall be laid open'. The sentence shall be justified by the consciousness all persons shall have, that they themselves, in what bodies soever they appear, or what substances soever that consciousness adheres to, are the same that committed those actions, and deserve that punishment for them.[7]

To anyone who believes in God's Last Judgement this may be an adequate justification of the unitary self lodged in its body, but it fails to convince anyone who does not believe in God and it should not weigh with one who believes in God, but doubts a Day of Judgement. The link between the self and its body is not an academic issue. Modern transplant surgery makes real life pressure on the connection. The question of transfer of the self from one body to another becomes a practical issue which throws our habits of thought into disarray. It may become necessary to admit that it is neither logically absurd nor practically irrelevant to conceive of transferable and disembodied selves.

Daniel Dennett has invented a story that illustrates the weaknesses of contemporary thought on the body–mind link.[8] In the story he has agreed to go on a dangerous mission, leaving his brain behind. Surgery would completely remove his brain, which would then be stored in a life-support system; each input and output pathway, as it was severed, would be restored by a pair of microminiaturized radio transceivers, one attached precisely to the brain, the other to the nerve stumps in the empty skull. When the hero has had the process explained he says:

> At first I was a bit reluctant. Would it really work? The Houston brain surgeons encouraged me. 'Think of it', they said, 'as a mere *stretching* of the nerves. If your brain were just moved over an *inch* in your skull, that would not alter or impair your mind. We're going to make your nerves indefinitely elastic by splicing radio links into them.'

The operation is successful, and when he comes out of the anaesthetic he is taken to see his own brain floating in a liquid, and covered with little electrodes, circuit chips and other electrical paraphernalia. To test whether it really is his own brain, he hits a switch connected to it, and collapses from the blow. When he comes round, he thinks to himself:

> 'Here I am, sitting on a folding chair, staring through a piece of plate glass at my own brain. . . But wait,' I said to myself, 'shouldn't I have thought, here am I, suspended in a bubbling fluid, being stared at by my own eyes?' . . . 'When I thought "Here I am", where the thought occurred to me was *here*, outside the vat, where I, Daniel Dennett, was standing staring at my brain'. (pp. 311–12)

Eventually he leaves his brain in the vat in Houston and goes on his dangerous, subterranean mission. At all times he can call operation control and receive instructions. While he is working underground on dismantling a warhead the cerebral links break. He finds himself blind and deaf and dumb in a radioactive hole a mile underground. It takes him some time to realize that the realization that his poor body is dead underground miles away is taking place in his brain in the vat in Houston. But where is he, really? Or which is he: the dead body, or his brain? As the story goes on, having been disembodied, he is given by the skill of the scientists a new body. Then all the problems of the legendary Hindu sages transformed into outcasts or kings, or of kings transformed into women, or of outcasts transformed into kings, are implicitly before us in our own vernacular philosophy.

Dennett's funny story makes the point that personal transferability between bodies is not necessarily inconsistent with our space–time theories. So why do philosophers resist the implications of Hume's analysis? Why can we not accept a number of self theories, involving multiple selves, passive selves, invaded and possessed selves, each serving different forensic purposes? Are we to conclude that all other civilizations are wrong if they encourage notions of transfers of the self between one body and another? Philosophers cannot say that they are wrong, except on the forensic grounds that they would make society unworkable, but in fact many societies built upon these ideas work well. The objections we read are based more on morality and political acceptability than on feasibility. They argue that there has to be a unitary self, because the individual person has to be able to be held accountable. Thus is John Locke's religious argument secularized. Instead of the Last Judgement, the coherent, unitary self is validated by the demands of the secular law courts and by moral principles. Terence Penelhum waxes indignant on 'the moral trickery' of anyone who would represent his desires as external to himself.[9] Parrotting Locke in a secular vein, a unitary, responsible self-agent must be supposed to exist because it is intellectually, juridically, and morally necessary. This is the prevailing forensic model of the person that best suits our culture.

## INTENTIONAL SYSTEMS

The secular forensic model is an invitation to attend to the tension between self and the judges to whose penalties and awards the self is having to conform. The judges and jury are the other members of the culture, who have set up its standards and enforce them. If we could compare alternative ideas about the person we would be half way to getting past the intellectual block that prevents us from reasoning about selves in general. The forensic model of the person affords a possibility of setting up an external, empirical method of comparison. To this end, we look round for ideology-free, science-like descriptions of persons. The utilitarian model of the self purports to be one such, but as we have shown, it is loaded with ideological assumptions. Furthermore, it has only one person, and no way of taking account of other persons except to make a simple aggregation of their satisfactions. It does not incorporate the results of politicking except by pushing into the negotiations the same analysis of costs and benefits which carry the burden of explanation for the selection of satisfactions. Being content with an individualist method is part of its ideological burden. Always focused on one actor, it can analyse human social behaviour as if all the other individuals were organized as a market, in other words as if there were no community. If we are looking for a culture-free approach, we have to bracket away the utilitarian account of persons as a forensic model generated by a strong cultural bias. We want a method of finding alternative forensic models.

Daniel Dennett has proposed an all-purpose, minimal model of the person which he describes as an 'Intentional System'. The awkward language testifies to the effort to be free of adhering cultural bias. For lack of a better theory of the self he has had to invent a new way of thinking about the neuron pathways in the body to the individual brain, and about the pathways between the brain and the society, and he means the same model to do as well for thinking of the communication between communities. National states trying to calculate the intentions of other nation states and making inferences useful for foreign policy count as intentional systems.[10] An intentional system needs three conditions: rationality, intentions, and a reciprocal stance towards and from other intentional systems.[11] Persons are rational beings whose actions are to be understood in terms of their intentions, these being construed from the logical relations between their beliefs and desires. Intentionality is a capability which persons attribute to one another. Since it works only in an environment of other persons this is radically different from methodological individualism. The 'intentional stance'[12] expects to predict how other persons are going to behave, and makes this knowledge the basis for strategies.

Predictions in terms of intentions are different from predictions in terms of physical laws. He uses the word intentions to include hopes, fears, intentions, perceptions, expectations, etc. We ascribe intentions to dogs and fish, or even to trees, so the intentional stance does not only include persons.[13] When he ascribes beliefs and desires to the computer chess player Dennett is not saying that the machine really has beliefs and desires, but that its behaviour can be explained and predicted by ascribing to it machine equivalents for beliefs and desires. Thus he can describe a computer in the same terms: it is much easier to decide whether a machine can be an intentional system than it is to decide whether a machine can *really* think, or be conscious, or morally responsible.[14]

A larger intentional system includes others, the community includes the person, the person includes the neurones. Dennett does not specify the relation between one level and the next. How is a level determined? The levels are supposed to connect and interact, but his model does not say how this happens. We can improve his model quite simply by incorporating the forensic process as the connecting medium and by giving cultural equivalents of person's beliefs and desires. Change his term 'beliefs' to 'theories' about the world; then change his term 'desires' to 'claims', so as to pay attention only to that part of intentions which enter the forensic process because they can be formulated as claims on others; then postulate that the claims invoke the theories in their support. These three slight adaptations give an abstract context of interaction between individual members of a community. Then the higher level or community can be presented as a system of claims sorted out by logic applied to negotiations and deals. Claims are the very substance of the higher level IS. At the community level the equivalent of individual claims are collective claims, or claims made on behalf of and in the name of the collectivity. The community equivalent of individual beliefs are collectively held beliefs, public knowledge, and generally accepted theories, or culture. Self-perception of a community will correspond to what its members think proper, and likewise, the knowledge of the self that is available to members will be limited by the forensic process.

## CLAIMS

The project of this essay is to find a way of evaluating the claims about the self in the enterprise culture. This involved noting the strong resistance to subjecting the idea of the self to reasoned argument, evidence, if evidence was needed, for its ideological embeddedness. The idea of the self is made to sit upon huge blank spaces of missing evidence. Admittedly this is the case for all ideas, so it is not the evidence that is missing but the theory that would indicate what would count as evidence in an argument. We have no such theory of the self because (for good reasons) we have deliberately put it into that inaccessible limbo that cannot be opened for theorizing. A theory of knowledge based on claims does not intrude into that domain. It does not pretend to reveal anything about the inner experiences of the self, only about its uses in negotiation. A theory about claims made on the self has the advantage of not being grounded on an appeal to the transcendental. It is limited to knowledge that is made public, specifically to culture.

Transform, for the sake of argument, the judgement seat of God and the formal judgement seat of tribunals into the informal judgement of peers. In Dennett's terms they are intentional systems continually monitoring your behaviour and trying to make predictions about what you are going to do. The word 'claims' refers to demands that a person makes on the time or other resources of others. Acceptable claims at any point in time are equivalent to society. Claims include all kinds of pretensions, requests, entitlements, expectations, demands. The gamut of claims runs from great confidence that an established claim exists and will be honoured, to a very tentative request for consideration. Disputes about claims on a person's time and property if not quickly resolved are always put to some testing of the condition of the world. Whoever can dispute a knowledge claim used as backing by his opponents can escape from the charges they seek to lay on him. As I have argued, the two kinds of claims, on persons and on knowledge, establish each other.[15] Dennett's model needs to insert the connection between responsibility and theories.[16] The gamut of theories runs from facts well established to very tentative hypotheses.

If there is a sustainable pattern of claims it is a cultural system. Culture is the point at which claims and counter-claims come to rest and where authority is attributed to theories about the world. The context of claims and counter-claims sets up a pressure for consistency. Only a vigilantly maintained set of reasoned statements about the self will hold off the claims of others who will pounce on the least sign of contradiction, intellectual or moral weakness. To be able to invoke the self is an indispensable forensic resource for living in society.

# INTERACTION BETWEEN INTENTIONAL SYSTEMS

Keeping a new concept free of content is a good strategy for starting an investigation at an abstract level. Dennett is careful not to be saying anything at all about the content of consciousness beyond the beliefs and desires and the power of inference. He never treads on the forbidden ground of subjective experience. His account is always from the outside, never risking a speculation on which beliefs or what kinds of desires could be found within. This is how he avoids importing unwanted metaphysical and political biases into his account.[17] A test of his theory about persons would have to be the same as the test that persons normally apply to their own theories about persons: predictive power.

Dennett's empty slots for beliefs and desires would be useful for predicting theories of the self if only the said beliefs and desires could be qualified a bit more. He does not try to assess the influence of the containing intentional system over its elements. He does not show how its internal relations are articulated. He cannot (and does not aim to) develop a critique of folk psychology, still less provide the basis for a critique of the self in the enterprise culture. But he does provide the beginnings of a model free of ideological adhesions that cultural theory can amend and use.

As a heuristic, set up four kinds of culture[18] each sustained by its members actively invoking a particular idea of the self. One of the four types will be the enterprise culture, one, the hierarchical culture, one, the culture of the dissident minority enclave. In each of these cultures power and authority are actively contested. The fourth is the type of culture in which the members are not involved in the dialogue about power. Each culture is carried in a community, an intentional system connected by claims with its own sub-systems, the persons. Each culture produces, in the process of negotiating claims, its own compatible theory of the world and the self. It also calls forth the desires from the persons at the same time that it defines good and wrong behaviour. 'Society prepares the crime' as Quetelet said,[19] and at the same time it defines the persons, as Durkheim said.

Consider hierarchy as one type of higher level intentional system. The test of a hierarchy is not stratified ranks but the overarching whole which contains them. It may be necessary to remind readers that every bureaucracy is not hierarchical. Nor does every king reign over a hierarchy; nor is a great industrial corporation a hierarchy if the chiefs, whom Horkheimer calls 'totalitarian cartel lords',[20] treat its members as transient, dispensable resources. An individualist culture can have huge bureaucracies which make no moral claims on their own behalf, which are treated as private assets, stripped if possible by their members, treated as a kind of scaffolding or natural advantage which can be disposed of when it suits the individual member. Other bureaucracies, just as big, may be hierarchies, according to the meaning of the term, that is units whose parts contribute to the maintenance of the whole and which never abandon responsibility for members. By definition, hierarchy is maintained by claims accepted on behalf of the whole community; because claims overriding those of individual members are acceptable, authority can be exerted on behalf of the community; its member persons perform public ceremonials, invest in public goods, and justify a high degree of organization in order to strengthen the public claims they cherish. One result is that a well-run hierarchy has a lot to offer its members, and in consequence it is not worried lest they secede. Loyalty being secure, the main concern is that the up-down structure be not weakened.

In contrast, consider the dissenting minority enclave culture, which often tends to be sectarian. The main concern will be the fear of secession: anxiety lest the faithful leak away weakens authority and encourages a tendency to egalitarian organization. Here, to be acceptable, claims should invoke the principle of equality. Third, the enterprise culture is distinguished from both of these by the weakness of the claims of the community over those of its members. Fourth, isolates who are not involved in economic or political or social competition, either having been forced out, or having chosen not to be involved, also have a typical culture characterized by absence of attempt to explain or influence events, freedom from the ideological commitments which control so much of other persons' lives. It is as hard to find a pure hierarchy or a pure type of enclave culture as it is to find an extreme kind of enterprise culture or completely isolated members of the isolates' culture.

We look now for simple tests to show how incompatible cultures rest on distinctive, incompatible patterns of claims. One test should concern the claims that links the levels. How does a person become a member of a larger intentional system? It is easier to answer the question from the other angle: how does exclusion work? A second test should show the way the higher level system shapes individual desires conformably to its acceptable claims. A third test should show how the bundle of acceptable claims affects theories about reality, and particularly about the self. If we can develop a discussion on those lines, we can start to argue about persons in a way that includes their ideological bias.

## DOWNGRADING AND EXCLUSION FROM THE CLAIMS SYSTEM

The distinguishing feature of hierarchy is that every decision is referred to the well-being of the whole. A whole transcending its parts is what hierarchy means.[21] It is a claims system from which it is very difficult for anyone to be dropped. Everyone is there forever, and their claims are to be kept alive in some form or other. Inveterate disloyalty and unrepentant disobedience disqualify. Incompetence and infirmity do not. In the hierarchy the lobby of the weak is powerful since it is a good strategy to claim to represent it. (In consequence much distinctive regulation is entailed – for example, the protection of pension schemes will have priority over risky profits.) By what administrative arrangements is this result procured? By maintaining the influence of distinct sectors in the overall decision process. Each person in such a hierarchy has to be enrolled within a recognized sector to have any claims at all, and the sectors have to be formally related to the whole. Since no one can be eliminated, all have to be assigned places in the system, and the claims of the places have to be recognized. This type of higher level intentional system, the hierarchy, would be suffocated by the mutually conflicting claims between lower level systems unless it had ways of grading and reconciling them. Inequality of status and inequality of claims is built in to the constitution. Successful claims are backed by reference to some expected good for the whole, and in this system, though some can claim more and others less, all have claims. The distinctive point is that people can drop down, but not out.

On this issue there is little difference between a hierarchy and an enclave. In the latter, membership is theoretically for ever.

However, it is generally an egalitarian claims system,[22] so there is no lower level for incompetents to drop down to. Disloyal traitors and subversive elements may be expelled from such a system of claims, but completely expelled. They will not be seen hanging around because neither incompetence nor infirmity will have caused their exclusion, only political animosity.

In an individualist market-oriented society incompetence disqualifies. The system tends to honour the person who organizes effective networks. As exchange theory shows, there have to be failures in such a system, persons whom it is worth no one's while to count as an ally. Falling into infirmity or otherwise showing weakness is a sure way of falling out of the network of worthy partners.[23] In the enterprise culture appalling black spots of poverty should not provoke surprise, especially in face of immense private wealth. Though it needs to include the rising generation, and tries to reincorporate them into the competitive network, the claims of older failures and the demands for safety nets for the weak are incompatible with the doctrine of undiminished personal responsibility. The strength of the enterprise culture is the creation of wealth by a self-reliant meritocracy. Inevitably it has a large class of rejects. They are not the low-grade citizens of the bottom echelons of hierarchy, but disfranchised derelicts who cannot be reincorporated into the system which excludes for poor performance.

## DESIRES

As to desires, consider how consumerism has been misjudged. In all societies consumption is enjoyed, but consumerism, the unlimited private demand for commodities, is part of the individualist culture. Other cultural types impose restrictions on desires. The hierarchy certainly encourages conspicuous display, but requires that the show be on behalf of the community. The public affluence of palaces, cathedrals, law courts, and public parks, depends on the willingness of the taxpayer to fork out for civic benefits. The hierarchical person has been encouraged, by all the devices which give a sense of belonging and loyalty, to make personal desires subordinate to the claims of the community. Like the hierarchy, the culture of the enclave puts strong community constraints on spending. The idea of what is a suitable standard of living in an enclave is partly developed by opposition to those of the mainstream society, whether it is market-individualism or hierarchy: thrift is more elegant, more appropriate, than vulgar display. Consumerism is impossible in either of these types of higher level intentional system, and if a new habit of conspicuous private spending appears it can be taken as a symptom of a cultural shift.

The persons whose behaviour is condemned as consumerist are wrongly blamed if consumerism means private competitive consumption. They cannot help themselves; they are living in a social environment in which they must compete or risk being omitted from convivial lists, which will lead to being omitted from other important lists on which their livelihood depends. No one really wants to get so involved in a consumption rat race, but one person cannot put a lid on the pressure to compete with display of goods and hospitality. Only community disapproval can impose limits to competitive display, but this kind of culture is continually stripping the community. Persons in an individualist culture question authority, believe that censorship in all its forms is wrong, and disapprove of sumptuary laws and other such controls on individual freedom of choice. The weight of their cultural consensus is thrown behind the work of liberation. It is part of the definition of the fully responsible individual to be sovereign in choice. For better or worse, consumerism rampages within the enterprise culture. It is inconsistent for its subscribers to berate consumerism and at the same time to subscribe unreservedly to the individualist values.

## THEORIES ABOUT THE SELF

Now we can return to those bizarre foreign ideas about the person. This essay started out by explaining the kind of claims that are sustained by the theory of the unitary, rational, responsible self. They are claims that are tested at law. The resulting idea of a forensic self is well adapted to a culture which demands complete accountability from its members, the right idea of the self for an individualist culture. If elsewhere zombies and demonic possession and transfers of self are publicly standardized ideas, we can be sure that they are also being employed in the making and testing of claims. Folk psychology is not just speculative, but used for predicting, explaining, and preparing claims. This is the weakness of Daniel Dennett's little story about the brain transplant: it has interesting confrontations but nothing about conflict of claims. Only by seeing how the theory of the self is used in dealing with conflicting claims can we have the rational conversation about persons and selfhood that is so difficult in our Western culture.

Start with a hierarchical culture where, as we have seen, the claims of fellow members of the community cannot be rejected out of hand. Each person belongs ideally to a sector that makes effective claims on their behalf. In the enclave culture likewise, members are anxious to avoid a schism. The outsiders can carry the full burden of responsibility for what they do, but insiders are easily let off the hook. In both cultures, because of the desire of members to honour the claims of the community, instead of pressure to pin responsibility on individuals, there is pressure to alleviate it. Pinning blame on weaklings will achieve nothing: so long as they are loyal, they cannot be eliminated. When they err, it is a better strategy to relieve them of too much responsibility, and work for them to be reincorporated. Split personalities, passive persons, zombies, ghost-haunted, bewitched, and cursed persons may be theories that pass the blame on to some other person, but they may also serve in kindly, forgiving theories which show the sinner as a victim.

Side by side with the forensic model, a therapeutic model of the self develops. The therapist does not want the patient to suffer from a sense of guilt or rejection. So he does not rub salt into the sores by insisting on unambiguous personal accountability. He diagnoses misfortune as an attack on the unwitting patient by a demon who can be fairly easily exorcised.[24] No one in the community is to blame, the misfortune was caused by a capricious spiritual being. Or the patient learns that his own self in a prenatal stage of existence chose trouble.[25] In this usage the theory of the multiple self diffuses responsibility. A verdict that the patient brought his troubles on himself means that other people are not to blame, yet at the same time the patient cannot feel too responsible since the self that made the bad choice was not himself as he is now.

## GUILT AND RESPONSIBILITY

The context of therapy and consultation is more practice-oriented than the context of philosophical enquiry. Passive modes of conceiving the person permit the patient to join the therapeutic project as an independent agent. They distance him from moral responsibility but they do not necessarily absolve him from responsibility in the law courts. Our own psychiatrists use the idea of the passive self, by way of not forcing blame. In his account of the language of psychoanalysis Roy Schafer criticized the over-use of what he called 'passive voice' language instead of 'action language'.[26] The analyst will say: 'Your chronic deep sense of worthlessness comes from the condemning voice of your mother'; or 'You are afraid of your impulse to throw caution to the winds', both passive forms, allowing the patient to think of himself as a victim, without bearing responsibility for what he is.

In personal contexts where we want to evade blame, we also work happily with the philosophically nonsensical ideas. We talk about being beside ourselves with rage, or out of our minds; objects slip away from our minds or enter them, as if the mind was a house with rooms. We are evidently quite able to entertain and to make everyday use of the idea of multiple personality. In other contexts, we are determined that each shall bear the costs of his actions. Accused by the traffic warden or the speed cop the sinner will do himself no good at all by citing his therapist's remissions of responsibility. The therapeutic model of the blame-free self works where the contexts of blame are segmented. The different selves are active ideas in different patterns of claims. For the context of healing, the law is peripheral. For the context of justice, healing is peripheral. There need be no problem about using the idea of multiple selves in one context and the single, continuous self in the other context, so long as the contexts can be distinguished. Thus far we have exonerated the foreign civilizations which operate with ideas of the self repugnant in our own. We are not more rational than they, and they are more forgiving than we. But that was not the main objective for this essay.

The first objective in taking seriously a range of alien ideas about selves is to complete Daniel Dennett's model by linking ideas about the self, through claims, with the larger intentional system. The latter is the community without which the self is meaningless. The community is the locus of ideology connecting the idea of the person to the culture which its members are making. It is interesting to compare the trade-offs for each cultural type. In economic terms the individualist (enterprise) culture raises the standard of living all round. The hierarchical culture is stronger on solidarity and stability. The enclave culture is good for pricking the conscience of both the other types[27] but not very good at raising the material standard of living. It tends to have a lot of worry about the loyalty of its members,[28] but the latter would seem to have a good opinion of themselves. There has been as yet no research combining assessments of cultural bias with psychological assessments of personality. In default, a guess suggests that the isolate would be most contented with his lot and least ridden with guilt, while the culture that tends to give its members a sense of irredeemable guilt and inadequacy is the enterprise culture.

It has long been recognized in psychoanalysis that modern industrial society is hard upon the person's self-image. Perhaps for lack of a discourse in which self-concepts can be studied as aspects of culture, rather facile explanations of psychological stress have been proposed, such as consumerism, bureaucracy, inhumanity, fascism, industrialism. The barely articulated diagnosis is part of the thought style[29] of the enterprise culture. That the self-reliant, autonomous, responsible self should be its ideal is understandable, but cultural theory can give better explanations than psychology for why the ideal is so hard to achieve. First there is the burden of responsibility, often unfair. Failure to carry it meets with none of the kindly exonerations that failure meets in a hierarchy. The culture is so organized that incompetence and weakness cannot be compensated for. Rewards go to performance and merit, there is less readiness to carry mediocrity, there is more failure, and punishment for failure is more severe. In the enterprise culture exclusion can be a silent process, almost imperceptible, by simple exit as in the market, not by complaining voice[30] as in enclave, or by formal edict as in hierarchy. In the enterprise culture the person excluded need not know what has happened until some time after. No one else needs to notice either: the enterprise culture just waves a wand and its rejects become invisible.

In conclusion, the public idea of the self is part of a cultural commitment, and so is determined by a thought style which will vary according to the thought collective, to use Fleck's terms. Because of the active role played by the claims of the self in the making of culture it is difficult to put a sceptical bracket around it. Our culture stalls on enquiry into the nature of the private self so as to protect the freedom of persons from ideologized coercion. It is presented to us as something we should not and cannot analyse. But now we have entered the claims of the community into the account of the person the idea of the self turns out to be something which can be and ought to be critically examined. Both self and community have to be examined together. Refusing to go into details about the ideological construction of the self is not the best way to resist the would-be tyrant's claims. Far safer to practise being articulate about the external and ideological bases of selfhood, because this leads to straight talk about the kind of community and the kind of culture we want to protect.

## ACKNOWLEDGEMENT

The first version of this article was written for *The Enterprise Culture, Themes in the Work of Mary Douglas*, edited by Shaun Hargreaves Heap and Angus Ross (Edinburgh University Press, 1992), pp. 41–62. This version was presented at the Berliner Institut für Vergleichende Sozialforschung, 11 December 1990. I am grateful to Jonathan Miller for advice on the philosophy of the self.

## NOTES

1 Ludwik Fleck, *The Genesis and Development of a Scientific Fact* (first published 1935, translation, Chicago University Press, 1979).

2 Mary Douglas, *How Institutions Think* (Syracuse University Press, 1986).

3 T.W. Adorno and M. Horkheimer, *The Dialectic of Enlightenment* (Trans. John Cumming, NY, Herder & Herder (1972); edition quoted, Verso, 1979; original German, *Dailektik der Aufklarung*, New York Social Studies Assoc., 1944).

4 Stephen J. Gould, *The Mismeasure of Man* (New York, Norton, 1981).

5 Isaiah Berlin, 'Two Concepts of Liberty', in *Four Essays on Liberty* (Oxford University Press, 1969).

6 Derek Parfit, *Reasons and Persons* (Oxford, Clarendon, 1984).

7 John Locke, (1694) *Essay Concerning Human Understanding*, 2nd edn, section 26. Cited in John Peery (ed.) *Personal Identity* (University of California Press, 1975).

8 Daniel Dennett, 'Where am I?' in *Brainstorms: Philosophical Essays on Mind and Psychology* (Cambridge, Bradford Books, MIT Press, 1981), pp. 310–23.

9 Terence Penelhum, (1971) 'The Importance of Self-Identity', *Jouranl of Philosophy* LXVIII:670–2, quoted in Harry Frankfurt, 'Identification and Externality', in Amelie Rorty (ed.), *The Identities of Persons* (California University Press, 1976), pp. 238–51.

10 Dennett uses this abstract scheme to bridge the various sciences dealing with the mind, artificial intelligence, game theory, neurology, psychology, and philosophy. It is meant to apply wherever the theorizing is about the predictions that logical beings in a particular system are making about each others' behaviour from deductions about their beliefs and desires. 'A particular thing is an intentional system only in relation to the strategies of someone who is trying to explain and predict its behaviour' (Daniel Dennett (1971) 'Institutional Systems', *Journal of Philosophy* 68:87).

11 Daniel Dennett, *Brainstorms, Philosophical Essays on Mind and Psychology* (Bradford Books, MIT Press, 1981), pp. 268–9.

12 Daniel Dennett, *The Intentional Stance* (MIT Press, Bradford Books, 1988).

13 Daniel Dennett, in Amelie Rorty (ed.), *The Identities of Persons* (California University Press, 1976), pp. 178–9.

14 Daniel Dennett, 'Where am I?', in *Brainstorms: Philosophical Essays on Mind and Psychology* (Cambridge, Bradford Books, MIT Press, 1981), p. 16.

15 This argument is a development of that broached in Mary Douglas, *How Institutions Think* (Syracuse University Press, 1986).

16 Max Gluckman (ed.), *The Allocation of Responsibility* (Manchester University Press, 1972).

17 B. Hannam (1990) 'Critical Notice, The Intentional Stance', *Mind*, xcix:394, April: 291–2.

18 Michael Thompson, Richard Ellis and Aaron Wildavsky, *Cultural Theory* (Westview Publications, 1990).

19 Quetelet, quoted in Ian Hacking, *The Taming of Chance* (Cambridge University Press, 1990), p. 116.

20 T.W. Adorno and Max Horkheimer, *The Dialectic of Enlightenment* (Verso, 1979), p. 87.

21 Louis Dumont, *Essais sur l'Individualisme* (Paris, Seuil, 1983).

22 Mary Douglas, *How Institutions Think* (Syracuse University Press, 1986).

23 An example of systematic rejection in an individualist world is given by Gerald Mars of the society of longshoremen in the Port of St. John's, Newfoundland, Canada: 'Longshore drinking, economic security and union politics in Newfoundland', in Mary Douglas (ed.), *Constructive Drinking, Perspectives on Drink from Anthropology* (Cambridge University Press, 1987), pp. 91–101.

24 Bruce Kapferer, *A Celebration of Demons* (Bloomington, University of Indiana Press, 1983).

25 Meyer Fortes, *Oedipus and Job in West African Religion*, with an essay by Robin Horton (Cambridge University Press, 1983).

26 Roy Schafer, *A New Language for Psychoanalysis* (New Haven, Yale University Press, 1976).

27 Mary Douglas and Aaron Wildavsky, *Risk and Culture, An Essay on the Selection of Technical and Environmental Dangers* (California University Press, 1982).
28 Mary Douglas, *How Institutions Think*, Chapter 3 (Syracuse University Press, 1986).
29 Ludwik Fleck, *The Genesis and Development of a Scientific Fact* (first published 1935, translation, University of Chicago Press, 1979).
30 A.O. Hirschman, *Exit, Voice and Loyalty, Responses to Decline in Firms, Organisations, and States* (Harvard University Press, 1970).

# 13

# CREDIBILITY

Although many religious minds are attracted by Pascal's argument for believing in the existence of God – it has been derided by logicians. So it seems good to draw the attention of the American Academy of Religion to a modern philosopher who defends it on purely logical grounds. This is Ian Hacking, expert in the theory of probability.[1] According to Hacking the principles of decision theory which Pascal used three hundred years ago have only recently been formulated, but even so, Pascal's logic is still impeccable. Betting on the probability of God's existence, wagering the constraints of religion against the libertine pleasures open to an unbeliever, betting on the incommensurability of a chance of heaven and a chance of damnation, Pascal stands centuries ahead on game theory and the technical analysis of rational choice – the founding ancestor of modern decision theory.

Pascal recognized that the metaphysical proofs of God were based[2] on logical implication so remote from ordinary reasoning that they have little persuasive power against scepticism. He was specially concerned to argue a case for belief that would not rely on the authority of church doctors, nor upon the witness of the faithful, since these were already discredited by the sceptic. So he invented his wager. Modern decision theory requires an exhaustive list of the possible hypotheses of the way the world is, an inventory of possible decisions plus the different benefits from making a decision in all the possible various states of the world: from this the analyst can determine the decision most likely to pay off best. But Pascal ruled out observations of experimental data, since he would not consider reports of miracles either: this is the case of decision-making in face of uncertainty when no experiments are possible. To solve the problem he correctly used three separate arguments, called in the jargon, 'dominance', 'expectation', and 'dominating expectation'. Dominance applies when one course of action would be better, no matter what the world is like: there is more utility in preferring course A–1 than any of the other actions: then course A–1 is said to dominate. To bet that God does not exist, and to live as if that is what the world is like, will bring damnation if the bet turns out wrong. Since salvation is infinitely better than damnation, the dominance rule directs the bet in God's favour or rather in favour of living a life that is reckoned to win salvation – an important difference. Similarly for 'expectation' and 'dominating expectations', all three arguments indicate the decision to live by the rules of religion. All three arguments are valid in the sense that the conclusions follow from the premises. It is the premises that are hard to defend.

This essay that starts with Pascal's wager has two objectives, both rather different from Pascal's. One is to persuade some contemporary religious thinkers to be less disdainful of sociological principles and even to include them in their theological constructions of the world. The second is to use a sociological argument to locate the sources of scepticism. For these purposes, we do not need a survey of all the possible kinds of scepticism. It will not be necessary to distinguish the healthy scepticism of everyday life nor the methodological doubt of epistemology, nor the scepticism that underlies empirical enquiry in science. These are partial scepticisms that do not threaten discourse, rather they make it possible. The scepticism at issue is the same overall questioning of reality that Pascal himself attacked under the name of 'pyrrhonisme'. He used his decision-theory technique to found a reasoned basis for distinguishing reality from illusion. It was a foundational problem in philosophy which he sought to solve by defining first the nature of man, second, the certain prospect of death, and third, a testing of all the different available paths for establishing a realist view against an acceptance of uncertainty. He included as hypotheses about possible states of the world the teachings of Judaism, Islam, Montaigne, the 'dogmatists' and 'academicians'. Sorting them through, he decided that Christianity best meets the facts he finds established about the nature of man (a monster mixed of vileness and glory) and about the certainty of death. It was beside the point for Diderot to have remarked that the method of the wager could be used just as well to justify Islam. Pascal had carefully gathered up all the versions of the world and partitioned it exhaustively into two options: either there is no God, or there is a God whose characteristics are correctly reported by the Catholic Church. Hacking remarks that the strength of his logic is no help to his decisions if the partitioning of the universe is not well done. Is his list of possible hypotheses about the alternative states of the world exhaustive? Supposing God was a Protestant? Suppose He was not impressed by holy water and sacraments (or even suppose He disapproved of betting altogether)?

The argument below will focus not on God but on an anterior aspect of Pascal's partitioning: the issue of either believing in reality (especially in the reality of death) or of living in uncertainty about everything in life. He says: you are here, you are engaged in the game, you have to wager. To be indifferent, to try to withdraw from the game, is in itself a wager. Either conviction is possible or an all encompassing doubt wins the game. His real enemies are not the Protestants, Jews, or Muslims, nor even the Jesuits and academicians against whom he inveighs, but the pronouncements of radical sceptics. In this choice of problem, he poses an option which is more contemporary than the choice between denominational religious forms. He thought that those especially charged in his time with expounding the claims of reason would never succeed without a modern argument. This essay assumes that scholars of today specialized in religion and philosophy will never even clarify their aims without a modern argument. Religious thinkers are not the only ones who shudder at the mention of sociological factors. Here it will be argued that their defence against historic waves of general scepticism loses its best arm by ignoring the sociological dimension.

Many students of religion display a bias against the idea that an individual human being receives and sustains his religious beliefs in a social medium. But can they seriously discount the possibility that God, having made man a social being, allows His Face to be seen only through a distorted lens, through the medium of the society which men themselves create? To say Yes, belief and society go together, to concede this, would endorse a further element in Pascal's argument. For he did not think that belief comes by a decision to believe. At issue in his wager is the idea that belief comes by living in the company of believers. He did not discount social influences. So there is a further implication

237

for theology: could it be that the virtuous activity of avoiding damnation could entail the activity of making the society which best images God? It might also suggest that theology could not get far along its special path without studying that social medium through which God is known. And finally, on another tack, it is often remarked that an effect of the special distorting medium of our own contemporary society is to show each person related to God as an isolated individual. Theologians could well be under social constraints in this day and age to ignore the social support of belief and to emphasize the individual. If that seems plausible, then, paradoxically, those who most vehemently deny sociological determinism are by that very fact demonstrating their own intellectual dependence on shared prejudices of their society.

Religious thinkers in our times agree in taking the difference between Eastern and Western traditions as the most distinctive variation in approaches to the divine. Pascal is highly relevant on this score. For the most striking difference between the two hemispheres is the strength of the sceptical tradition in the East and its weakness in the West. Different writers on religion have selected different elements to present the contrast of East and West, yet none has hitherto focused on this fundamental point. With the publication of *Dreams, Illusions and Other Realities*,[3] the focus is placed where it needs to be if discourse in the history of religion is not to remain in a separate sacred enclosure, fenced off from other major concerns of our times. In this book, Wendy O'Flaherty takes her own work on the interpretation of Hindu mythology to a new depth by starting from the questions formulated by Ernest Gombrich:

> Do all cultures make the same radical distinction between 'appearances' and 'reality' which ours have inherited from Plato? Are their hierarchies the same? In other words, do they necessarily accept the demand that contradictions must be ironed out and that all perceptions that clash with beliefs must force us either to change our views of the 'objective world' or declare the perception to have been a subjective experience – an illusion?[4]

She sees the history of dealing with this question in the West as a long and serious combat between Platonic idealism and Humean empiricism in which our legal system keeps coming in on the side of Hume. Here it will be argued that 'What think ye of dreams?' is the contemporary way of facing Pascal's two-pronged choice. Pascal's argument took the division between dreaming and waking as the touchstone.[5] To the reader in the Western tradition this always seems a little far-fetched: in sleep, we think that we are awake; since we dream a lot, and since in dreaming, one dream often nests in another, is it not plausible that the other half of life in which we think we are awake is itself only a dream nested in the other dreams? Then death will be a wakening. All the flow of time and the flow of life and the sensation of various bodies, these different thoughts which disturb us, perhaps they are all illusions like the flow of time in our dreams. Who knows whether this other half of our lives in which we think we are awake is another sleep a bit different from the first? These are the very questions which the Indian literature on dreaming poses dramatically and worryingly. That tradition presents to us the logical development which Pascal wished to refute.

In Hindu and Buddhist thought, the doctrine of illusion is the single, clearest, distinguishing mark setting apart the Eastern and Western traditions. Western philosophers have been arguing with radical scepticism from the beginning of the philosophical record. But here it is a suppressed vein of thought, while in the East it is a dominant one.

Often the sceptical question is presented to us as if it only concerns the reality of particular experiences, something about stubbing toes on hard objects and feeling it hurt. Such a presentation is but a prelude to a facile dismissal. More fairly, the question is not about particular realities or certainties; it is Pascal's question of how to have confidence in speaking about reality in general. It is a technical question about how to establish a position without depending on another position that equally needs defence and that defence depending on another and so on, opening up infinite regress.

Of course, if you want discourse to proceed, it is easy to agree to avoid the whole issue of foundations. Some truce between the sceptic and his opponent can always be arranged if they so desire. They can easily agree on a conventional appeal to authority or to self-evidence. But it is a patched up truce liable to break down. The Western philosopher's favourite recourse tends to be the announcement that it has to be possible: to deny the possibility of discourse is to fall into absurdity. Or else the matter is settled by convicting the sceptic of inconsistency. The sceptic is repeating

Parmenides' ancient paradox: if he says that all utterances are empty, then his own utterance is empty too. Hilary Putnam, who takes these questions seriously, seems to feel that it is a strong argument to declare that total relativism's inconsistency is a truism.[6] He quotes for two kinds of inconsistency: Quine and Davidson argue that a consistent relativist has excluded the possibility of treating others as speakers or thinkers at all, while Plato and Wittgenstein argue that a consistent relativist is not even entitled to treat himself as a speaker or thinker. Reading these philosophers, it is clear that the power of total relativism and of other radical forms of scepticism should be easy to defuse. The logical arguments against allowing a conversation to be interrupted in their name are strong.

However, if the sceptic does not particularly want there to be a discourse, or at least does not want to assert any thesis of his own, his sceptical position is unassailable. As Dr Matilal remarks, quoting the Buddhist sceptic, Nagarjuna: radical scepticism is feasible, but not stateable: if it is stated, it falls into contradiction.[7] But in the Eastern tradition, there is nothing wrong with being silent. Buddhism applauds silence. This sceptical philosophy is compatible wth religious doctrines of non-commitment or non-attachment. Scepticism itself cannot be a doctrine; it can be a practice which is valued explicitly in the Eastern tradition because it leads to religious insight. It makes way for a mystical experience of the grounds of truth.

In the West, we have Hume's philosophical scepticism, but as Wendy O'Flaherty says, it is usually worked on behalf of empirical reality. Whatever else may be said of Hume, it cannot be claimed that he laid the cornerstone for a great mystical tradition. Something has been at work in the Western religious experience and its philosophical history that directs our sceptical resources into different channels.

We can try to construct some sort of overall scheme for comparing religions of the world. Some scale that relates the degree of scepticism to the desire to maintain a community of discourse would be a start. First, at one end of the scale we would place unquestioned belief: here we would expect to find many so-called primitive religions, and also many parishes and dioceses of so-called advanced civilizations. The basic idea is that questioning and doubt can be held in check only by a strong institutional structure. Here, by definition then, religion would be directly engaged with the social order, legitimating the social machinery, making community commitments manifest.[8]

In the middle of this scale, we would place those religions whose teachings are both contested and defended in a pluralist society. The challenge to explain and define forces axiomatization. Loose doctrinal threads will be stitched back, concepts stretched, and new verbal formulae sought to meet the needs of dialogue. In this middle part of the scale, the religion stands in sophisticated engagement with the social world. In its historic controversies, Christianity gives abundant instances of how the pressure to create one unified church authority is related to the pressure to axiomatize the elements of belief, allowing for private doubt but requiring that the community of discourse be protected by a political effort at consensus.

The last point in the scale would be represented by full scale scepticism. By this reckoning, the Eastern religions would be way ahead of Christianity. Sustained scepticism is a feasible stance for those who do not expect to command or unify society, but stand apart from it. Belief/scepticism patterns have much to do with the claims of power and revolt against its claims.

The rest of the argument leads us to examine the social conditions which foster general radical scepticism. Then we should take account of sceptical movements in the West at this present time. Then, finally, we can raise questions for religious philosophy. Peter Berger[9] maintains that Jerusalem (made to represent Western Religion) should now turn towards Benares (representing Eastern Religion). Louis Dumont[10] holds that Western political thought suffers by having let go of the concept of hierarchy which is still understood in the East. But neither recognizes that the critically distinctive element of Eastern philosophy, its scepticism, has arrived here in the West already and is thriving.

Espousing a fully sceptical philosophy leads to non-attachment, and vice versa, non-attachment permits a sceptical philosophy. In recognizing this we have a principle for tracing the wavering movements in Christianity away from or towards scepticism. In theology the crucial relation is that held to obtain between divine and human life. If the teaching is that they are very remote from each other, the divine an altogether unreachable, unknowable element, impossibly distant from and superior to humanity, then we have the beginning of a religious discourse that can move to a second doctrine, that the human experience is necessarily so inferior that it can hardly be credited with reality compared with the divine; then, the latest stages of the religious discourse can progressively downgrade the human sphere so that nothing that happens in it is of any significance except in so far as it enables the human being to escape into the superior element, at whatever cost. This religious discourse can proceed either apart from, or at the expense of, the political community to which it can lend no support.

Our scepticism scale for comparing religions draws on a relation presumed to hold between the believer and the source of agreed authority. In the first (and the lowest) class, that of unquestioning belief, there are no cracks in the consensual system; in the second class, that of challenged and defended belief, emerging threats to community authority are seen as such and battened down. In the third and last class, belief just stands apart from authority.

Let us glance now at the subversive energies that lie dormant in religious doctrines on the nature of reality. Anyone new to this line of reasoning may question whether the protagonists in religious controversies fully recognize that authority is at stake. There is a tradition in the Humanities that assumes that ontological doubts are purely intellectual. To answer this tradition, ask whether a debater who proposes even a small doubt about the line separating reality from illusion can know that he has his hand on a powerful weapon. The answer is Yes, everyone knows and knows at once. Just imagine yourself in the unlikely situation of being confronted by a student who is never rebellious or even rude, but who seems to lack commitment to his studies. All he says to counter your rebukes is that sorrows and joys are ephemeral; grades and reports likewise; all material things are passing or illusory. Then nothing you can say matters. As an experienced pedagogue, you can see a mile off that if you concede, you have lost your grip on your class. No need for the gentle student to accuse the teacher of being materialist, or to be impolite in any way; it is disruptive enough to authority to insist on the supremacy of spiritual values.

This is the context in which to appreciate the Christological debates of the second century. Witness, for example, the contest between Irenaeus of Lyons against the Gnostics: Irenaeus clearly knew that loss of concreteness and materiality meant loss of authority. On every issue, the Gnostics would spiritualize, philosophize; they also knew that a shift away from the direct personal relation between God and his people, that is the distinctive feature of biblical Judaism, would be a strategic shift in evading control. Laeuchli, in *The Language of Faith*,[11] says that the concept of God the Father is used four hundred times in the New Testament. In Gnostic discourse the term is expanded to include Mother as well as Father; thus it loses some rather definite cognitive contours. When Fatherhood/Motherhood becomes part of the scheme of cosmic layers in which the universe is evolving, the discourse is also moved up into higher levels of abstraction. Again, in the New Testament the term 'righteousness' is equivalent to Justice. The Gnostics give it a different sense in which Justice means equality and equality means universality: thus justice becomes separated from day-to-day ethics and non-ethical justice is absorbed into the abstract theorizing about natural cycles of the universe. And again, in the Old Testament God addresses Israel as a nation, as a political unit, as a land. But the Gnostics would not accept the Old Testament verse (Psalms 24:1): 'The earth is the Lord's and the fullness thereof.' For the Gnostic, the earth was definitely not the Lord's, quite the contrary. The whole idea made no sense to one who thought of salvation as mental and mystical redemption. Irenaeus argued against their over-philosophizing and over-cerebralizing. He was defending a more directly concrete and personally immediate religion. Laeuchli shows him to be fighting for each word, not so much for the word but for its particular placement in the structure that was even then perceived as the essentially Christian doctrine.

The early and continuing Christological crises are never finally settled. What think ye of Christ? Man or God? Is it obscenely blasphemous to suppose the two natures, divine and human, spiritual and material, could be combined – or is it an inoffensive, central, necessary doctrine? Historians who trace the parting of the ways between Eastern and Western thought write as if both traditions once shared a common primitive viewpoint and at a critical moment diverged. The scepticism scale which I am here inviting you to use suggests that the major issues of authority and resistance are always capable of being translated into a choice between spiritualizing and concretizing philosophies. The question then is not to search for the historical origin but for the best analysis of the political conditions which enable one vision to win over its opposite.

In a great essay on the genesis of the distinctive Western attitudes, Louis Dumont[12] goes back to the very early Church, noting the views of the Fathers on the state, on slavery, and private property. He finds in the early Church an ambivalent attitude to secular life: to the faithful soul embarked on life's pilgrimage the world is both an obstacle to, and a necessary condition of, salvation. The life of the world was neither denied nor rejected, just relativized by comparison with the beatific vision of God in paradise. The hierarchical scheme allowed great latitude in principles of government. The spot on which Dumont wants to put his finger, the defining point for the beginnings of our Western tradition, is the point at which the relation between persons and persons yields pride of place to the relation between persons and things. In the early view the things can only be means of or hindrances to salvation; they hardly counted in the hierarchy compared with relations between persons, sets of beings made in the image of God. In our own days the crucial relationships have become economic (that is the relation between persons and things) and the hierarchy of values has disappeared under a homogenizing common denominator – material wealth. This trend is an instance of the many philosophies which dichotomize the universe between spiritual and material: sometimes a balance is held, sometimes the spiritual comes out on top, sometimes the material wins.

At the beginning of the fourth century, the emperor Constantine converted to Christianity. Then Christian thinkers (I am still following Dumont) were faced with a formidable problem. They could no longer devalue the state and the world as they had done heretofore. The state made a step towards the Church, and the Church had to take some responsibility for the secular world. Then followed frictions, disputes about doctrine, the pressure to axiomatize, resolved by denouncing heresy or by efforts to reconcile the different traditions of Alexandria and Antioch. There appears a dominant social and political concern to unify. Dumont writes:

> Il est remarquable que la plupart de ces débats aient été centrés sur la difficulté de concevoir et de formuler correctement l'union du Dieu et de l'homme en Jésus-Christ. Or c'est là ce qui nous apparait rétrospectivement comme le cœur, le secret du christianisme considéré dans tout son

développement historique, soit, en termes abstraits, l'affirmation d'une transition effective entre l'au-delà et ce monde,
entre l'extra-mondain et l'intra-mondain, l'*Incarnation de la
Valeur.*[13]

In its distinctive unfolding, Louis Dumont sees two crucial
moments in the turning of the Western tradition away from
hierarchy. The first was the fourth-century conversion of the
Roman Emperor and the consequent establishment of the Church.
This in itself did not cause the hierarchical doctrine which balanced priestly and kingly power to be abandoned, but caused it
to be very carefully enunciated. But at the second point, in the
mid-century, the Pope conferred on the Frankish king the role
of protector and ally of the Roman Church: almost a treaty
between princes; and then in 800 AD, Leo III crowned Charle-
magne emperor in St Peter's, Rome. The Popes now arrogated
to themselves a supreme political function; they made territorial
claims on their own behalf; in a later stage they could be conceived of as delegating temporal power to the emperor. By taking
over this material world in the name of the spiritual one, by so
nakedly throwing in its lot with political power, the Church led
Western thought to abandon hierarchical principles. Paradoxically, it started the West on the slippery slope of subordinating
the spiritual to the material which Dumont elaborately traces out,
culminating in the rise in the eighteenth and nineteenth centuries
of economic theory, our own special contribution to the cultural
history of the world.

Something about the commitment to ordering and organizing
other people is incompatible with nihilism, relativism, romantic
idealism, and radical scepticism. Commitment in itself explains
nothing, it is that which is to be explained. Weberian sociologists
are often content to explain religious variation by reference to the
spirit of the culture. But this tautology does not help to explain
the great divergence between the Eastern and the Western traditions. If we are to follow up the explicit connection between
the Western experience of empire and the Christian Incarnational
theology,[14] we should take account of the sheer physical difficulty
of laying the Indian subcontinent under unified control. There
can be physical conditions so hostile to sustained political order
that dominion is virtually impossible however strong the commitment may be. The Moguls had a great period of Empire; then,

between their reign and the British Empire, there was a history of numerous local princedoms; of ephemeral, arbitrary power; a history of local dynasties under attack and overthrown. We should also recall the sanskritizing success of the Brahmins,[15] their universal spiritual hegemony and their self-denying exclusion from exercise of power.

After a hundred years of Marxist criticism of ideology, the beliefs and values of Western intellectuals are rather well documented.[16] Their tendency to cerebralize and spiritualize the glaring social abuses of the day, though tempting a comparison with Eastern philosophy, is generally given separate treatment from the Brahmin: the differences seem overwhelming because one is the product of the Capitalist and the other of the Caste system. If we compare the position in which the Brahmins express their commitment to hierarchy, we see them in helpless contemplation of arbitrary power, wedged between rulers and exploited masses. These are the conditions of the intellectuals of Western Capitalism against whom Joseph Schumpeter inveighs.[17] Their discontent and unrealism sprang, he argues, from their being trapped without esteem or dignified employment between the ruling class and the populace whose cause they espoused in furthering their own quest for higher status. Harsher than Schumpeter's measured condemnation, George Orwell[18] reviles the English 'highbrow with his domed forehead and stalklike neck', and the 'irresponsible carping of people who have never been and never expect to be in a position of power', and the 'emotional shallowness of people who live in a world of ideas and have little contact with reality', and above all – 'their severance from the common culture of the country' – their lack of concern for injustice. His diagnosis also depends on the relative shift in opportunities for employment: while the empire was expanding there were rewards for ambitious men. In the stagnation of empire when the educated found themselves unesteemed, they denied political realities, espoused contradictory and impossible projects and cherished ultramontane loyalties.

Compare these fragmentary images of the post-First World War intelligentsia in Europe with Isaiah Berlin's great essay on the young Russian radicals of the 1830s and 1840s.[19] This is too early a date for Capitalism. The framework is the sheer weakness and arbitrary cruelty of the political system. The Russian intelligentsia were members of a dedicated order, almost a secular priesthood. On the one hand, they had glimpsed a new social order in the West, on the other, the government of the nation became progressively more difficult. As the gulf between people and rulers widened, the repression by the ruling elite became more harsh. Between the oppressors and the oppressed, a small, cultivated French-speaking class became painfully aware of the gap between Russia and the West, and of the difference between justice and injustice and of their own stake in the regime which too hasty reform might easily overturn: 'Some were reduced to cynicism, some to noble eloquence and futile despair.' Berlin identifies three social categories under Tsar Nicholas I: a dead, oppressive government hindering change, the vast mass of the population, wretched, weak, and ignorant peasants, and this small, educated class, the intelligentsia. Their ideas came to them from German Romanticism.

> For anyone who was young and idealistic in Russia in 1830 and 1840, or simply human enough to be depressed by the social conditions of this country, it was comforting to be told that the appalling evils of Russian life – the ignorance and poverty of the serfs, the illiteracy and hypocrisy of the clergy, the corruption, inefficiency, brutality, arbitrariness of the governing class, the pettiness, the sycophancy, and the inhumanity of the merchants – that the entire barbarous system, according to the sages of the West, was a mere bubble on the surface of life. It was ultimately unimportant, the inevitable attribute of the world of appearances which seen from a superior vantage point, did not disturb the deeper harmony. (Berlin, in Hardy and Kelly (eds) op. cit.: 142).

A dominant element in the German romantic movement was to transpose Spinoza's science into aesthetic terms, to conceive of life as an artistic creation of some cosmic deity – to convert it from a scientific to a mystical or transcendental view of life and history.

What do these varied scenarios imply about the conditions for sceptical philosophy? Radical scepticism may flourish where an elite, educated and privileged, is faced with unacceptable arbitrary power, and is helpless to challenge it. Any equilibrium between spiritual and temporal authority is probably a precarious ideal, precarious in the East where it topples over to a fully idealized philosophy and precarious in the West where it topples to a materialist individualized philosophy. On this approach, the top-pling could be reversed temporarily in either direction, according to the scope for effective responsibility by the educated elite.

At this point, looking round at ourselves, we find the whole Western scene is changed. Instead of a repressed minority, the idealists – sympathetically drawn by Berlin, excoriated by Schum-peter, derided by Orwell – are now in the ascendent. When a pragmatic ruling class governed the inarticulate masses, the mainstream philosophers denounced radical scepticism wherever it reared its head: absurd, inconsistent, impossible, incoherent, unfeasible, nihilistic, and so on. Thus they saved the cause of reason. But now those philosophers say those same things in vain.

Anthropologists have always been attracted to cultural relativ-ism and I do not doubt that they have relished the iconoclastic threat.[20] Their doubts were never really threatening to the estab-lished order. The cutting edge of relativism today, as Hilary Putnam puts it,[21] derives explicitly from Marx, Freud, and Nietzsche. They taught us that 'Below what we are pleased to regard as our most profound spiritual and moral insight lies a seething cauldron of power drives, economic interests, and selfish fantasies.' All ideology is now dubbed as culture-relative, with a set of unconscious, guiding assumptions whose determinants are non-rational. In vain does Putnam protest: 'If all argument were mere rationalization, it would make no sense either to argue for or to hold any views.'[22] He is accusing the relativists of the most fundamental paradox of all. Naming Kuhn, Feyerabend, and Foucault as the leaders, Putnam frankly identifies the politically subversive intent:

> . . . while Kuhn has increasingly moderated his view, both Feyerabend and Michel Foucault have tended to push it to extremes. There is something political in their minds: both Feyerabend and Michel Foucault link our present insti-tutionalized criteria of rationality with capitalism, exploita-tion, and even with sexual repression. Clearly there are many divergent reasons why people are attracted to extreme relativism today, the idea that all existing institutions are bad being one of them.[23]

Without going to the extremists in the philosophy of science, we cannot avoid hearing a parallel tale in every branch of social knowledge. Economics experiences a profound methodological upheaval. Tests of scientific method are applied to economic theory and it fails; its once vaunted predictions are mocked; its assumptions severely exposed to philosophic doubt, its proofs relegated to mere rhetoric.[24] Historiography now holds a more important place than straight history. Political philosophy finds its theory of representation built on Arrow's inescapable paradox. Jurisprudence is ferociously engaged in a debate on the legitimacy of law.[25] Literary theory would transform all human experience to the status of texts – an extreme idealist position.[26] The philosophers of science are at the centre of the storm. Science is based on a collection of provisional statements. The logicians themselves have abandoned their claims to be able to found rational discourse in reason, and also the claim to identify analytic self-evident truths. On all sides radical scepticism is advancing. Scholars in religious studies would be recluses indeed not to have heard that a crisis of epistemology is here. What think ye of dreams? What do scholars in religion feel about secular scepticism? They ought to feel liberated. It is as if they have been imprisoned since the sixteenth century behind a wall built to keep out the dragon of scientific objectivity. But now science and religion are no longer polarized by two distinctive kinds of reasoning. Not only the religion lacks rational foundation – but every intellectual enterprise whatsoever is exposed to the merciless, sceptical enquiry: 'How do you know? By what authority?' And the answers lead back in infinite regress or run in self-referencing circles. The dragon has expired in its own poisonous exhalations. But there is no victory. Radical scepticism could yet defeat us all.

Should we rejoice at being liberated by the triumphal on-sweep of radical scepticism? Does not more sophistication seem preferable to less? Is it not a position of advantage to throw doubt on earlier scholars' simple-mindedness? Do they not seem like schoolboys, scrambling for grades in a well-defined world of textbook heroes and comic baddies? 'Never glad confident morning again!' Clifford Geertz seems to sigh, half regretfully, comparing his own doubts with the earlier generation of British anthropologists who worked, after all, in a framework of empire.[27]

On the one hand, Western incarnational theology, with its will to consecrate institutions and make them work, tips easily towards materialist values. On the other hand, the Eastern doctrine of illusion, despairing of good institutions, easily tips towards privileged withdrawal. Choose the more sophisticated path if you will. As you do so, we shall hear you invoking metaphors of ritual cleanness. You will separate yourselves from dirty politics, and look down on those crude officers of public administration, whose minds such complicated doubts would never cross. They have a vested interest in legitimacy and so in the possibility of rational discourse. It is only the excluded elite who seriously entertain radical doubt and allow it to subvert the enterprise of communication.

In what sense do we form an excluded elite? If discourse be possible, that is the first question to ask. Have we chosen to withdraw from the murky paths of politics and power? Or do inherent processes in the machine of government exclude us, as they excluded the Russian intelligentsia and the European intellectuals? If we are excluded against our will, then who are the tyrannical rulers squeezing us between their minions and the toiling masses they oppress? At the national level the parallel does not hold up well. But new communications technology has expanded the boundaries of effective influence from nation state to hemisphere. From the north facing southward, we cannot miss the inarticulate, miserably poor millions of oppressed. From north to south the analogy is startling. Yes – we are as keenly attached to our privileged status as any Brahmins; aware of collective guilt and indulging in idealist rhetoric as much as the Russian intelligentsia and just as despairing about the injustices committed in our name. I am not sure if we are excluded involuntarily, though I can see the imponderable machineries which we individually cannot influence. We are wedged between inhuman rulers and suffering masses. I am also convinced that if we all choose the path to subjective idealism there will be no sustained intellectual support or 'group-wise'[28] intelligent effort to heal the widening divisions.

There is another choice. Philosophers of religion could take philosophy seriously. At this point, highly accredited enquirers into the nature of reasoning converge in a new kind of response to radical scepticism. There is no way for protecting the claims for rational foundations of discourse. The ground rules (that is the conditions for knowledge) cannot be tested and proved in the same ways as discourse itself is tested. The step-by-step construction of a logical argument, correctly performed, leads to valid conclusions. But though valid, the conclusions may not be accepted as true. (Remember how Pascal was criticized for the way in which he categorized the universe.) The question of foundations is about acceptable categories, not about valid logic. So what does acceptability depend upon?

One by one the great logicians of our day are reluctantly coming out with the same kind of answer. The ultimate and only authority for the way the universe is divided up has to be the community. For Wittgenstein it is the community making rules for its life in common. For Quine it is the speech community which settles issues of sameness and identity by assigning items of the world to words and words to classes.[29] Putnam admits appeal to cultural acceptability: '. . . our world is a human world, and what is conscious and not conscious, what has sensations and what doesn't, what is qualitatively similar to what and what is dissimilar, are all dependent ultimately on our human judgements of likeness and difference.'[30] Nelson Goodman says of acceptability that since it 'involves inductive validity, which involves right categorization, which involves entrenchment, habit must be recognized as an integral ingredient of truth'.[31] Each of these philosophers is laying emphasis on the community processes for shaping the building blocks for its own logical discourse. First there begins a community engagement in a form of social intercourse: its usages entrench certain categories or ways of sorting; the entrenchment in community life gives rise to acceptable categorization upon which logical arguments are founded. Community is not separable from logic: the mistake was to suppose logic had an independent existence, held up by its own bootstraps.[32] The foundations of rational discourse are found in community commitment to stability and coherence.

The argument seems to point in terrifying directions. We know that historical communities have founded their logic upon an utterly reprehensible categorization of the world. Is this a reason for not daring to look at the process by which acceptable categories are shaped and then entrenched? One can forgive the logicians for stopping, having come thus far. But the scholars in religion should surely see the advantages to their work of following it through. Their own professional interests should encourage them in a programme of researching into how the faces of God are formed in the social process of sorting out the world. In that process there is always some fiduciary element, underwriting the prior assent which discourse needs. It is not only assent to arguments. Anyway arguments can be and are publicly contested by logic. Assent to the kinds of building blocks that logic can use emerges from hidden social processes that anthropologists uncover and which are of prime relevance to the study of religion.

Logicians' reflections on the grounds of reasoning are not so remote and specialized that philosophers of religion can credibly stand aside. In a new context, Pascal's argument holds still. If they stay within their protective fortress, still imagining the fight between science and religion is being waged outside, they will likely be overwhelmed by the great waves of scepticism and they will not even recognize the new argument about religion that is pressing to be formulated.

If Pascal felt that the metaphysical proofs of the existence of God were too complicated, he would feel the same about current attempts to prove the foundations of rational thought. How would he constitute the terms of a modern wager? I am not sufficiently skilled in decision theory to marshal the arguments for a bet on reality versus illusion, on the likelihood of a sharp difference between waking and dreaming. To my naïve eye the probable value of deciding to live by a simple faith in reality seems high. Finally, Pascal's bet was not about deciding to believe, as is commonly thought, but about deciding to live as if one believed, to live in the community of other believers. Either way he considered the decision would be validated to the extent that belief or disbelief would follow upon the choice of human company.

## ACKNOWLEDGEMENT

I thank Wendy O'Flaherty for the invitation to give the first version of this to the American Academy of Religion at its meeting in Dallas, December 1983, and Michel Cartry and Luc de Heusch for the invitation to give the second version to the CNRS Laboratoire, 'Systèmes de pensée en Afrique noire', March 1984. I am particularly grateful to Germaine Dieterlen and to Jeffrey Stout for hardhitting criticism.

This paper was first published under the title 'Pascal's Great Wager' in L'Homme XXV, 1 (1985), and in Power, Action and Belief: A New Sociology of Knowledge?, edited by John Law, Sociological Review Monograph No. 32 (1986), London, Methuen.

# NOTES

1 Ian Hacking, *The Emergence of Probability* (Boston, Cambridge University Press, 1975).

2 Blaise Pascal, *Pensées sur la religion et sur quelques autres sujets*, edited by Louis Lafuma (Paris, Éditions du Luxembourg, 1951), Fragment: 190–381.

3 Wendy Doniger O'Flaherty, *Dreams, Illusions and Other Realities* (Chicago, Chicago University Press, 1984).

4 E. Gombrich, 'Illusion and Art', in E.H. Gombrich and R.L. Gregory (eds), *Illusion in Nature and Art* (London, Duckworth, 1973), pp. 193–243.

5 Pascal, *Pensées sur la religion*, Fragment: 131–246.

6 Hilary Putnam, *Reason, Truth and History* (Cambridge, Cambridge University Press, 1981), p. 124.

7 Bimal Krishna Matilal, 'The Logical Illumination of Indian Mysticism', an Inaugural Lecture delivered before the University of Oxford (Oxford, Clarendon Press, 1977). See also *The Navya-Nyaya Doctrine of Negation*, and *The Semantics and Ontology of Negative Statements in Navya-Nyaya Philosophy* (Cambridge, MA, Harvard University Press, 1968). Matilal demonstrates that the Indian philosophers who founded a school of logic on the principle of negation were as rigorously rational as the analytic shools of the West and that their philosophy, by challenging other schools, forced them to organize their thought systematically. The Indian 'mystical philosophers' were serious professionals whose writing was intended to be available to rational discussion, and whose logic is inherently the same as Western logic.

8 There are many situations in which neither the words 'believe' nor 'disbelieve' apply. See Jean Pouillon, 'Remarques sur le verbe "croire" ', in M. Izard and P. Smith (eds), *La Fonction symbolique. Essais d'anthropologie* (Paris, Gallimard, 1979) ('Bibliothèque des Sciences humaines').

9 Peter Berger, *The Heretical Imperative: Contemporary Possibilities of Religious Affirmation* (Garden City, NJ, Anchor Press, 1979).

10 Louis Dumont, *Homo hierarchicus. Essai sur le système des castes* (Paris, Gallimard, 1966) ('Bibliothèque des Sciences humaines').

11 S. Laeuchli, *The Language of Faith: Introduction to the Semantic Dilemma of the Early Church* (NY, Abingdon Press, 1962).

12 Louis Dumont, *Essais sur l'individualisme. Une perspective anthropologique sur l'idéologie moderne* (Paris, Le Seuil, 1983), pp. 46–7.

13 Ibid.: 51.

14 Marcel Gauchet (1984) 'Fin de la Religion?', *Le Débat* 28:155–75.

15 M.N. Srinivas, 'A Note on Sanskritization and Westernization', *The Far Eastern Quarterly* (1956) XV, 4:481–96.

16 Edward Shils, *The Intellectuals and the Powers and Other Essays* (Chicago, University of Chicago Press, 1972).

17 Joseph Schumpeter, *Capitalism, Socialism and Democracy* (New York, Harper Bros, 1942).

18 George Orwell, 'Your England', in Colin Bell and Sol Engel (eds), *Inside the Whale* (New York, Pergamon, 1978).
19 Isaiah Berlin, in Henry Hardy and Aileen Kelly (eds), *Russian Thinkers* (New York, Viking Press, 1978).
20 Elvin Hatch, *Culture and Morality, The Relativity of Values in Anthropology* (New York, Columbia University Press, 1983).
21 Hilary Putnam, *Reason, Truth and History* (Boston, Cambridge University Press, 1981).
22 Ibid.: 161.
23 Ibid.: 126.
24 Donald McCloskey, 'The Rhetoric of Economics', *Journal of Economic Literature* 21:481–517.
25 Stephen Presser, Rorschach Lecture, 1983.
26 Richard Rorty, 'Idealism and Textualism', in *Consequences of Pragmatism* (Minneapolis, University of Minnesota Press, 1982), Ch. 8:139.
27 Clifford Geertz, (1983) 'Slide Show, Evans-Pritchard's African Transparencies', *Raritan*, Fall: 62–80.
28 Schumpeter's word for the kind of social know-how he felt was so often lacking in the European intellectual.
29 Saul Kripke, *Wittgenstein on Rules and Private Language* (New York, Blackwell, 1982).
30 Putnam, op. cit.: 102.
31 Nelson Goodman, 'Notes on the Well-Made World', *Erkenntnis* 19:99–107, and *Of Mind and Other Matters* (Cambridge, MA, Harvard University Press, 1984).
32 S.B. Barnes, 'Reference', unpublished paper for the Edinburgh Science Studies Unit, 1982.

# 14

# A CREDIBLE BIOSPHERE

I have chosen to talk about credibility and reflexivity because this is (I imagine) the sort of thing you expect from an anthropologist. They used to say that the big difference between anthropology and sociology was not method, or history of the discipline, so much as focus of interests; sociology, they would say, is driven by its concern for current social problems, anthropology falls only too easily into metaphysics and collectibles, erotic and exotic. To do honour to this occasion, I have picked one problem on which to fasten my professional speculations: the biosphere. The question is whether it is endangered and if so whether we should do anything about it? On this topic I will ask whether the bad prophecies of the scientists are credible. From credibility in general my speculations will be led to culture and to reflexivity.

During the last few hundred years human action has drastically modified the natural environment. No one is going to doubt the transformations that we have effected, as to the disappearance of forests, as to the drainage of wetlands, as to irrigation of dry lands, the extension and conversion of grazing lands. Given this agreement among scientists (and ourselves) as to the past, what I find really interesting is the disagreement about the future.

Is there really a global catastrophe ahead of the world? Some say 'No'; most scientists say definitely 'Yes', but the response from lay people is very divided. I want to examine today the distribution of belief and unbelief. Like anthropologists we can distance ourselves from the case, considering which scientists we should credit, the soothsayers or the doom sayers, as if it were the same kind of problem as that of the credibility of medicine, or of religious scepticism and fundamentalism in the modern world.

How are we to give an account of unbelief? When it is a matter of harm from carcinogens, there is the excuse that the scientists are divided.[1] When the question is whether to be for or against nuclear power for peaceful purposes, again the scientists are divided.[2] But in the case of the harm we are doing to the biosphere they speak with remarkable unity. Their consensus is all the more impressive in that science in general has become much more cautious. It is less confident of its claims than it was fifty years ago.

The problem of the greenhouse effect takes us through the long sweep of human history. It is partly a question of scale. What used to be local incidents of pollution or damage now involve many nations. The choice between ecological conservation and economic growth now reflects complex linkages. Energy and agriculture feed back to deforestation and climatic change.[3] We have moved from a regional to a global scale. The new integrative perspective emphasizes biogeochemical processes and their connections with climate. Parallel to the scientific effort, the broad patterns of human development have been studied in the world-system view of modern history. The modern world supports three times the human population and a hundred times the industrial activity that it did one hundred years ago. That is rapid change. As William Clark says in his introduction to *Sustainable Development of the Bio-sphere*, a new intellectual mood 'has focused on the interplay of institutions, technologies, and resources over what Braudel has called *la longue durée*, thus providing fertile ground for the collaboration of economists, historians and geographers'.[4]

Presumably individual sociologists are engaged in this fervent discussion of the future of our globe. But I do not hear loud or clear professional voices. In every scientific overview I read some tribute to what is called 'the social component', but I do not see that the sociologists feel bound to engage professionally on what this social component is and how it works.

Most scholars treat the relevant period as the last three hundred years. That is approximately from the bloodless English Revolution of 1688 through the bloody French Revolution, and on through the nineteenth century to today. In that time a number of processes have created our present world order and, it is widely agreed, have produced seemingly irreversible changes. Here I quote from J.F. Richards[5] for a wide-angle view of the historical trends.

1 Expansion of the European frontier of settlement into the New World, the great Eurasian steppe, and Australasia.
2 Steady growth in human population from 641 million estimated for 1700 to 4435 million estimated for 1980.
3 Dramatic growth in the spatial extent of cities and their population.
4 Increased use of fossil fuels and hydroelectric power, thus creating a revolution in transport, communications, and industrial production.
5 Development of scientific methods, institutions, and means for research and discovery.
6 Development of new weaponry with global reach and capacity for near-global destruction.
7 Dramatic increase in our ability to cure the body and curb disease.
8 Growth in scale, efficiency, and stability of complex organization (i.e. bureaucracies).
9 Emergence of self-regulating, price-fixing global markets for goods and services.
10 Emergence of a world division of labour between the North (or core) developed countries and the developing countries of the South (or periphery).

That sums it up, except for a drastic effect on the peoples whom anthropologists traditionally study. We have to add that along with all of this has gone the expansion of more intensive sedentary agriculture and in consequence the squeeze on tribal peoples engaged in shifting cultivation or in pastoral nomadism.

Evidently our cultural bias over this period has been towards expansion. We have made ourselves very efficient in exploiting natural resources. But these social and scientific trends have had the following effects on the environment.

1 World expansion of arable land: for every region an enormous and unreversed growth of arable land, to match the demand from swelling populations, and resulting in a near doubling of the pace of soil erosion in the world.
2 Deforestation, woods and forests in retreat before the advance of arable land.

As early as the seventeenth century the forested plains of eastern Germany and Poland underwent steady clearance and plowing as the market for eastern European wheat expanded. By the eighteenth century New World lands in eastern North America and in coastal Brazil felt pressures for marketable wood and arable land. By the early nineteenth century forested covers in India and the midwestern USA were being felled for development purposes, and in the mid-nineteenth century rapid deforestation had begun in Himalayan India, Australasia, Southeast Asia, South Africa, Manchuria, Taiwan, and elsewhere. The end of the century brought east and west Sub-Saharan Africa, the American far west and Siberia into this process. The twentieth century has seen a nearly global onslaught on woodlands, with, after World War II, swelling pressures for economic development in the era of decolonization.

3 The drainage of wetlands, especially with use of new technology since 1870, has dramatically increased. The drying up of marshes and swamps releases stored carbon into the atmosphere and changes water tables. When this type of habitat disappears, many plant and animal species retreat or disappear too, and tribal communities who used to live on them are forced to work as sharecroppers in the new agricultural regime.

4 Irrigation of arid lands is a major environmental change. The trend to controlled watering and cultivation of dry lands means that few rivers flowing through arid or semi-arid regions remain untapped by irrigation schemes, with effects on the world hydrological cycle. As Professor Richards says:

Making the deserts bloom corresponds to some of our deepest aesthetic and cultural instincts. The drama of towering dams, huge turbines, and massive canal systems has made large irrigation systems one index of modernity (p. 63).

5 Grazing lands of the world have been reduced in favour of arable and heavy, sustained grazing for supplying meat to the increased human population finally depletes the grasslands.

Summing up, Richards says that in the relatively short period since 1700 human control over the natural environment has transformed it into an anthropogenic or human-determined system: 'By far the most important reason for the changes that have occurred in the biota, the atmosphere, and the oceans is the growing efficiency and global scale of man's economic activity' (p. 68).

His wide-angled survey is a corrective to the way we usually hear of threats and disasters, which is one at a time, encouraging hope for item-by-item solutions. But the biosphere is one range of interlinked problems, not caused by car-drivers as such, nor now suddenly by domestic use of aerosol pumps, or even by recent cutting down of trees; the problems have been going on for a long time and are not to be solved so easily merely by giving up one or other of these activities. The trends are produced by very basic transformations of our social organization. He speaks for many other scientists when he says that he does not expect these trends to be diverted or reversed. We are going to have to live with them. In which case, the question is about the kinds of social organization best able to deal with the global threat. Such a question falls right into the court of the sociologists.

A biologist asks: 'What images are appropriate for thinking about an Earth transformed by human action?' (Clark: 11). One group of ecologists seems to use a model of the Garden of Eden spoiled by human misdoings; another prefers the model of a garden that needs a lot of care. Another asks what kind of society can be envisaged that will be able to deliver the care? To me and to many that question seems urgent. I am convinced by the evidence that, as far as we can tell, the biosphere is subject to unprecedented strains. I am afraid of holes in the sky and of global warming and floods and droughts, and I also take it for granted that we should be thinking of how to forfend such extremities. But I find that many of my friends mistrust these tales of doom; there have been too many in the past; nature has proved herself to be too robust for them to believe in the advent of a global disaster. Others are fatalists; they believe in the seriousness of the problems as sincerely as I do, but feel that we are totally impotent; we might just as well ignore the warnings, for there is nothing that we can do or ever could have done.

What about our diverse attitudes? What do the sociologists say? Are our views just randomly distributed? just psychological? Or is there an underlying cultural explanation for our respective optimism, fatalism, and pessimism? In an interesting set of surveys in the 1970s Stephen Cotgrove[6] found that the British public tended to fall into two groups taking opposite views of the stability and resilience of nature: on the one hand some respondents whom he dubbed the cornucopians believed in the unendingly lavish bounty of nature, and so could not get worried about rumours of resources drying up; on the other hand respondents whom he called the catastrophists believed that nature is fragile and unable to resist the crash that is just round the corner. Roughly speaking these divergent views of nature were interpreted as justifications for the correlated preferences expressed by the same subjects on political or economic issues.

The idea that polarized views of nature enter into any well-developed cultural debate is central to my own work as an anthropologist. I am about to argue that if sociologists wish to comment on the social component in the transformation of the environment they would do well to join the anthropologists and think systematically[7] about culture. First they might like to do a little auto-analysis and decide whether they are cornucopians, catastrophists, or fatalists, and having recognized their own position they might like to consider whether it enters their larger agenda for life and art. If their attitude to nature turns out to be not very relevant in upholding any of the rest of their serious thinking, I would be inclined to count them along with the fatalists, those who think it may or may not be true but in either case regard it as no concern of theirs. It will be a help in following the argument to have made up your mind as to where you stand.

Cornucopians! Catastrophists! Fatalists! As we listen to the biosphere scientists we match their narrative with our own narrative about how the world ought to be, and is. And so, according to its fit, we doubt or believe.

What is culture? I take it to be an ongoing, never resolved argument about rightness of choice. Following Pierre Bourdieu I take high culture to be an argument about taste, and I take low culture to be an argument about morals. In both the stakes are heavy.[8] In the debate one side is striving to capture and control legitimacy for themselves, the other to defend the control they have. Argument is too soft a word for the struggle. Since the winning side gains legitimacy, there is little left for the losers but drastic down-grading or exile. Both arguments (about taste and morality) take place within an existing framework of power and authority, consequently within a structured framework (that Bourdieu calls *habitus*). Being structured means of course that culture cannot affirm all things. Something affirmed means something else denied. Blindspots and unthinking rejection are just as essential to culture as seeing and affirming. The great merit of this view is that it systematically connects the cognitive and affective side of culture to the strategies of the contestants for legitimacy.[9] Their rhetorical and other strategies can be analysed as part of their struggle to create the good society.

We seem to be very short on models of the good society. Over the last three hundred years the winning side in the cultural debates of the world has successsfully presented a steady, cumulative argument in favour of expansion, individual freedom, the sloughing off of chains and shackles. As we saw, expansion has indeed taken place. The image of restriction is a menacing spectre of blind superstition and unreason. And yet, as I hear the ecologists, there will be a need for legitimate control on a global scale. While legitimacy is as hard as ever to achieve, the message of the scientists is that the social component in the matter of the biosphere is about legitimate authority. It goes almost without saying that to put the cultural machine into reverse after three hundred years is deeply counter-cultural. For some the prospect is so contradictory and unacceptable to their active role in the cultural debates that either they say nothing or they are forced to take the negative position of unbelief.

An expressive sociology speaks for the dominant culture to which the profession belongs. It speaks with a strong voice when it defends its cultural ideals. It can and must express the sorrows of the oppressed. It can and must denounce injustice. Far be it from me to imply even faintly that sociology should not be fully engaged in the cultural struggle of its time, and fully expressive. But it needs to wear another hat when thinking about the threat to the biosphere. To enter this debate we need a reflexive sociology. That would be a sociology temporarily detached from its normal expressive functions. Sociology would need to stand outside of itself and its cultural niche. It might need to consider what kind of society would be able to curb the cultural pressure which it faithfully serves under its other hat, the cultural pressure to delegitimize control and to license ever more exploiting, escaping, and expanding.

A reflexive culture that takes all sides at once is a contradiction, but I don't think that the idea of a reflexive sociology is absurd. It only needs to set a deliberate trap to catch the reflexive moments in which we privately indulge. Individually we are capable of great honesty and insight. We can see our postures as responding to institutional pressures. We are individually capable of recognizing ourself in the Other and, without losing sight of the quality of otherness, we are individually capable of embracing the stranger. Cultural analysis can try to do formally what we do informally and privately. Cultural analysis can make a gimmick to capture formally the coherence and rightness of other possible positions in any cultural debate. My platform today is to invite sociologists to join the exercise, and my task is to explain it.

Cultural analysis comes in several forms and deals with a whole range of questions. For the issue in hand I want to present some of the work of Michael Thompson and other anthropologists who have studied the ecologists' views of nature.[10] They find that for any position we might want to take about the fragility or the resilience of nature, there is a practical ecologists' view that we could cite to back our case. Certain 'myths of nature' circulate among natural resource ecologists who manage forests, fisheries, or grazing lands. The ecologists in question observe how the managed eco-systems are modified by the humans. Making suggestions about how to improve their own work they are particularly interested in management problems, that is, in how things go wrong. Thus their concern is on trying to avoid surprises. Four kinds of myths about nature's predictability emerge from their reports.

Nature is capricious,
Nature is fragile,
Nature is robust,
Nature is only robust within limits.

Each of these myths is represented by a little picture of a ball in a landscape (see Figure 14.1).

The anthropologists have matched the four myths of nature favoured by practical ecologists to four positions in the cultural struggle (see Figure 14.2).

Myth is not being used here in any derogatory sense. Each of the ecological views is as fully justifiable as the others. Each sums up an enormous experience and vast array of learning about humans interacting in eco-systems. There is no way that any of them could be proved right or wrong except in the event. The research that I am outlining much too briefly is a cultural theory of surprise.[11] These come out of two dimensions of social

1. The myth of capricious nature has the ball rolling anywhere on a flat plane. There is no knowing what it will do next, and no use theorizing about it. This gives grounding for the fatalist whose agnosticism is at least theoretically safe from surprises sprung by nature.

2. The myth of fragile nature has the ball on top of a mound, delicately poised in the only place it can be in equilibrium. The smallest shift will roll it off the landscape altogether. For an example of a theory based on·this kind of myth they cite the Malthusian prophecy of overpopulation.

3. The myth that nature is robust has the ball in the bottom of a curve; which ever way it is pushed off centre it can only roll back into position again. (For an example of this kind of grounding myth, Timmerman cites Adam Smith's theory of the invisible hand, where all perturbations will work out for the good.) This is the myth that encourages bold, individualistic experimentation, expansion, and technological development.

4. When nature is robust within limits the ball is in a dip between two hillocks; it can roll within specific limits and be expected to come back safely, but too big a push risks sending it over the edge of the containing frame. This is the myth to encourage risk-averse planning controls, government intervention, restrictions on the market.

*Figure 14.1*

relations,[12] collectivist/individualist, unstructured/structured. Each of the four positions combines a preferred pattern of social relations with certain values which justify and sustain the preference. The theory is that elements of each position form a distinctive, unified cultural package which cannot be unpacked or recombined without radical social change and which is in conflict with the others.

My own research interest has been in the recurrence of these stable cultural patterns and their associated social structures. The

Fatalists:
Nature capricious

Hierarchists:
Nature robust
within limits

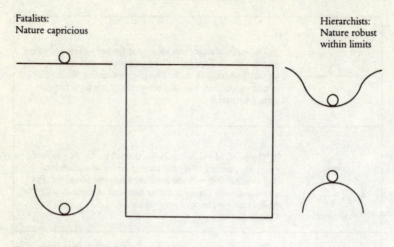

Entrepreneurial expansionists:
Nature robust

Communards:
Nature fragile

*Figure 14.2*

surprise theorists have taken it much further. They have reformul-
ated the cultural patterns in ecological terms. Working with biolo-
gists it was a step to mutual understanding to describe each
cultural pattern as a specialized use of resources, each using the
environment in ways that are incompatible with the needs of the
other cultural types; the grand cultural debate is comparable to
the struggle between species competing for ecological dominance.
The strategies deployed in the struggle by each cultural form map
on to an appropriate 'myth of nature'. Each myth is used as a
rhetorical resource in the cultural struggle. Furthermore, the use
of the myth feeds back to the persons who deploy it so that it
forms part of their view of the way the world is. This makes
good sense. People are not knaves and fools; they believe and act
upon their belief. The myth of nature comes as part of the package
that they have chosen when they opted for a cultural form. Within
that package it is totally convincing that nature is fragile; or
robust; or only robust within constraints; or just capricious,
whichever is the right myth for the rest of the argument. Consequently we can expect that, being sincere and clever, everyone
will have put their money where their mouth is. The commun-

ards will have been reducing their demands on nature as they beseech the rest of us to do the same; the entrepreneurs will have gone on with their expansionist policies; the hierarchists will have been trying to plan and control, while the fatalists stand back and mock their futile efforts.

For surprise research the object of trying to understand cultural bias is to work out the kinds of surprises that each culture lays up in store for itself. Supposing in the event nature turns out to be really ephemeral and the biosphere splits and slides away; then the communards will not be surprised. Saying 'We told you so' will be small comfort to themselves and to the surprise-holders, in this case the entrepreneurs and the hierarchists. But supposing in the event nature turns out to be robust enough to take all the punishment we mete out to her. Then the surprise-holders will be the communards. They will find that they didn't need to reduce their style of life, that they have gained little while their opponents have made large fortunes. And so it goes on. The only people who will get no surprise are the fatalists because they made no bets. I am always intrigued to know how they manage to remain so detached.

For today my main interest in the surprise game, as it is called, is its opening upon reflexivity. In this account what is said in the cultural debate is believed and acted upon and to some extent self-confirming until the big moment of surprise. My argument above led to the point at which I observed how few images we have of good societies. Staying inside the expressive culture, we can only see one good society, our own culture, and the Other as its bad opponent. For the present global problem we would do well to develop gimmicks for appreciating other forms of life, and for contemplating them without rivalry. Such a gimmick, I suggest, is this form of cultural analysis. It presents the social organization as a cognitive screen. What the social organization lets through its cultural meshes is seen, what it blocks are the blindspots. The finer the mesh, the finer the nuances. The longer the perspective, the more history can be held in mind. The more varied and numerous the elements, the richer the pattern, the more the variety of strangers, and the more levels of inclusion. The more self-conscious the awareness of our negotiators, the more hope for conciliatory and strong counsels.

At this point someone tells me that reflexivity is not a question that can be handled sociologically. Certainly in its literary, and philosophical and psychological aspects many doubts can be raised. Such as, how can we know that others know themselves as knowing subjects? What is consciousness? And self-consciousness? Among sociologists such issues have to be more open to inspection and counting. Even though self-knowledge be internal and private, most of the categories of the Other are public. There is nothing to stop us from comparing modern industrial societies on a count of the sheer number of kinds of people that they legislate for. There may be more or less of nested administrative categories, arranging for us to line up by age, immigrant status, gender, colour, birth, education, health, criminality. It should be illuminating to check the varieties of classifications and their numbers and other features of these classifications against other features of the culture.

One of the salutory effects of this gimmick towards reflexivity is that it pushes its practitioners to clarify their own preferences. My own preference has emerged as an idealized form of hierarchy. This has always given me to some degree the professional advantage of feeling out of kilter with the times. It gives me a standpoint from which to see that in this 300-year expansionary trend of Western civilization two kinds of cultures have come to dominate, two that are opposed to hierarchy. Today I am arguing that unless we learn to control our cultivated gut response against the idea of hierarchy we will have no choice among models of the good society to counter our long-established predatory, expansionary trend. By sheer default, among cultural forms hierarchy is the rejected Other. We take it for granted that hierarchy will always fall into traps of routinization and censorship; we see its dangers but have no clear model of how it would be if it worked well. Yet hierarchy is the social form that can impose economies, and make constraints acceptable.

I hope you heard me then. I was using the appropriate myth of nature, that she is only robust within limits, to support my preferred cultural form. I expect to hear you doing the same through this congress.

The argument started with the biosphere and with the question whether it is credible that it is in danger; and if it is, should something be done? And, at the very least, should not sociologists consider the kind of society that can best deal with global crisis? My use of cultural theory suggests that in each case the response is never purely individual. Trying to think of such basic issues taps into deep emotional reserves. The answers well up from attitudes to authority, to accountability and freedom, and from any other experiences that define the relation of one person to others. The principles tend to be inculcated in the school playground, if not at the mother's knee. We have each been making small choices of whom we like to consort with and how much competition we can bear. The little choices lead to big institutions in which we feel comfortable and to a way of life that we want to protect. There is no innocent answer to the question of what sort of good society would best cope with a fragile biosphere. So let us not pretend to be innocent.

Finally let me anticipate the disdain of the academic fatalists in our midst. To me, sitting with the hierarchs, convinced that we can and should do something, their disbelief is amazing. For them, my credulity is naïve, or my claimed concern is ideologically suspect. Their doubts come at two points: they are sceptical about knowledge and sceptical about effective action. Some of them doubt the possibility of knowledge about anything. They are not quite joining the brahmins and buddhist philosophers who teach that reality is illusion. For the fatalists in anthropology (I cannot speak for those in sociology) scepticism about comparisons and categories does not inhibit them from writing, for it leaves them scope for exploring the cage of their own consciousness. Others doubt whether trying to do something is going to be worthwhile. This in itself is a form of withdrawal from the world. Some of them are alone, and others belong together in sects or communes. How do they console themselves?

Our academic fatalists in their opting out of choice remind me of the intelligentsia of nineteenth-century Russia described by Isaiah Berlin[13] in his profoundly insightful *Russian Thinkers*. He describes how these radicals came to decide that there was nothing to be done to cure the evils of the time and so embraced the consolations of the Romantic movement. There they were, a small educated class, with a hostile, arbitrary government on the one hand and an uncomprehending, oppressed peasantry on the other: there they were, a few, cultivated people, sensitive to the gross injustices of the regime, and nervous of the dangers of reform, dangerous to the regime in which they held a privileged but ineffectual place. German romanticism was a liberation for them in the sense that a liberator doesn't solve problems but transforms them. In Berlin's words, romanticism was a new framework in which 'old problems cease to have meaning and new ones appear which have their solutions as it were, already to some degree prefigured in the new universe in which you find yourself. . .' (p. 123). The new universe was aesthetically refined, personal consciousness was cultivated to a high degree, it was sad but uplifting.

Berlin's description of the intelligentsia seduced away from their radical programme by speculations upon appearance and reality has a bearing on my theme. Following Napoleon's invasion, Russia became suddenly aware of Europe and of being in the middle of it (as we have become aware recently of the globe and ourselves in it). He describes the growth of patriotic nationalism (a growth we also know), and the collective sense of guilt for squalor, poverty, inefficiency, and chaos. (And we also know the sense of guilt.) His essay implies that the intelligentsia could have done something. His sardonic tone says that they didn't have to be liberated from their guilt and concern; they could have stayed with it and found ways of being effective for reform.

This is not the lesson I would draw. One cannot say that the young Russian radicals in the 1830s to 1850s shouldn't and didn't have to be fatalists. Cultural theory is not judgemental or determinist, not in the least. The example serves several purposes. For doing analytic sociology the intelligentsia of Tsarist Russia illustrate the social circumstances in which the fatalist position is attractive. There can be many reasons for opting out of pressing problems: one may be that they seem too overwhelming for correction, and another that thinkers occupy a totally peripheral niche in the distribution of power and influence, and another is that the same thinkers themselves are privileged in the regime they dislike. This response would explain the disbelief and apathy that some sociologists feel in face of the biosphere threat.

Still withholding judgement, we can recognize Isaiah Berlin himself as an example of another position. A centralist, avoiding the periphery, he clearly believes that concern can be transmuted into responsibility. This is the position from which the hierarchy looks at life. As far as biosphere doom is concerned, the hierarchists are practising believers. It is terrifying and something should be done. Right or wrong, they will do something. The prospect of the hierarchists determining what to do is of course distasteful to the fatalists. But they should argue the case for not believing from an analytic sociological theory and they should not merely perform the expressive functions of their own culture. This is the advantage of taking up cultural theory. And now I will move into the expressive mode myself.

The biosphere is too large. There are smaller worlds in which cultural analysis can be applied to disbelief, for example, the so-called social sciences which would do well occasionally to move out of their expressive mode, refraining from ardent defence of their cultural positions. To justify their role as analysts the social sciences absolutely need to get distance from their own commitments. Cultural theory is a tool to dispel the fog of expressive propaganda. Cultural analysis is a practice that forces argument on to a franker plane; disputants find themselves arguing directly about how they want decisions to be taken and what kind of society they want, and then how they expect it to function, and from there they are led to their own myths of nature. Is it a ball that might slide anywhere? Is it robust? Is it fragile? And human nature too: cultural theory will not let disputants espouse one view of human nature that is incompatible with their view of society and nature. In this perspective sociological argument loses none of its interest.

This being so, and cultural theory having so many merits, I find it hard to understand why you, the sociologists, can want to stand aside. I would like to persuade you out of your apathy and disbelief. Perhaps you regard the tasks of cultural theory to be impossible, the problems too overwhelming, the results too uncomfortable. Whatever the cause of your having so far refrained from joining in the practice of this method, I am standing within the branch of the social sciences that I have been trained in and speaking in the expressive mode, inviting you to be here too.

## ACKNOWLEDGEMENT

This paper was given at the Gemeinsamer Kongress für Kultur und Gesellschaft, Zurich, October 1988 and was first published under the title 'A Typology of Cultures' in *Kultur und Gesellschaft* (Frankfurt and New York, Campus Verlag, 1989, pp. 85–97).

## NOTES

1 Edith Efron, *The Apocalyptics. Cancer and the Big Lie* (New York, Simon & Schuster, 1984).

2 Mary Douglas and Aaron Wildavsky, *Risk and Culture, An Essay on the Selection of Technological Risk* (California University Press, 1982).

3 William Clark, 'Sustainable Development of the Biosphere: Themes for a Research Program', in W. Clark and R.E. Munn (eds), *Sustainable Development of the Biosphere* (Cambridge University Press, 1986), pp. 5–48.

4 Clark, p. 6.

5 J.F. Richards, 'World Environmental History and Economic Development', Ch. 2 in Clark and Munn 1986, op. cit.

6 Stephen Cotgrove, *Catastrophe or Cornucopia*? (Wiley, 1982).

7 The key word here is 'systematic'. There are plenty of schemes in circulation which purport to explain attitudes and behaviour; the logical connections between the scheme and what it explains are either very weak (as in the case of Maslow's model of social conscience developing when primary needs have been met), or absent (as in the case of 'Life Styles' and 'Values' models current in market research).

8 Pierre Bourdieu, *La Distinction: Critique sociale du Jugement* (Paris, Editions de Minuit, 1974).

9 Some anthropologists write as if culture were unanalysable and autonomous, but this is a professional stance close to fatalism, in so far as it denies the possibility of knowledge and the worthwhileness of trying to know.

10 Michael Thompson, 'A Cultural Basis for Comparison', (pp. 233–60) in Howard Kunreuther and Joanne Linnerooth (eds), *Risk Analysis and Decision Process: The Siting of Liquefied Energy Gas Facilities in Four Countries* (Springer-Verlag, 1983).

11 Michael Thompson and Paul Tayler, 'The Surprise Game: An Exploration of Constrained Relativism' WP–04, The Aston-Warwick Scale Papers (Institute for Management, Research and Development, University of Warwick, Coventry, 1986). Paul Timmermann, 'Mythology and Surprise in the Sustainable Development of the Biosphere', Ch. 16 in Clark and Munn, op. cit. C.S. Holling (ed.), *Adaptive Environmental Assessment and Management* (Wiley, 1978). Holling uses another set of terms: capricious, ephemeral, benign, and perverse/tolerant. The terms I have used are intended to convey the same meaning while fitting better into this present discussion.

12 Mary Douglas, *Natural Symbols, Explorations in Cosmology* (Penguin, 1970).

13 I. Berlin, *Russian Thinkers*, Henry Hardy and Aileen Kell (eds) (Viking Press, 1978).

# 15

# THE DEBATE ON WOMEN PRIESTS

## INTRODUCTION

Religious disagreement is the richest material for cultural analysis. Debates which originate in quite mundane issues tend to become religious if they go on long enough. Durkheim said that religion is the consciousness of the consciousness. Certainly a religious debate goes straight to first principles. It is a more conscious kind of debate than one in which the contenders first disagree about taxes or property rights and then go on to invoke justice, humanity, and God. A religious debate parades transcendental reasons at the outset.

A major policy disagreement, whatever the appearances, has to do with social forms. Each position is a defence of a distinctive idea about what the ideal society is like. The debate is inherently about the right model for organizing community life even when the debaters seem to have their minds on other issues.

I will illustrate the thesis by examining the current debate about the ordination of women priests. First I will summarize the main issues put forward on behalf of women priests. I will also summarize the grounds for rejecting their case, as laid out in the Declaration of the Sacred Congregation on the Admission of Women to the Priesthood (1976). Rome is not alone in her opposition, for the Eastern Churches, Greek and Russian Orthodox, and the others, are all agreed. But we can focus on this document because it is a formal (though not final) expression of objections. Third, I will review various forms of cultural analysis available, before introducing my preferred method. In the result, the analysis will sort out the debating positions into the camps that emerge in any major political conflict, whether it be about the environment, risks from technology, unemployment, or foreign policy.

We will find that Rome, in this Declaration, has replied to some of the women's claims, but not to all. Certain important points go unremarked. For their part, the women do not pay attention to the arguments given by Rome. We see the debaters speaking past each other.

## CLAIMS ON BEHALF OF WOMEN'S ORDINATION

### Vocations

The proper starting place must surely be with the women who seek to be ordained. Their claim is that they have received a divine calling. Deaconess Hilary speaks for many when she says that 'a vocation is not a choosing, but a response to an imperative call' (1975). To many Christians this would seem to settle the matter: there would be nothing more to say. But the Catholic Church has long experience of sifting through alleged vocations and telling devout postulants, male and female, that they are mistaken about their calling. 'The priesthood is not conferred for the honour or advantage of the recipient . . . it is the object of a specific and totally gratuitous vocation: "You did not choose me, no, I chose you; and I commissioned you" ' (John 15:16; cf. Heb. 5:4) (D:6). Indeed, in most religions of the world, where a sacerdotal office is distinguished from other religious roles, the practice is the same. No hierarchical organization is going to abandon control of admission to its responsible offices. In this case, however, the women are in a particularly prejudicial position. Only men constitute the jury which scrutinizes claims to a vocation. Moreover, there is no scrutiny. Women as a category are already pronounced ineligible. And there is nowhere else they can appeal. Of course they can always move out of the denomination which excludes them, and this is done by some.

The Declaration turns immediately to the gender obstacle, and reaffirms the doctrine that gender disables all women from entering the priesthood. It goes directly on to the main issue, which is why maintaining the gender difference is important.

## Injustice

Various and many claims come under the head of injustice. The women suffer from discrimination by an elitist, isolated, priestly caste of 'elderly Italian male celibates' (Gardiner 1975:199–298, quoting Ruether). They see the present as all of a piece with a heinous record of sex discrimination. Many feminists today subscribe to views expressed in 1893 by Matilda Joslyn Gage to the effect that Christianity is a justification produced by men to make acceptable their violent and barbarous treatment of women (Spender 1982:325). Through church history women have been humiliated, treated as defiled and defiling. The defilement issue is being examined by anthropologists as well as by historians. Sometimes theories of pollution have been used to oppress women, sometimes they have been used by women and by men to segregate spheres of gender control. Certainly women have been declared inadequate humans, incomplete humans, childlike humans by individual members of the Christian Church.

To these reproaches Rome replies by denial. Women have been officially honoured, they have often played decisive roles in the life of the Church, Saints Clare, Teresa, and Catherine of Siena have been officially recognized as great spiritual teachers; whereas it is true that offensive things have been said by individuals about women, this did not affect the pastoral concern which they received. Rome insists that her gender distinction is not discriminatory: masculine and feminine are distinguished because they play complementary parts in the divine plan of salvation.

The women have plenty of replies to these objections: it is not true that pastoral attitudes have not been affected by unthinking discriminatory bias; the Church of Rome's ruling on contraception and abortion exemplifies it. The women's movement will not accept that men, their historic exploiters, may dictate how their bodies shall be used.

## Misinterpretation

It is widely asserted by feminist theologians that the Church organization has built its discriminatory pattern of power by systematic misinterpretation of the gospels and of the Old Testament. To this complaint Rome does harken, and replies with its own list of crucial quotations from source. The whole argument here shifts to textual criticism, a subject beyond the present scope and deserving a separate paper.

## The evolution of doctrine

The women point out that doctrine is not a static thing: it has shifted before and it will surely shift again in tune with the cultural attitudes of the day. They cite the case of slavery, once condoned as a necessary evil and now condemned. They could cite the case of usury and other developments of doctrine which would support their case that the times are right for new thinking. The Declaration answers by distinguishing between doctrinal and disciplinary changes (DSC.4), allows that the latter occur, insists that the present issue is doctrinal not disciplinary, but does not meet the issue that doctrinal development has always taken place and must do so.

## Male appropriation of cognitive categories

The claim is that Catholic teaching and doctrine give women no scope for understanding their own experience. New historical scholarship has revealed how women's consciousness of themselves is stunted and deformed by a male-oriented conceptual apparatus. The epistemological attack is strongly supported in the women's movement (Friedan 1963; Daly 1973, 1984; Cixous 1981). The question of women's self-understanding is not taken seriously.

## Hierarchy is wrong

A cental plank in the women's case as it evolves is a principled objection to authoritarian institutions. 'Recognizing that deep damage has been afflicted upon consciousness under phallocracy's myths and institutions, continue to Name patriarchy as the perverted paradigm and source of other social evils' (Daly 1984:xii). Hierarchy is specially undesirable in religion.

Although Rome does not think it relevant in this context to justify her hierarchical organization, the Declaration reaffirms it. Citing Pope Innocent III at the beginning of the thirteenth century: 'Although the Blessed Virgin Mary surpassed in dignity and in excellence all the Apostles, nevertheless it was not to her but to them that the Lord entrusted the keys of the kingdom of Heaven' (DSC.2).

### Christianity has strayed

The women maintain that the gospel doctrines of love and freedom are not exemplified by Rome's present institutions and teaching; she needs to be led back to her own calling; admitting women to the priesthood will inaugurate religious renewal.

To sum up, what Rome does not hear, and what the feminists hear her not hearing, are the claims based on injustice. For her it suffices that entry to the priesthood is not on a par with entry to the learned professions. She says nothing about the evolution of doctrine. She pays no attention to the anguish caused by male appropriation of the categories of discourse. As to the doctrine of love and freedom, the Declaration asserts that realizing these is always her goal.

On their part women show little sign of hearing references to the divine scheme of salvation, to the Mystical Body, or to the Nuptial Mystery. If they do notice these doctrines marshalled against their case they evidently do not think they should be taken seriously.

## QUESTIONS AND ANSWERS

These are the bare bones of the debate. To show how the debaters are talking past each other. I will now use the rhetorical device of setting those seeking ordination as questioners, and those refusing them as objectors. This involves going beyond the Declaration, for the other denominations are in the debate, official and unofficial statements echo one another, with the Anglican Bishop of London as vehement as any in his rejection of women's ordination.

### First question

If women and men are equally important in the context of salvation, why cannot women serve as well as men in this ritual office? Why cannot they put on masculine dress and be symbolically assimilated to the other gender for the purpose of the rite? Among the famous Nuer of the Sudan a cucumber can substitute for an ox in a sacrifice (Evans-Pritchard 1956) and among the Mandari a ritual that requires a red ox to be sacrificed can be performed with a white ox if the right words are uttered (Buxton 1973). So why cannot a woman be transformed by an agreed incantation into a man?

## Answer of the objectors

The Declaration states that this symbolic system is not based on conventions. The signs are not arbitrary but natural. In the Eucharist a stone cannot be substituted for bread; the eating has to be real eating. The wine cannot be substituted by orange juice; it has to be 'fruit of the vine and work of human hands'. Without bread and wine the Eucharist cannot be celebrated. In some sense the word natural means real. The man officiating in the Eucharist has to be a real man. The priest is himself a sign.

## Second question

But in any system of signs there is always some room for play. At some time past the Eucharist used to be unleavened bread; now it can be leavened. Both are forms of bread for eating. Male and female are both humans for the purposes of salvation.

## Answer of the objectors

True, both are human, but we are not talking about humanity just now. The point at issue is the distinction of male and female in sexual reproduction. The sign has to be a natural sign, so that it can be readily understood. (Rome is using the idea of a system of signs, while the questioners are taking one sign at a time and asking what it stands for as if it were picture or label.)

## Third question

Natural signs, male and female! Is not this a harking back to magical ideas about the pollution of women? Beliefs in female defilement have been part of a strategy for heaping indignity on women and diminishing their value (Spender 1982). The Declaration refers to 'a difference of fact on the level of function and service' (DSC.5). This is read as a dark hint that the old beliefs persist. Clerical misogyny strikes the women as alive and well. The Catholic Church teaches that through women sin entered the world; she uses 1 Corinthians as warrant that women are not made in the image of God; Chrysostom is cited for having said that women are essentially inferior to men (Soskice 1986:222). Rosemary Ruether sums up the Church's older attitude (and she makes it sound as if it is still held): 'Women's body is described with violent disgust as the image of decay' (1983:81). The contemporary result of these ideas is a 'male-shaped church in which the ideal of humanity and the norm of humanity is male' (Soskice 1986:81). That Catholics hesitate to inaugurate a female priesthood is attributed by some to the 'feeling that women are somehow less appropriate vehicles than men for that ritual purity and spiritual authority which ordination symbolises' (Muddiman 1984). The women's movement has become sophisticated about arguments from female nature. What does 'natural' mean? they ask. You say that there is no question of male superiority, but is it an accident that the exclusion of women coincides neatly with an archaic ontology in which female defilement destroyed the efficacy of a sacrament? As we now understand the word, there is nothing natural in the exclusion of females from the highest ritual office. The attributes of male and female are largely given by cultural convention. Is it not naïve nowadays to invoke a 'natural' basis of sexual difference?

## Answer of the objectors

This third question gets the same answer as that provided for the second question. The Church's model does not make gender attributions but focuses on a process, a physical one, of sexual reproduction. This is an answer which is apparently hard to take in. It is part of the doctrine of the Nuptial Mystery which is a major point in Rome's argument, and which, considering their interest in ancient myths of sacred marriages (Rich 1977; Stone 1979), ought to interest the feminists, but it rarely features in the public debate and never in a well-informed way.

## Fourth question

Why should humanity be represented by males only? Robert, Archbishop of Canterbury, on behalf of the women, asks Cardi-

nal Willebrands whether those 'who represent Christ in the
Church would do so more perfectly if their number included
both males and female?' (*The Tablet*, 5.7.1986:718).

## Answer of the objectors

If the priest were representing the human race this might have
some force, but in this sacrament the priest represents Christ in
relation to the Church; in that relationship the Church is feminine,
therefore the imagery requires that the representative of Christ
be masculine. Willebrands here states the doctrine of the Nuptial
Mystery which has been more fully given in the Declaration:

> Feminine imagery is used to reveal the place of the human
> family in God's plan of salvation. In the Old Testament,
> the people of Israel is depicted as the Bride of Yahweh. In
> the New Testament St. Paul speaks of the Church as the
> Bride of Christ. In its tradition the Church has understood
> itself in terms of this feminine imagery and symbolism as
> the Body which received the Word of God, and which is
> fruitful in virtue of that which has been received. . .

In elaborating the imagery of sexual reproduction Rome is
explaining how the Church experiences its own identity. It is
saying that it needs this symbol for understanding its experience
and mission. This is quite well parallel with the women's concern
about the appropriate categories of discourse and of self-understanding. Unwarily, Cardinal Willebrands says not only that the
sacramental ordination of men takes on its significance because
of the masculine person of Jesus Christ, but he refers to 'the
symbolic and iconic role of those who represent him in the
Eucharist'. What the Declaration says about representation is very
complex, but the word iconic triggers an anxious response.

So this is the answer. So the men are better icons of Christ
than we are. The women look at each other: what did we say
about a male-shaped church?

## Fifth question

Does this mean that femininity is only a pale version of masculinity? Is a man more of a person than a woman? (Morley 1984).
Some writers see this part of doctrine as an elaborate metaphysical

structure whose main object is to defend against arguments for women's ordination (Baker Miller 1976).

Though a lot of discussion in England has focused on the idea of the icon of Christ, and recoils at the teaching that only a male person produces an accurate icon of Jesus, there is no answer to this question from Rome, for she had never committed herself to any notion of accuracy or adequacy in males as representing Christ to the Church. This misunderstanding signals a recurrent difficulty that prevents the debaters from hearing one another on the subject of symbols. Rome is talking about real signs from a theory of sacramental empowerment. The questioners are talking about valid signs from a theory of symbolic representation; they are challenging Rome as to whether a sign correctly represents the thing it is supposed to stand for . . . one sex, one gender, or humanity as a whole. Rome is talking about signs within a symbolic system, and the questioners are talking about signs as commodities or prices; their concern is whether the correct values have been assigned, whether the correct equivalences have been matched, sign to thing signified, value for value. For them, a sign is a word with its correct signification. Not surprisingly they, and all of us who are used to looking for the fixed meanings of a sign, are completely thrown when the Declaration goes on to mix up gender so that at one point the priest has to be a male, because Jesus Christ was (and is) male, and at another point the same priest is representing males and females, all humanity. This dodging about seems to be sheer prevarication over which the friends of Rome ought to draw a polite veil. Yet the commoditizing of signs (a diagnosis developed by Marilyn Strathern in her study of symbolic systems in New Guinea) is exactly one of the ways of thought rooted in capitalist, commercial ideology that the feminists are trying to escape. A sign is not like a label on a can of beans. It is a part of a system of signs and such a system cannot function unless it is capable of transformations. Note how Julian Pitt-Rivers (1983) needs to trace a switching of gender between the toreador and the bull when he interprets the transforming symbols of the Spanish bull-ring. Marshall Sahlins also testifies to the inadequacy of any analysis of symbolic systems that does not incorporate dynamic transformations within the structure that is made of signs (Sahlins 1985).

## Sixth question

Should not the Christian tradition have female as well as male metaphors of godhead (Wren 1982)? Should not the all-male pantheon be changed so as to include both male and female gender? This thought takes up a lot of feminist Christian discussion. Ruether, for fairness' sake, takes care never to refer to God, but to God-ess. Others may need to answer this question, Rome expects to go by this criticism unscathed: she has never subscribed to an all-male pantheon: her heaven has a queen who is the mother of God. This would be an answer for which the feminists are ready. Marina Warner has noted that the cult of the Virgin Mary is generally used to make women more compliant to the masculine world and more passive in the face of exploitation (Warner 1976). So it turns out that this question does not make any difference to the main issue.

## Seventh question

Could the fact that Jesus was born a male be a historical accident with no special significance? In the Year 1, in Galilee, a woman could never have founded a church or been taken seriously as a preacher. It obviously helped his mission on earth that Jesus was born a male, but it was a purely contingent detail, without further meaning (Bailey 1954; Harries 1986).

## Answer of the objectors

The Bishop of London replies that if it is true that the cultural tradition of the first century made it impossible for our Lord to appoint women apostles, we are still faced with the question: why did God choose that time and place for the Incarnation (Leonard 1986)? The Declaration also says that 'if Jesus did not call women to become part of the Twelve it was not in order to conform to the customs of the time, for his attitude towards women was quite different from that of his milieu. . .' (DSC.2)

## Eighth question

What about the maleness of Christ? Too much importance is being attached to it. The very importance of maleness in this theology is suspect: 'The relationship of Christ's maleness to priesthood becomes an untouchable mystery on a metaphysical and symbolic plane' (Baker Miller 1976: Hoad 1984).

## Answer of the objectors

The same as for question seven, in a revealed religion nothing that is part of the revelation is fortuitous. A neat argument tries to turn the Bishop of London's argument in the women's favour: yes, Jesus was a male; but how little did his masculinity exemplify the dominating masculinity from which women have suffered through the ages: himself oppressed and humiliated, he subverted the gender polarity of his day. Rowan Williams makes Jesus's suffering into a version of masculinity which works for women's admission to the priesthood (Williams 1984: Ch. 1).

On this question the women are seeking to undermine the idea of nature, especially sexual nature, as having any fixed attributes. This arrow would miss its target if Rome's case were not based on gender attributions except only as they are part of a model of sexual reproduction, as this model is nowhere disputed, but gender is deeply involved.

Thus the debate emerges into the late twentieth century with an extraordinarily archaic content. The summary indicates that a large chapter on symbolism, another on the idea of nature, and another on textual interpretation would be needed to lay the groundwork for a serious meeting of minds. How are we to understand it as a major policy debate?

## ANALYSING THE DEBATE

At first view the women's case seems strong. Rome is blind and deaf and sunk in obscurantism. Her answers express an institutional death wish; she faces a big schismatic movement but still persists in outdated sexual discrimination. Her attitudes are apparently as incapable of modernizing as her thought. She is demonstrably an organization that is incompatible with North American political institutions. Most of the usual theories for interpreting a policy debate will follow these lines, pitting goodies against baddies, two contenders, the right and the wrong. Such one-sidedness smacks of local, historical bias. The anthropologist needs to get outside the debate.

Some analyses separate contenders only into two sides. The women's movement is extraordinarily diverse, with self-styled androgynists, separatists, millennialists, ERA promoters and other groups to be distinguished from would-be ordinands, consecrated nuns, priests and bishops, all on the same side.

For example, there is a strong vein of Marxist thinking in the women's movement. The Marxists would divide the camps according to who is doing the exploiting and who is the exploited. They cannot cast this debate into the mould of a class war over control of the means of production in the ordinary sense, since the voice of the workers is never heard . . . it is a rich country's and a rich person's debate. Nonetheless the notion of means of production can be expanded to fit this case, as the Liberation Theologians have shown in their protest to Rome that she has alienated the worshippers by separating them from the means of spiritual production. The claim that the means of intellectual production have been monopolized is exactly the women's complaint. Back in 1895 Elizabeth Cady Thompson observed that the Bible was not written for nor intelligible to women: 'Theology itself is an institutional activity monopolised by men' (Staunton 1895). Though the idea of the largest part of the church, having been made mute (Ardener 1978) is very important, this charge of monopoly does little more than redescribe the line-up of exploited and exploiter. It fails to identify the point at issue.

The women have said it often enough: many of the most vocal have a rooted objection to authority and hierarchy as such. Writing of the Christian Feminist Groups Sara Maitland says: 'Within certain variations, all these groups reject leadership and hierarchy and specifically reject tightly organised structures and channels of command; they proclaim the absolute parity of all members' (Maitland 1975:28). These extreme individualists want no part of a church that presents God as indifferent to equality.

Frequently this argument from the women's movement is raised on behalf of the ordination of women. Its perspective is very sympathetic to the original conception of Luther: it maintains that a church that sets up mediating institutions between God and his creatures is fundamentally and theologically wrong. Such a church allocates to selected humans the right to loose and bind, to include and expel; it is open to the very worst kinds of corruption; God can be left to speak his mind direct to his people. Gail Chester says:

If you are against hierarchies and elites, how can you partici-
pate in practices which accept belief in a supreme extra-
terrestrial being of either or no gender which employs
earthly intermediaries (of either gender) to interpret its message for you and guide, nay, lead you in the paths of
righteousness? Most of us have to fight to have an argument
heard in the market place where ideas are exchanged. How
can we compete with those who claim divine inspiration,
irrefutable knowledge from the highest authority? . . . I do
not understand how people who aspire to radical change,
especially feminists, can claim to be rabbis (or any other
sort of religious guru). (Chester 1983)

Another two-contender analysis lifts us clear away from the
particular doctrines, directing us to the structure of societies.
Marshall Sahlins distinguishes two social orders, each with its
distinctive mode of dealing with the past. He employs the well-
tried distinction between open and closed societies. One type,
open, he calls performative: it deals lightly with its own past; the
categories of its thought are open to negotiation, like its moral
and political options. This suggests our own society. The other
type, closed, he calls prescriptive: it is composed of corporate
groups which transmit ascribed statuses to their members; everything which ever happens is absorbed into the existing categories;
the social order partakes of the eternal as it projects itself forward
and backward in its entirety. Its style of discourse is dogmatic,
unlike the pragmatic style of the open system. Its own stability
guarantees the validity of its version of the world, while its
version of reality upholds its stability. It protects the established
categories of its thought by forcing events into their pre-existing
forms. With this type nothing that can happen can be completely
new (Sahlins 1985: 103).

The Catholic Church in Rome fits very well into the closed
type as shown by the arguments we have been rehearsing. The
focus of its law is not upon individual exchanges but upon corporate memberships and inter-corporate relations and on the authority that upholds them. However, the women's movement is much
too varied to fit into the other side. Only some, those who are
pressing for equality on principle, and those with purely pragmatic and political arguments, fit the system of unlimited nego-

tiability. This analytical scheme has no niche for the women who want to be priests, nor for the millennialists, etc.

More promising for this debate is the form of explanation developed by Pierre Bourdieu, which he calls *habitus*. This is a dynamic model of public discourse and aesthetic judgement. It starts by locating the legitimized holders of power and authority in a given social field. This fortunate category of people is blessed with two forms of capital, economic and symbolic. Symbolic capital is everything the possession of which ratifies privilege. A house in the right street, the right class of pictures on the living room wall, liking the right music and books, and supporting right-minded politicians; all aesthetic and moral judgements are signs of having or not having symbolic capital.

*Habitus* makes several advances on the two-contender confrontational model. Some objectivity has been achieved because the feminists and Rome are equally presented as adopting the best strategies available to them in the contemporary *habitus*. Neither party is made more attractive or less reasonable than the other. This may account for the limited enthusiasm so far displayed by academics for using Bourdieu's model. Another advance is that it distinguishes three positions instead of two. Rome corresponds with the holders of symbolic and economic capital; the women claiming equality are seeking to dislodge her monopoly of symbolic capital; the women wanting to be priests, having neither and wanting a little of both, seek to join, not to attack, the central institutions. They are the equivalents of the petite bourgeoisie, disadvantaged followers.

Here is the case against ordination pronounced by Rome, drawing on all the legitimacy of which she is possessed:

> The Catholic Church has never felt that priestly or episcopal ordination can be validly conferred on women . . . the Church intends to remain faithful to the type of ordained ministry willed by the Lord Jesus Christ and carefully maintained by the apostles. The Church's tradition in the matter has thus been so firm in the course of the centuries that the Magisterium has not felt the need to intervene or to formulate a principle which was not attacked. . . (DSC.1)

And clearly the feminists are making a bid to grab symbolic capital by disengaging it from the economic and political institutions in which it inheres. Rome is said to have lost legitimacy by falling away from the true, original traditions . . . the role of the feminists is to bring Christianity back to the Gospel message of love, equality, and freedom, even to save the Church of Rome from her self-destructive alienation of the faithful. Rosemary Ruether delves heavily into the Old Testament and the gospels and asserts the true norm for Christianity: an egalitarian, counter-cultural vision which has been overturned by the patriarchal Church (1983:34; 1977).

Though *habitus* is richer than the two-contender models, it only begins to explain all we need to know. As their ribald style implies, not all who speak for the feminists sympathize with the would-be priests; many who speak on behalf of the right to be ordained in the Church of Rome do not like the Roman faith at all and many who join the debate on their side are not even Christians. They are clearly not trying to grab symbolic capital, yet we cannot put them outside a debate in which they speak with passion. Nor can we class them with those who take the other option and go for economic capital without worrying about signs of legitimation.

Another weakness of the *habitus* model is that it only has one dimension on which to rank those who dissent from the Church of Rome: they are either more or less extreme in their rebound against Rome and in their readiness to embrace purely spiritual capital. There should be some way of explaining their different positions. Before embarking on this, we do well to carry forward from the Marxists the idea that major debates are about control. Taken by itself the idea has little value for the present topic. There is no time when it has been easier to evade the control of the Roman Catholic Church. You only have to drop out; the Pope still doesn't have any battalions. That is one of the bizarre things about this debate.

From Bourdieu we can carry forward the dialogue about symbolic capital. Though this idea is indispensable, by itself it does nothing to explain the sudden wish of some women (not a great number, to be sure) to be ordained priests. For there never was a time when the priesthood was a profession less well rewarded and lower in esteem. Why now? This is the most bizarre of all. Why would anyone want to be a priest just now, or even a bishop? Bourdieu's model completely fails to explain why so much effort is expended to gain so little in the way of symbolic capital.

From Marshall Sahlins' comparison of prescriptive and performative societies, we will need to carry forward his image of the closed system, holding protectively to all its categories, unwilling to let them be subverted by new events. This reads like good sociological sense. The community that puts its categories at risk puts itself at risk. The institution and the categories by which it knows itself are one. On this showing, Rome is acting like all closed societies would do, and justifiably so. Its part in the debate becomes easier to understand.

## CULTURAL ANALYSIS

The method that I am advocating requires certain assumptions to be made about culture. First, there is the assumption of voluntarism. We make a diagram of possible types of social environments and assume that those who by their words and deeds would seem to be situated in a particular spot on the diagram have made a choice to be there. They are assumed not to be automatons guided to where they are by inexorable social and economic forces. It is possible that individuals stay where they find themselves because they see no alternative, or because the alternative seems too costly. Bourdieu's argument explains why the cultural costs become prohibitive, and nothing in the rest of the argument is deterministic. Further, we assume that their heaviest emotional investment is in some situation where they are trying to go or trying to make happen or to keep as it is. These assumptions taken together explain something that needs to be explained, their entry into debates that do not concern them directly.

Another bunch of assumptions is about the stability of social forms and the possibility of classifying them. If all social forms are in perpetual flux, anthropologists, sociologists, political scientists, and a lot of literary critics might as well pack up their books and go home. This may be no more than a heuristic, a device to allow the conversation to continue – but it is absolutely necessary to assume that there are some social forms that will stay sufficiently still for us to recognize them when we go back later to have another look. Another assumption necessary to cultural analysis is that it is the legitimizing symbols that hold the social form steady.

This leads to working out a typology of the stable social forms and their legitimizing procedures. In Western political thought, we have become accustomed to thinking in contrasted pairs. The favourite contrast distinguishes the openness of the market system from the closure of hierarchies. But we have already seen that two parts are not enough for a typology. The method starts by ascending to a higher level of abstraction. We need to transcend the concrete here and now of markets and hierarchies so as to reach a plane of generality that will encompass closed and open and other forms in different times and places. To do this we set up two dimensions: for one, the dimension of control, take the presence or absence of prescription; for the other, the dimension of closure or group, take the presence or absence of group boundaries (see Figure 15.1). Now we have a 2 × 2 matrix which can be used to characterize social forms and the legitimizing symbols that make them stable.

This is a static picture. But it does encourage us to look for the legitimizing process that explains how a community lives by the kind of arrangements that put it, as a hierarchy in the C corner, with strong ascription and strong closure, or in A, the open type of society in which anything can be negotiated, or in D, which, having closed boundaries and consisting of equal individuals, is sect-like in organization and symbolic life, or in B, where the individuals neither belong to any group nor enjoy autonomy.

C clearly fits Rome's position in this debate about women priests.

Position A is for persons who like to be free to negotiate for themselves. Equal rights is an obvious ethical value accepted here. It needs no explaining. Anyone who is oppressed or imprisoned is deserving of their support. By definition this corner is not the place for firm loyalties, for they involve constraints. Nothing is

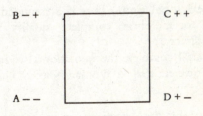

*Figure 15.1*

firm here and no one wants anything firm. They live by brokerage and opportunism. They broker ideas, they broker defences,
they challenge victimage of all kinds as part of their active
expression of their preference for a certain way of life. The structure of the modern economy puts more and more of the population into occupations which encourage these values. When they
enter the women priests debate they speak their feeling against
constraint and serfdom. As Sally Barnes relays the message of
the academics to the readers of the *Hampstead and Highgate Express*
(referring to the intransigence of Rome regarding the women
priest problem):

> By continually defining and controlling women's place in
> the manner they do, they are behaving like proprietors of
> an all-male club, using women's crucial servicing to under-
> pin its foundations, while maintaining their position.
> (Barnes 1986)

At first I supposed that the women who fought for the ERA
would also be in this corner. Then I read Jane Mansbridge's
scholarly book, *Why We Lost the ERA*. From her vivid account
of strongly entrenched boundaries between hostile forces, I now
see that they cannot belong here at A. She describes a cell-like
structure, different small groups selecting slightly different
themes, only weakly united by their shared campaign. Unlike the
women who formed the STOP THE ERA lobby, they had no
hierarchical structure. From Jane Mansbridge's chapter comparing
the ERA with inward-turning sects one must agree with her that
it belongs at D.

Who else fits D? Mary Daly's followers, organized in small,
consciousness-raising groups, passionately egalitarian, apocalyptic
and millennial, they fit the sectarian corner. They come out in
defence of women priests because they are thereby supporting
their chosen, ideal social form. That is a bounded group, with
no prescriptions for members, complete equality, no dominion
of anyone over anyone.

To illustrate this I complete the quotation already begun from
Gail Chester's article entitled 'A Woman Needs a God Like a Fish
Needs a Bicycle':

> I am staggered by the arrogance of it, by their lack of
> awareness of the incongruity between wanting to be a

leader, claiming to know better than all the rest of us, and supporting the struggle for the egalitarian society we want to bring about. (Chester 1983:82)

What about corner B? The women who want to be ordained are mostly nuns, or women who would have been nuns if the organization of convents presented a more attractive vocation. This may help us to answer the question, why do they want to be priests?

Before Vatican II a convent was organized as a little hierarchy, and not so little either. It was partly autonomous within a larger hierarchy, the diocese, the order, the church. If there is something that a hierarchy is really good at providing for its members it is meaningfulness. It deploys all the symbolic capital it can collect in order to create and maintain a high level of meaning. It has developed the art of self-justification to a high degree. Each legitimation rests on the others; the symbols refer back and forth to the same structure of metaphors, resonating to one another as in an echo chamber. In a well-established hierarchy none of the rituals is meaningless and the life of an individual is impregnated with shared thought structures. Much of the amassed symbolic capital is invested in the meaningfulness for the whole of the life of each individual member.

Vatican II invited the religious orders to experiment with new forms to suit the conditions of today. Thereupon the nuns lowered the convent walls, stripped off the once revered uniform, freed up the routines, and even left the warm, affectionate community. Piece by piece they took down the structure of legitimation. The result, in the terms of our diagram, is that they moved themselves across from right to left, away from the bounded group, and down the board away from the prescribed lifestyle toward the place where the individualists live. Life there tends inevitably to be competitive, generally disappointing except to the most successful, and short of meaning even for those.

So no wonder the nuns who have disbanded their communities, and the women who might become nuns if they could only discern a difference between belonging and not belonging . . . no wonder they miss the meaningfulness of the old hierarchical structures. If they could be priests they would feel they belonged to something, that they were of value themselves, a part of a larger whole that is valuable. Whereas now they are sensitive to

the charge of 'accepting traditional male theological consciousness, and of serving up "what Mary Daly calls male ideas in
drag" ' (Mollenkott 1975).

# CONCLUSION

Very much is incomplete in this argument. But incomplete as it
is, the analysis suggests several questions we could address to the
contenders in the debate.

Two questions could be put to Rome: one about the discrepancy in her assurances of high respect toward women in the
Church on the one hand and the lack of formal provision for
their views to be heard and heeded (for example on contraception
and on the doctrine of marriage). Where is the place of the women
in the Magisterium (Neal 1975)? Although we learn that the
women are the Church, that they are the body of Christ and the
bride of Christ, these meanings of their estate are not made
available in the initiations and celebrations and public consul-
tations which a hierarchy usually employs for transmitting its
shared meanings. Rome seems to be saying that the imagery of
the nuptial mystery is central to ecclesiology and to other fundamental fields of theology. Perhaps the nuptial mystery could be
shown to be a crucial link in a coherent chain of doctrine, so
essential, as the 1976 Declaration claims, that the other categories
and distinctions would collapse if this doctrine were weakened.
After all, she says that this has been for millennia her way of
understanding herself. If that is the case, then presumably this is
a more deeply entrenched set of doctrines than that which forbids
contraception, which is based on the theory of natural law. It
should be extremely interesting for Catholic women to know
which of the two prohibitions, the one against women priests or
the one against contraceptive practices, is the most precious to
Rome. The comparison needs to be made, as part of a reply to
a well-presented case on behalf of the women. It is possible that
the reserving of the eucharist as a sacrament for male gender is
more defensibly coherent and central in the theological scheme
than the ruling about contraception.

To the women's various constituencies some questions could
be addressed. Do the women who seek admission to the priesthood want to join a hierarchical system or an egalitarian one? If
the answer is that they have strong feelings against hierarchy,

they might well consider whether they have chosen the right church. This could be put to the hundred American women seeking ordination to the priesthood in the Roman Catholic Church who answered that they did not seek to 'join' the priesthood but rather to change it (Maitland 1975:107–14).

For the pragmatists in the women's movement, those who are more concerned with women's rights to equal status than with details of theology, there is a delicate problem about their support of the cause of women priests. When democrats adopt a suffering category that needs to be liberated, the usual question is how to help the victims to escape from an oppressor, as for example, in the case of rescuing Soviet dissidents. The victimage of the would-be woman priest is just the other way round: the exploited want to enter, not to escape from the circle that is excluding them. Supposing the strategy worked, supposing that Rome's defences were to cave in, suppose the inner circles of control were to open up, and the existing hierarchical authority were to bow itself out in favour of a participant democracy, then there would be no priesthood for the women priests to join. In so far as they have an imperative vocation to be Catholic priests this result would not help them one bit.

As to the corner of the debate that is occupied by the sectists, millennialists and small, consciousness-raising groups, they are contributing only indirectly. They are like a sounding box that amplifies the power of words. They are not particularly interested in the problem of the women who wish to be priests. For them the debate is just one more medium through which to enjoy and contemplate the sect itself. The sect cherishes the fight for its own sake, regardless of objectives. However, there is a question that should be put to them, one of consistency. We have noted that their primary conviction is against domination of all kinds. Any dominion over anyone is a scandal to them. This is a position that can be maintained with perfect consistency if no attempt is made to stop anyone from doing anything. No one and no institution can be denied the right to exist. Consistency prohibits those who are against domination of any kind to dominate. It even requires them to allow other forms of life to flourish. So their tirades against hierarchy have to be taken as sheer self-expression, not as a plank in a serious programme of reform. On reflection, the Christian feminists would not wish to reduce to sameness the wide spectrum that now comprises the variety of Christian institutions.

To sum up, cultural analysis suggests how the public debate on women priests could be shifted to less repetitious channels. Those who are concerned might speak more directly to each other. Rome would acquire a tremendous agenda of rethinking the ecclesiological doctrines based on gender enactment. She might understandably feel that she has too many poor countries' problems pressing on her to be able just now to attend to a theological problem that has arisen in the West. Here the whole structure of the modern economy has freed women from their household ties and the high level of public health has freed them from the terrors of infant mortality. A church which expects to be here until the day of judgement may also be excused from wondering whether the conditions will endure which newly prevail in the West. Thinking of this debate as a little local perturbation might enable her to face one more schism with calm. But if she were to take it seriously she should note the discrepancy between the verbal dignities accorded to womankind in her statements and the absence of effective institutions for enrolling them in positions of shared authority. If the women are the Church in some fundamental way, and if the Church is the bride of Christ, presumably the wedding day passes and the bride eventually grows up to be the wife.

## ACKNOWLEDGEMENT

I am grateful to many who have discussed this with me and thank for her research assistance Christine Novy. This paper first appeared in Anne Marie Blondeau and Kristofer Schipper (eds) (1987), *Essais sur le Rituel I, Colloque du Centenaire de la Section des Sciences Religieuses de l'Ecole Pratique des Hautes Etudes*, Bibliothèque de l'Ecole des Hautes Etudes, Section des Sciences Religieuses, vol. xcii, Paris, pp. 173–94.

## REFERENCES

Ardener, Edwin (1978) 'The Nature of Women in Society', Introduction to Shirley Ardener (ed.), *Defining Females*, Oxford, Blackwell.
Bailey, Sherwin (1954) 'Women and the Church's Lay Ministry', *Theology* LVI:322–30.

Baker Miller, T. (1976) *Toward a New Psychology of Women*, Harmondsworth, Penguin.

Barnes, Sally (1986) 'Challenge for the Church: Divide or Heal', *The Hampstead and Highgate Express*, 11 July:24.

Bourdieu, Pierre (1971) 'Genèse et structure du champ religieux', *Revue française de Sociologie* 12:295–334.

Bourdieu, Pierre (1972) 'Esquisse d'une théorie de la pratique', *Revue française de Sociologie*, 12:295–334.

Bourdieu, Pierre (1979) *La distinction, critique sociale du jugement*, Paris, Les Editions de Minuit.

Buxton, Jean (1973) *Religion and Healing in Mandari*, Oxford, Clarendon Press.

Cantuor, Robert Archbishop, Letter to Cardinal Willebrands, 18 Dec. 1985, published in *The Tablet*, 5 July 1986:716–17.

Chester, Gail (1983) 'A Woman Needs a God like a Fish Needs a Bicycle', in Joe Garcia and Sara Maitland (eds), *Walking on the Water*, London, Viking, Virago, pp. 148–53.

Cixous, Hélène (1981) 'Where is She?', in Elaine Marks and Isabelle de Courtivron (eds), *New French Feminisms*, Brighton, Harvester Press.

Daly, Mary (1973) *Beyond God the Father; Toward a Philosophy of Women's Liberation*, Boston, Beacon Press.

Daly, Mary (1978) *Gyn/Ecology, The Metaethics of Radical Feminism*, Boston, Beacon Press.

Daly, Mary (1984) *Pure Lust, Elemental Feminist Philosophy*, Boston, Beacon Press.

Douglas, Mary (1970) *Natural Symbols*, New York, Pantheon.

Evans-Pritchard, E.E. (1956) *Nuer Religion*, Oxford, Clarendon Press.

Friedan, Betty (1963) *The Feminine Mystique*, New York, W.W. Norton.

Furlong, Monica (1984) *Feminine in the Church*, London, SPCK.

Gardiner, Anne Marie (ed.) (1975) *Women and Catholic Priesthood, an Expanded Vision*, New York, Paulist Press.

Harries, R. (1986) 'On Women Priests, an Open Letter', *The Tablet*, 8 Feb. vol. 240:158–9.

Hilary, Deaconess (1975) 'The Argument from Vocation', in Canon H. Wilson (ed.), *Women Priests? Yes Now*, Redhill, Surrey, Denholm House Press.

Hoad, Anne (1984) 'Crumbs from the Table', Ch. 7 in Monica Furlong (ed.), *Feminine in the Church*, London, SPCK.

Howard, R.W. (1950) *Should Women be Priests? Three Sermons Preached before Oxford University*, Oxford, Blackwell.

Leonard, G., Bishop of London (1986) Letter, 22 Feb., *The Tablet*, vol. 240.

Maitland, Sara (1975) *A Map of the New Country, Women and Christianity*, London, Routledge & Kegan Paul.

Mansbridge, Jane J. (1986) *Why we Lost the ERA*, Chicago, University of Chicago Press.

Marks, Elaine and Courtivron, Isabelle de (1981) *New French Feminisms*, Brighton, Harvester Press.

Mollenkott, Virginia (1975) 'Topic: Religion, Author: Female, Outlook: Troubled', quoted in Maitland (1975):104–7.

Morley, J. (1984) 'In God's Image?' Lectures for the Movement for the Ordination of Women (MOW).

Muddiman, J. and G. (1984) 'Women, the Bible and the Priesthood'. Lectures for the Movement for the Ordination of Women (MOW).

Neal, Sister Mary Augusta, S.N.D. (1975) 'Models for Future Priesthood', Ch. 13 in Anne Marie Gardiner S.N.D. (ed.), *Women and Catholic Priesthood, an Expanded Vision*, New York, Paulist Press.

Pitt-Rivers, Julian (1983) 'Le Sacrifice du taureau', *Le Temps de la Réflexion*, IV Gallimard.

Rich, Adrienne (1977) *Of Women Born*, New York, W.W. Norton.

Ruether, Rosemary (1977) 'Women Priests and Church Tradition', Ch. 31 in Leonard Swidler (ed.), *Women Priests: Catholic Commentary*, New York, Paulist Press.

Ruether, Rosemary (1983) *Sexism and God Talk; Toward a Feminist Theology*, London, SCM.

Sacred Congregation for the Doctrine of the Faith (1976) *Inter Insigniores:* 'Declaration on the Ordination of Women'.

Sahlins, Marshall (1985) *Islands of History*, Chicago, University of Chicago Press.

Soskice, Janet Martin (1986) 'Viewpoint', *The Tablet*, 1 March, vol. 240– , No. 7599:222.

Spender, Dale (1982) *Women of Ideas (and What Men Have Done to Them)*, London, Ark Paperbacks.

Spender, Dale (ed.) (1983) *Feminist Theories, Three Centuries of Women's Intellectual Traditions*, London, Women's Press.

Staunton, Elizabeth Cady (1895) *The Woman's Bible*, republished 1985 by Polygon Books, quoted in Spender 1982.

Stone, Merlin (1979) *The Paradise Papers, The Suppression of Women's Rights*, London, Virago.

Strathern, Marilyn (1985) 'Dislodging a World View', *Australian Feminist Studies*, 1:1–25. Edited by Susan Magarey.

Strathern, Marilyn (1986) 'The Study of Gender Relations: A Personal Context', forthcoming in Deirdre Meintel (ed.), *Anthropologie et Société (Issue sur les rapports hommes-femmes)*.

Swidler, Leonard (ed.) (1977) *Women Priests: Catholic Commentary*, New York, Paulist Press.

Warner, Marina (1976) *Alone of All her Sex, The Myth and Cult of the Virgin Mary*, London, Picador.

Willebrands, Johannes Cardinal (1986) Letter to the Archbishop of Canterbury, 17 June, *The Tablet*, July: 718–19.

Williams, Rowan (1984) 'Women and the Ministry', Ch. 1 in Monica Furlong (ed.), *Feminine in the Church*, London, SPCK.

Wren, Brian (1982) In the Methodist Recorder, quoted in J. Morley, *In God's Image* (1984).

# 16

# THE HOTEL KWILU
## A model of models

The friends that I consulted on how to do honour to this occasion made various suggestions. Some said of course I would be expected to talk about Gender and what it has been like to be a woman anthropologist in America. But for the last decade I have not been located in an anthropology department so it would be hard to take up that idea. Others said that Gender is too risky a topic and advised me to stick to travelogue. But travelogue is too trivial. I have compromised and will talk about a recent visit to the Lele in Zaire (the travel part) and what cultural anthropology looks like, seen from the windows of religious studies departments, whose hospitality I have now enjoyed for many years.

In the privileged perspective of religious studies at Northwestern and Princeton, both theology and anthropology look surprisingly alike. But perhaps it is not so surprising since both have been engaged in something of the same kind of quest, the quest to know the Other. The New Testament scholars have centred their work on Jesus, the Divine Other, a human with something plus. The anthropologists have centred their whole work on the Savage, the Primitive, the Native, call him what you will, the Other, a human with something minus. My long-term reasons for comparing anthropology with nineteenth-century German New Testament studies have to do with my sense of the importance of anthropology and of its intellectual responsibility. The immediate choice is inspired by my conflicting emotions on returning to Zaire, emotions of admiration mixed with sorrow and concern.

## THE HOTEL

First I start with the travelogue. Last year, forty years after my first visit, and after a very long absence, I revisited the Lele of the Kasai, in the company of a young Lele anthropologist, Dr Pierre Ngokwey. On the way we stopped for a night at the Hotel Kwilu. The hotel sits in the town of Kikwit on the banks of the Kwilu River, in Zaire. It is reached by a 450-km drive due east on a superb motorway, well-metalled and well-cambered, all the way from Kinshasa over bare, burnt hills. Kikwit is the end of the road going east. Here it turns due south and apparently continues its fast, high style all the way to the diamond mines. For the traveller going east for another 450 km to the rural areas inhabited by the Lele, there are only rough tracks, over eroded gullies and deep sandbanks. When we set out, the head driver engaged us all in prayer. Until we got to Kikwit the praying had seemed unnecessary; afterwards, when we left the metalled road, I saw the point.

The Hotel Kwilu looks like a modest version of the Sheraton or the Marriott or any of a number of well-standardized airport hotels: modest by comparison, but grandiose in its setting. As I remember, it is a handsome building made of solid stone, with broad steps up to the front entry, a reception desk on the right, a big glass-roofed atrium in front, potted palm trees around, a bar to the left, and a restaurant beyond that, all calm, cool, and inviting. Before looking in I asked to see the bedroom. It was still in the accepted Sheraton style: clean, big, huge mirror, air-conditioning, twin beds, twin pictures on the wall, the telephone, the reading lamp, well carpeted, the bathroom en suite. Inside the bathroom, again: perfectly in style, the bath, the gleaming fittings on the hand basin, shower, hairwashing spray, the lavatory. Everything was there, not forgetting the bottle of drinking water. The only thing I thought was odd was that the bath was full of cold water. I wondered if the last guest had not left them time to clean it, but no, I was told this was to economize water. The candle and matches by the bed I took for an extra courtesy in case of emergency. The window looked out onto the hotel garden where a children's playground was crammed full of swings and roundabouts and climbing frames, all piled up in a small space around a fountain that was not playing.

The receptionist asked me to pay in advance so that they could procure the diesel fuel needed for refrigeration and electricity. He also said that the electric lighting went out at 8 o'clock, to save diesel. Dinner was good. We chose the only available dish off a huge menu that looked like a diploma. So far so good.

However, when I got upstairs I found, with the help of the candle, that the taps did not run, the lavatory did not flush, the phone was not connected, nor the air-conditioning. But I rejoiced in the huge bath full of water, and a dipper for carrying water to the hand-basin and the lavatory. I slept well and wanted nothing.

## THE VILLAGES

When we reached the Lele territory the villages were in the same places roughly; some had dwindled, some had grown. Some of my friends had died, young had grown old, children were now adult. But I was appalled at the underlying change. They had been poor enough before, but self-sufficient. They used to make their own clothes and containers, baskets and pots and boxes; their houses were made of forest products, they ate their own crops and the meat of game they hunted. Now they had arrived in the cash economy of Zaire, without any cash. Their forest had disappeared, their grassland was burnt, their soil looked to my (inexpert) eye like dust. They were groaning under the exactions of their chiefs. The market economy around had entrapped them. They tried to sell surplus grain, but transport conditions do not serve the growth of a food market. Their old work for Unilever's oil palm plantations had ceased; the company is pulling out. I gathered that the uncertainties are too great for industry in a country so dislocated and corrupt that no funds can be sure of reaching their destination, and where the infrastructure of communications (posts, telephone, roads, boat, air, train) is crumbling. All this made me very sad.

On the return journey the driver wanted to drive straight through Kikwit so as to reach Idiofa before dark. But I rebelled. I wanted to spend one more night in that hotel. It was not just for the comfort. I had some curiosity to satisfy, particularly about the bath water. How did it get there? Did twelve women slink in barefooted, gracefully bearing calabashes on their heads? Or did they make a file all the way from the river bank, passing buckets from hand to hand? In either case, why did I never see them, or their footprints, or hear them? Or did the hotel find the cash to buy diesel and switch on the pump, making the taps really work for an hour? And where did the hotel get cash from anyway? We were almost the only guests in the place.

I never found the answers. I suppose a diamond consortium maintained the hotel for their occasional comfort.

## THE METAPHOR

I fear you may be inclined to mock at the pretensions of this hotel. You may think it quite inappropriate to have a perfect little model of the Sheraton in the middle of the bush. You may well accuse me of liking my creature comforts more than is right on safari. Perhaps I should have risked the bedbugs and smells of an Idiofa inn, so as to get a more authentic experience of real African travel. Perhaps you despise me for going to such an exclusive place, where I would be surely cut off from the populace and able to forget their needs. My elitism stands revealed. Alas for that!

I describe this inn to you because it strikes me as a rich parable. The truth is that I specially like it for its pretensions. True, none of the modern accoutrements of the hotel functioned, but the hotel actually functioned very well. There were the candles for light, the bath had water, the door had a lock. When I look back on all the other overnight stops we made, the Hotel Kwilu glimmers in my imagination more and more seductively as the most comfortable, the most secure, the most light and spacious; the whole thing worked. True, it could only make symbolic gestures toward the normal connection of a hotel to national communications and energy supplies. But this was not the Hotel Kwilu's fault. The central communication grid had broken down in Zaire.

All buildings lend themselves to metaphor. I take the Hotel Kwilu for a metaphor of functionalist theory, and for theory in general. Just as the Hotel Kwilu is an advantage for the traveller who can use it, so theory is an advantage for thinking. Theories give support to ideas. Ideas are fragile and to live at all, and to travel any distance, they need support. Theory is their temporary resting place, their necessary short respite from the road. Theory is always full of pretension, even scientific theory. The philosophy of science has made us used to that. Decorative cross-references to other, grander theories are part of the genre. You shouldn't mind that. The little, harmless attempt at chic should not make you reject theory as such. Theories never draw their authority entirely from logical deduction. There is usually an effective hidden line, somewhat like the role of women carrying in the water, supporting the male receptionist, and making the machinery look as if it really functions. There are always unanswerable questions, and grey areas where it is better not to probe. But why reject theory just for that? You can't really do without it. For thinking about Africa anthropologists need more theory, not less.

## DEVELOPMENT

My friends who have been regularly returning to Africa tend to smile at my concern about development. They have got used to it as an impossibly complex problem. Some are cynical: Africa is hopeless, they say, shrugging. I consult someone in an international agency about the endangered forest: the only sure way to save a forest, he says, is to get the people out of it. I look in the anthropology journals. Applied anthropology still has a sense of being a marginal sub-discipline, but that of course is absurd. Where there is no core there is no periphery. In anthropolgy we all do different things; on the social side there is urban anthropology, industrial anthropology, anthropology of food, disaster anthropology; these are only slightly connected with each other, and even less connected with the biological side of our subject, which is nonetheless very relevant.

There is a Kwilu effect in academic life. It means being cut off, self-sufficing, comfortable at a modest level, and exclusive. The mirrors into which we can gaze to see our own reflections are big, the windows look onto an enclosed garden. In anthropology there are a number of separate resting places where ideas can be cleaned up, nourished, and settled into an appropriate discourse.

In anthropology there are lots of local discussions about development and the environment, but I am missing some connecting up of ours with other serious discourse on the subjects we deal in – for example, culture, conservation, development. In the social sciences there are a number of well-energized central grids of communication. There are sustained debates that should concern us very closely, on solidarity, ethics, risk. But I doubt whether we anthropologists are connnected up enough to any central grids of discourse to be satisfied with the power of our own.

Please don't get me wrong. I am not against Kwiluization to a mild extent; it has benefits for an intellectual discipline. It protects local autonomy and promotes innovation. But now, when the problems of development have become so overwhelming, sure supplies of energy and communications are good too. It is possible for anthropology to become too cut off to be able to deal effectively with its traditional concern for the Third World.

## THE OTHER

I would like to talk to you about the things we have at heart. For me that means our belief in the value of anthropology, and because of this, the need for us to have a critical access to the best theorizing about our own society. If anthropologists think the savage, the primitive, or the native – the inhabitants of the Third World – are fundamentally 'other' than we are, I suppose we could study them as a thing apart, from our own anthropological expertise, without benefit of social theory. But, in general, anthropologists do not subscribe to the idea that there is a basic, natural difference between people called primitives and ourselves; the difference is cultural. Some may consider our work to be so much specialized upon the marginal peoples of the world as to be irrelevant in industrial conditions. With this I totally disagree. The best that social theory can do for us is not too good for thinking about the civilizations which our own civilization has marginalized. Social theory is in turmoil and change: risk has emerged as a new field; solidarity is a big theoretical issue; economic theory is being remade, institutions re-examined; even philosophy is being socialized. Anthropologists ought to be there, helping with the new thinking about human society in general. There is no fundamental difference between kinds of humans; the whole history of anthropology has been an affirmation of the unity of human society.

This affirmation takes me from travelogue to anthropology seen from the Department of Religion. In their common engagement in the quest of the Other, religion and anthropology went through similar crises of interpretation, similar doubts, and similar controversies. Though anthropology has come to it so much later, we have both tapped the same sources of postmodernity.

Cultural anthropology draws inspiration from the theologian, Heidegger. Stephen Tyler has said that in respect of its interpretive practices, postmodern ethnography's polyphonic chorus of witnesses is modelled less on 'the newspaper but that original ethnography – the Bible' (Tyler 1986:127). As Tyler shows, interpretive anthropology is a late-coming member of a European movement that took a sharp turn against science.

Personally, I have always wondered at this disdain of science in French and German philosophy. Science is the distinctive feature of our own civilization, one we ought to watch closely and critically. It may be all right in theology not to be interested in the philosophy of science, though even there I am not sure. In anthropology, where many of us are physical scientists, we neglect it at risk of splitting our discipline apart.

## SIGNS REVERSED

Historically, in their quest of the Other, the two disciplines moved in opposite directions. For the theologian of the nineteenth century the question was the truth of the messianic claims. Was Jesus indeed the messiah, God as well as man? Rationalists rejected the claim; theologians tried to defend it, using historical criticism to protect the plus sign with *yes*, he was and is God, other than us by nature.

In the beginnings of anthropology the Other (the native) was placed on the lower branches of the evolutionary tree, somewhere nearer the apes than we. Claims that the native is 'other' by nature were a diffused influence; the psychologists extended development theory to explain the different ways of thought, the administrators and missionaries and traders were apt to say: 'The native is like a child.' The 'orientalists', as Edward Said showed, portrayed the Oriental as a slave to his passions, easily distracted, sensual, ineducable. Darwinian theory supported the view; the mood of the Torres Straits expedition (1898) was expecting to discover samples of our early ancestry marooned but still alive on Pacific Islands.

By 1906 the New Testament scholars had reduced the otherness of Jesus to practically nothing. The plus sign was dismantled. Jesus was represented as just like us. For our part, contemporary cultural anthropology, after following the very same trajectory, has folded away the question of otherness along with mistrust of representations of any kind (Tyler 1986:128).

I now ask you to follow me in tracing the parallels between the two quests, taking the religious one as far as 1906 and the anthropological one to the present day. It is worth doing because the methodological issues in the religious debates are precursors of ones that trouble us still. A minor Kwilu effect has hidden the affinity.

## ALBERT SCHWEITZER

In what follows I am depending heavily on Albert Schweitzer's *The Quest of the Historical Jesus*. In 1906 it marked the end of an era of theology (Robinson 1959:32). As a Central Africanist I am familiar with Albert Schweitzer's work in his famous hospital at Lambarene and also with his fund-raising concerts in the West. I regret that until I began to prepare this paper I only knew his critical work through his autobiography. The latter was so modest that I discounted him as an intellectual heavyweight. When I read *The Quest of the Historical Jesus* I was amazed by the vigour, subtlety, and sustained control of his history of two hundred years of controversy about the New Testament. Surely never was so much destruction wrought with such bland courtesy. In the genre, Clifford Geertz's *Works and Lives* has a similar devastating brilliance, but its destructive range is relatively small. George Stocking's splendid *Victorian Anthropology* is nearer the mark for scope and for picking the central issue out of hundreds of volumes of confused controversy, but Stocking is not sardonic. In scale alone we anthropologists are bound to suffer by the comparison. We are just much less well staffed than the theologians were.

Schweitzer felt strongly that a theoretical movement which had succeeded in presenting Jesus as a nice middle-class Victorian should be brought to a close. His book was an attack on the theological establishment. The strategy he followed was to put haloes round the heads of the rationalist opponents of Christianity, only indicating vaguely the massive professional opposition which they encountered. He insisted that they, the rationalists, had the right questions, they saw the real issues. Established theology's villains were his heroes even if their great achievement was to bring about the present disastrous state of theology, so that it had to make a new start.

## Magic and miracle

I will take up the comparison with anthropology on several of Schweitzer's main topics, beginning with the miracles of Jesus. Schweitzer starts off with a tribute to Reimarus (1694–1788), the first to have tried to form a historical conception of the life of Jesus:

> Thus there has been nothing to prepare the world for a work of such power as Reimarus . . . there was nothing to indicate to the world what a master-stroke the spirit of the time was preparing. (1968:14)
> His work is perhaps the most splendid achievement in the whole course of the historical investigation of the life of Jesus. (1968:23)

Reading such elaborate compliments, you can be sure that Reimarus is usually made out by theologians to be the arch felon. Reimarus simply proposed that the miracles had never happened and that the claims of Jesus to be the messiah were invented by the apostles: they, having expected a messiah to establish an earthly kingdom, and being disappointed in their ambitions by Jesus's death, stole his body and made up the story of his resurrection and of his miracles. Schweitzer said that though this was an offensive argument for believing Christians, it had the great merit of focusing on the messianic ideal. Schweitzer insists that after such a clear perception that the problem has to do with eschatology, the theology which rejected it for more than a hundred years was just retrograde (i.e., until Johannes Weiss, *Die Predigt Jesu vom Reiche Gottes*, 1892).

Our counterpart to Reimarus's teaching that the apostles were imposters and the Christians over-credulous to have believed in the alleged miracles is Lévy-Bruhl's teaching that the primitive's credulity about magic is due to fallacious reasoning. The response of theology tried to rescue Jesus and the apostles from the charge of fraud. One form of response from anthropology to the question of magic has been to show that magical thinking is only symbolic thinking, and not peculiar to the natives. Before Reimarus and also after there were numerous rationalist accounts of the miracles, explaining each one as something that could have occurred naturally. Raymond Firth might be counted our nearest counterpart to Ernst Renan, giving a natural explanation for Tikopia rituals. Firth showed that though the beliefs seem irrational and difficult to justify, they provided incentive for economic effort and so have a certain validity in that they contributed to survival (1939:168–87). This is a simple functionalist argument that I appreciate, since functional arguments are often necessary. But it has flaws (see Douglas 1986). A better counterpart would be our president's, Roy Rappaport's, more elaborate naturalist account of ancestor worship which functions to maintain the ecological resources in balance, and thereby earns a certain validity (Rappaport 1968).

## Mythology

After the supernaturalist and the rationalist stages, there came the mythological stage of interpretation. The argument that the gospel narrative is not to be treated as false or true history but as mythology raised the whole question of the relation between myth and history, still vital in anthropology. You can tell that Schweitzer is going to make David Friedrich Strauss (b. 1808) the most outrageous anti-hero in his whole gallery from the way he starts: 'In order to understand Strauss one must love him. He was not the greatest, and not the deepest, of theologians, but he was the most absolutely sincere' (1968:68). And the chapter on David Strauss's *Life of Jesus* starts:

> Considered as a literary work, Strauss's first *Life of Jesus* is one of the most perfect things in the whole range of learned literature. In over 1400 pages he has not a superfluous phrase; his analysis descends to the minutest details, but he does not lose his way among them; the style is simple and picturesque, sometimes ironical, but always dignified and distinguished. (1968:78)

Before David Strauss there had been some tradition for treating parts of the gospel as mythological, especially the beginning and the end; that is, the story of Jesus's coming into the world and his departure from it. Strauss applied myth to the whole corpus. His predecessors had hesitated, asking themselves how much of the historical Jesus would remain as a foundation for religion if they dared a consistent application of myth. But Strauss had been liberated from such worries by Hegel's philosophy. For him everything is myth and so is all our experience. A historical life of Jesus would therefore be impossible; instead we should be aiming to understand the gospels as:

> a creative reminiscence acting under the impulse of an idea which the personality of Jesus had called to life among mankind. And this idea of God-manhood, the realisation of which in every personality is the ultimate goal of humanity, is the eternal reality in the Person of Jesus. (Schweitzer 1968:80)

By this move the miracles are no longer a stumbling block, and a lot of other problems disappear too.

Bound to follow from the mythologizing movement were competing structural analyses of the gospel texts. These resonate with our own competing analyses of myths and legends once Claude Lévi-Strauss introduced structuralist analysis, which also has its Hegelian inspiration. (Cf. Clifford Geertz's account of the Hegelian idealism in Lévi-Strauss's anthropology (Geertz 1988:Ch.2).)

Lévi-Strauss, Roland Barthes, Lacan, and others have similarly shocked and then pleased by treating all sorts of texts as myth, and all sorts of behaviour as texts that can be analysed like myths. But it is salutary to remember that the inspiration via Heidegger from Hegel is one they share with the nineteenth-century theologians. On the other hand, though so much is shared, Lévi-Strauss is not our modern anthropological counterpart to David Strauss. He is not so thoroughgoing. David Strauss made a wholesale mythological onslaught on his subject-matter allowing no space for history at all, whereas Lévi-Strauss distinguishes cold cultures from hot, those closed to history and those open to it, thus raising many interesting questions about the nature of historical evidence.

The Johannine gospel had been supposed, along with that of Matthew, to be the report of an eyewitness. David Friedrich Strauss showed that the Gospel of John is structured by theological and apologetic interests: arguing that it is too theoretical, too abstract, he threw suspicion on its eyewitness status. He then turned to Mark, and undermined the priority which it had hitherto enjoyed. He regarded the Synoptic discourses as composite structures. If they were the work of many hands they must have been created by later tradition. So the idea of the gospel as history was left with no credentials.

These interpretations depend on minute fractioning of bits of the text. Here is a sentence that echoes our own structural analyses of myths:

> From the comparison we have been making, we can already see that the hard grit of these sayings of Jesus has not indeed been dissolved away by the flood of oral tradition, but they have often been washed away from their original position and like rolling pebbles have been deposited in places to which they do not properly belong. (Strauss, in Schweitzer 1968:90)

Naturally this is taken by subsequent historians as a straight invitation to try their hand at finding the proper places where the sayings do belong. What Schweitzer deplores is that Strauss's critical tools leave the Synoptics as 'mere bundles of narratives and discourses' with no clue as to what if anything is supposed to be going on behind the curtain of myth. The feeling that the analysis has missed the meaning is all too familiar.

Schweitzer commented caustically on the impassioned debate which followed on Strauss's *Life of Jesus*: 'Scarcely ever has a book let loose such a storm of controversy; and scarcely ever has a controversy been so barren of immediate result. The fertilising rain brought up a crop of toad-stools' (1968:97).

## Authenticity

The distress which Strauss roused in the hearts of his fellow theologians is understandable. The sacred texts themselves were being manhandled, snipped up and rearranged by one who did not believe in miracles at all. The fury reminds me of our recent controversies about authenticity of reporting. In questioning the accuracy of particular texts about the Nuer or about Samoa, only the author's reputation is at stake, and those not affected can stand on the sidelines and jeer. Standards of reporting are a normal professional matter, and they are relatively easily dealt with by a professional enquiry. For example, William Arens (1979) dared to argue that perhaps cannibalism did not exist; examining the reports, he had found many of them to be secondary, relying on others, and these allegedly primary texts he again found suspect, very much on the same principles as Biblical Form Criticism: either they repeated the same details and so betrayed a common source, or they did not agree with one another and so indicated a fictional origin. The slur on ethnography was met by a special panel of the AAA on cannibalism, and an important book firmly vindicated the beliefs under attack (Brown and Tuzin 1983). Again, Adam Kuper asserts that lineages don't exist and never have, even in Africa (1988:201–9); in short, the descent side of descent theory is based on a fiction. If the anthropologists have any professional pride they will do as they did about cannibalism: investigate, set up criteria for a conclusive decision, and publish the results.

What is much more difficult to deal with, because it goes beyond any possible professional competence, is the total mythologizing of all discourse. The debate about the Marcan hypothesis corresponds to the current concern about truth in ethnography. Once the Johannine Gospel had been recognized as an artist's creation, the search for a true historical basis had to focus on the Synoptics. This is because the quest for the historical Jesus had always assumed it needed an unembellished chronicle. Then it became accepted that Luke and Matthew are based upon Mark and this made Mark the only remaining anchor for a historical version. But when Mark too was found to be written by an artist's hand, a highly structured literary creation, this threw the New Testament scholars into new disarray. But who nowadays would expect true history to be a simple record without any aesthetic or theoretical structure? The theologians who wanted to establish a history of Jesus from pure data not processed by any theoretical concepts anticipated those among us who still want to find pure, unmediated ethnography.

## Consciousness

In default of historical proof, the search turned to what the texts could reveal about the consciousness of Jesus. If the project of the Christian Church could not be grounded historically, perhaps the question could be settled by a clue as to what was going on in Jesus's mind. If he was conscious of being human plus divine, was he conscious of it all his life or did it only gradually dawn on him? Did he change his mind about who he really was or about what kind of kingdom he was to bring about?

Reflecting on his consciousness led to assimilating the object of study more completely into the consciousness of the investigators. This is how Jesus came to be presented as the nineteenth-century bourgeois, sensitive, kindly, practical, weak, vacillating, ambitious, and so on. Hermeneutics starts with conceding the difficulty of establishing any certain knowledge of external things. From here it turns attention to knowing subjects and to the conditions for communication between them. For anthropologists this problem is taken to be a special one for their discipline, the problem of communicating between two cultures. Some find this exacerbated by the inequalities in power and wealth between the fieldworker and the Other being studied (Geertz 1988:144). Personally I think this is mistaken. Communicating with anyone whomsoever is fraught with all the same difficulties as communicating with the Other designated by fieldwork. Anthropologists are not privileged by a special difficulty of their own. The wonder is that we can communicate with each other at all, and sometimes we have to be content with something less than perfection.

Focus on communication is so all-absorbing that it leaves no space for contemplating Otherness. Hermeneutics gives a shift of ground which solves problems by losing them. It did this in the same way for the New Testament controversies about the messiahship of Jesus as it does now for cultural anthropologists. Schweitzer regarded the work on Jesus's consciousness as not just a waste of time, but destructive and essentially wrong-headed. He grounded his objection to the work on its inbuilt methodological bias.

## Time and timelessness

The historical quest for Jesus by its method posited that he could be treated as a Being in time; for Schweitzer this invalidated the whole exercise because it assumed away the supernatural element about which the first questions were posed. The quest required Jesus to be brought into our times, treating him and his message as if they were like our everyday selves and our messages. The gospel was tacitly robbed of its supernatural claims, quite incidentally, even unintentionally as a by-product of the method of enquiring into their validity. How could we extrapolate from our knowledge of our own consciousness to assess a consciousness of divinity? 'The mistake was to suppose that Jesus could come to mean more to our time by entering in to it as a man like our-selves. That is not possible. First, because such a Jesus never existed' (Schweitzer 1968:397).

From his own study of the history of the subject, Adam Kuper has come to the parallel conclusion: the primitive culture never existed; it had been profoundly misconceived; there was no orig-inal 'primitive society'; the search and the goal were illusory (1988).

The theologians' mistaken attempt to place the Other, the human plus, into the stream of our history is ironically matched by anthropologists' attempts not to exclude from our history the other Other, the human minus, or the savage. The case for not excluding has been forcefully put by Johannes Fabian (1983). He has pointed out that the long-standing attempt to present the primitive culture as timeless has the effect of putting it to the periphery of our Darwinian evolutionary model of civilization, beyond and below where we are. So he is arguing that our anthropological Other should not be treated as a Timeless Being, but as being in time like ourselves; Schweitzer argues that the theologians' Other should not be treated as a being in time, but as a Timeless Being, quite unlike ourselves.

This is difficult because we seem to have a confusion of epochs: Darwin meets Thomas Aquinas. The timelessness of God is an ancient philosophical idea about eternity. The timelessness of primitive culture is indeed partly based on a nineteenth-century evolutionary model. But I suspect it to depend for its opprobrium more on Hegel than on Darwin, because it implicitly refers to Hegel's idea of historical consciousness. In the nineteenth-century perspective, not to have historical consciousness might mean miss-ing out on the general human destiny. Historical consciousness was the dialectical movement of the spirit's self-realization in the world and very little to do with how individuals remember their past. To treat the primitive society as so much less than human because not part of the spirit's actualization sounds like an insult. And Renato Rosaldo (1980) starts to cancel it, with a fascinating probe into the historical consciousness of the Ilongot. But if the whole Hegelian conception of History is dubious there will not be much point in working to remove from the primitive the reproach of not having that non-existent, impossible experience. It might be better first to have a theory about how our own historical consciousness is constituted, and so my survey brings me back full-circle to the state of social theory concerning ourselves.

So here we are, anthropologists, arrived at the point to which Schweitzer took his readers in 1906. We have all succeeded in diminishing the Otherness of our subject. Not just the rationalist critics who denied that Jesus was God, but also the theologians who tried to save the Christian project by making him a person in nature. And for their part, anthropologists have wiped the slate clean: primitive society was a myth. Good, Schweitzer welcomed the chance to start again, and so do I. We need to do better in considering the Other. Other people are persons with their own selves and their own others. Third World writers, however much they dislike the way in which we have represented their culture, do not see themselves as just like us. There are aspects of our civilization which they profoundly dislike. For them, *we* are the *Other*. Conversely, it is our business to recognize how they differ from 'we'. They are the marginal peoples of the world, marginalized by us. They are poor. They suffer famine. We put pressure upon them to cut their forest, plough up their grassland, drain their waterways to pay their debts to us. At the same time, we tell them that they must not plough or burn or drain, because their environment (which they thought was theirs), is actually a common resource. It belongs to the whole globe and is slipping away for lack of the care which we know how to administer. Other resources which they thought were held in common, turn out to be parcelled out among the nations.

What can anthropologists think about this? Can we think at all?

## Objectivity

As cultural anthropologists try to think, ambivalence about theory sets in. From what solid ground can we start? Where can objectivity be found? Incidentally, this is not a problem that besets biological anthropologists very hard.

Schweitzer faced the problem in an interesting way. His strategy has a Bayesian feel about it. Texts are infinitely suggestive; they are infinitely able to suggest probable interpretations. As he said, 'an able man who has sworn allegiance to John will always find a thousand ways in which the Johannine data can be reconciled with those of the Synoptics' (1968:87). His strategy is to set up the field of interpretive probabilities in the framework of his own assessment of how the world is. For his work, 'the world' is the New Testament; his assessment starts with a strong probability that it is an eschatological document. So his examination of the texts begins with an explicit hypothesis, that Jesus was talking about the spiritual kingdom of God. Crudely, he starts by asking himself: Do I think that Jesus is by nature Other? and he answers, Yes, I do. Then he goes on to look at the texts from the assumption that Jesus's kingdom was a spiritual one. This gives him a very different set of answers and new kinds of problems from everything that had been done since Reimarus.

For our part, doing the same exercise, our world is ethnography. We would need to ask ourselves, in counterpoint to Schweitzer, crudely: Do we think that the primitive is by nature Other? and we answer, No, we don't; culturally, yes, other, but by nature, no. Then we should look at our texts from that assumption, and decide whether cultural variety makes irrelevant our thinking about our own society. The challenge will be to connect up our thinking about exotic culture with the most exacting self-knowledge that we can achieve. For anthropologists to work on their own would be a pity.

This is where I revert to the image of the Hotel Kwilu. Considering that it depends on its own generators, and that it has not enough credit with the Bank, and considering everything else that makes it difficult to use its medium technology appurtenances, it does remarkably well. Its management is to be congratulated on providing a comfortable, self-contained place for privileged travellers to rest. It tempts them to abandon the voyage. The Hotel Kwilu could do much better if it were connected up to the national communications grid. Each separate branch of cultural anthropology is liable to enjoy the Kwilu seduction. Still more comforting is the wall that separates cultural anthropology from the rest of social theory. But how to link up, where to stand? The only place to stand is where we are. The theory has to start with ourselves; it has to be a slow, bungling process; theory is not a flying machine. As the poet said of wanting to get away from an earthquake: 'The heart of standing is we cannot fly' (Empson 1956).[1]

## ACKNOWLEDGEMENTS

The Spencer Foundation generously financed the visit to the Lele. I also owe grateful thanks to Pierre Ngokwey, who organized the voyage, and escorted me. Without his staunch support I would never have reached the Hotel Kwilu. Without his humour and philosophy I would have missed the confrontations surrounding us. The idea that we could learn about our own methods and assumptions from the comparison with Biblical studies I owe to David Bloor. He advocates the famous 'strong programme' in the sociology of knowledge, which requires fairness between beliefs and no point of view to get privileged protection from the enquiry. In pursuit of this ideal he compares the resistance of some scientists to the sociological enquiry into their assumptions with those of the nineteenth-century Bible scholars ('Rationalism and the Sociology of Knowledge', forthcoming in Proceedings of the Vezprem Conference, edited by Imre Kronsky (D. Reidel, publisher)). I am also grateful for much help from Princeton graduate students, especially Kate Cooper, Noriko Ouchi, and Richard Lim, in the Department of Religion.

This paper was delivered as the Distinguished Lecture at the 87th annual meeting of the American Anthropological Association 20 November 1988, in Phoenix, Arizona and was published in *The American Anthropologist* December 1989.

## NOTE

1 But as to risings, I can tell you why.
   It is on contradiction that they grow.
   It seemed the best thing to be up and go.
   Up was the heartening and the strong reply.
   The heart of standing is we cannot fly.

## REFERENCES

Arens, William (1979) *The Man-Eating Myth: Anthropology and Anthropophagy*, New York, Oxford University Press.

Brown, Paula, and Tuzin, Donald (eds) (1983) *The Ethnography of Cannibalism*, Washington, DC, Society for Psychological Anthropology.

Douglas, Mary (1986) *How Institutions Think*, Syracuse, NY, Syracuse University Press.

Empson, William (1956) *Collected Poems*, London, Chatto & Windus.

Fabian, Johannes (1983) *Time and the Other: How Anthropology Makes Its Object*, New York, Columbia University Press.

Firth, Raymond (1939) *Primitive Polynesian Economy*, London, Routledge.

Geertz, Clifford (1988) *Works and Lives: The Anthropologist as Author*, Stanford, CA, Stanford University Press.

Kuper, Adam (1988) *The Invention of Primitive Society*, New York, Routledge.

Rappaport, Roy (1968) *Pigs for the Ancestors*, New Haven, CT, Yale University Press.

Robinson, James M. (1959) *The New Quest of the Historical Jesus*, Philadelphia, Fortress Press.

Rosaldo, Renato (1980) *Ilongot Headhunting, 1883–1974: A Study in Society and History*, Stanford, CA, Stanford University Press.

Schweitzer, Albert (1968) (1906) *The Quest of the Historical Jesus: A Critical Study of Its Progress from Reimarus to Wrede*, New York, Macmillan.

Stocking, George W. Jr. (1987) *Victorian Anthropology*, New York, The Free Press.

Strauss, David F. (1968) *The Life of Jesus Critically Examined*, trans. Marian Evans, Leamington Spa, Scholastic.

Tyler, Stephen (1986) 'Post-Modern Ethnography', in James Clifford and George Marius (eds), *Writing Culture: The Poetics and Politics of Ethnography*, Berkeley, University of Califonria Press, pp. 122–40.

Weiss, Johannes (1892) *Die Predigt Jesu vom Reich Gottes*, Göttingen, Vandenhoeck & Ruprecht (*Jesus' Proclamation of the Kingdom of God*, London, SCM Press, 1971).

# NAME INDEX

# SUBJECT INDEX